Regional Policy in a
Changing World

ENVIRONMENT, DEVELOPMENT, AND PUBLIC POLICY

A series of volumes under the general editorship of
Lawrence Susskind, *Massachusetts Institute of Technology*
Cambridge, Massachusetts

CITIES AND DEVELOPMENT

Series Editor: Lloyd Rodwin, *Massachusetts Institute of Technology*
Cambridge, Massachusetts

THE ART OF PLANNING
Selected Essays of Harvey S. Perloff
Edited by Leland S. Burns and John Friedmann

BREAKING THE RULES
Bureaucracy and Reform in Public Housing
Jon Pynoos

CITIES OF THE MIND
Images and Themes of the City in the Social Sciences
Edited by Lloyd Rodwin and Robert M. Hollister

THE FUTURE OF HOUSING MARKETS
A New Appraisal
Leland S. Burns and Leo Grebler

HERE THE PEOPLE RULE
Selected Essays
Edward C. Banfield

NEIGHBORHOODS, PEOPLE, AND COMMUNITY
Roger S. Ahlbrandt, Jr.

REGIONAL POLICY IN A CHANGING WORLD
Niles Hansen, Benjamin Higgins, and Donald J. Savoie

Other subseries:

ENVIRONMENTAL POLICY AND PLANNING
Series Editor: Lawrence Susskind, *Massachusetts Institute of Technology*
Cambridge, Massachusetts

PUBLIC POLICY AND SOCIAL SERVICES
Series Editor: Gary Marx, *Massachusetts Institute of Technology*
Cambridge, Massachusetts

Regional Policy in a Changing World

Niles Hansen
University of Texas at Austin
Austin, Texas

Benjamin Higgins
Australian National University
Canberra ACT, Australia

and

Donald J. Savoie
Canadian Institute for Research on Regional Development
Université de Moncton
Moncton, New Brunswick, Canada

Plenum Press • New York and London

Library of Congress Cataloging-in-Publication Data

Hansen, Niles M.
   Regional policy in a changing world / Niles Hansen, Benjamin
Higgins, and Donald J. Savoie.
       p.   cm. -- (Environment, development, and public policy.
Cities and development)
   Includes bibliographical references.
   ISBN 0-306-43300-1
   1. Economic development. 2. Regional planning.   I. Higgins,
Benjamin Howard, 1912-   . II. Savoie, Donald J. III. Title.
IV. Series.
HD82.H276   1990
338.9--dc20   89-29566
                                                             CIP

©1990 Plenum Press, New York
A Division of Plenum Publishing Corporation
233 Spring Street, New York, N.Y. 10013

Printed in the United States of America

Preface

During the summer of 1987, the authors of this book found themselves together at the Canadian Institute for Research on Regional Development, at l'Université de Moncton in Moncton, New Brunswick. All of us were, of course, interested in regional development, regional policy, and regional planning. However, the geographic areas of our concentrated experience in these fields varied a good deal: for Niles Hansen, the United States and Western Europe; for Benjamin Higgins, Australia, Canada, and a number of developing countries in Asia, Africa, and Latin America; for Donald J. Savoie, Canada and the United Kingdom. In our virtually nonstop discussions, comparative analysis of these widely differing areas was inevitable. In addition, we were conscious of the fact that in 1987 we were living in a period of extraordinarily rapid and dramatic change—technological, economic, social, and political—that affected all of these areas. As we talked and thought, we also became aware of a surprising similarity in the changes occurring in all major regions of the world. With our shared special interests, we were especially fascinated by the conjunction of the politico-ideological pendulum. Then, we noted another striking phenomenon: swings in the regional policy pendulum seemed to have little to do with economic situations, either at the regional or at the national level, but are synchronized instead with swings of the politico-ideological pendulum. Generally speaking, swings of the latter to the Left bring more activist and more interventionist regional policy, whereas swings to the Right are accompanied by retreat from positive regional policy, whether the socioeconomic situation in the relatively disadvantaged regions in any country, or in the country as a whole, has improved or deteriorated.

Once we had arrived at that point in our thinking, there was no escape from our obvious obligation to write a book together elaborating this thesis.

v

The present volume is the result. The book is very much a joint effort and product. There was a good deal of cross-fertilization and mutual criticism along the way, although there was no real disagreement about the questions to be addressed or as to the conclusions reached.

As always at the Institute, our work at all stages benefited greatly from the assistance and support of the Institute's stalwart, loyal, and efficient "Ms's": Colette Allain, Ginette Benoit, and Louise Robichaud. We also profited from the comments and suggestions of our colleagues Maurice Beaudin and Rodolphe Lamarche. Finally, we had helpful suggestions from the reviewers of the manuscript and from the editor of this series, Lloyd Rodwin. To all of these we extend our heartfelt thanks, but none of the blame for the book's shortcomings.

Niles Hansen
Benjamin Higgins
Donald J. Savoie

Contents

CHAPTER ONE

Introduction

ECONOMIC DEVELOPMENT: THE REGIONAL DIMENSION

What? How? For Whom? These are the standard questions raised in all introductory economics courses with respect to the production and distribution of goods and services. Only rarely does one find in the basic textbooks any appreciation of the *whereness* of economic activity. With the exception of the topic of monopolistic spatial price discrimination, basic microeconomic theory unfolds in an essentially spaceless world, where disequilibria become equilibria through marginal adjustment processes. Macroeconomics analyzes the economy as a whole, at the national level, but despite admonitions that what may be true of the whole may not be true of the parts, it implicitly treats the nation as a homogeneous entity. Various schools contend with one another concerning whether or to what extent monetary and fiscal policies can or should influence *the* unemployment rate or *the* inflation rate, but in any case the student can only surmise that *the* rate is the same all over, though later he or she may find some perfunctory mention of "structural" problems, including those of a geographic nature.

In this volume, we argue that geographic space is an essential element in the performance of any economy. When one treats national economies as the bundles of more or less integrated regional economies that they are, one is led to an approach more akin to biomedical research than to the deductive, physics-inspired, models of neoclassical economic theory. A healthy body and a healthy economy both have many feedback mechanisms that serve to preserve equilibrium or to restore equilibrium when marginal adjustments become necessary. But bodies and economies can also experience major disequilibria that cannot be reversed by "natural" marginal processes of adjustment. Some people die of cancer, and some economies—national and regional—stagnate

1

and even decline over long periods of time. Medical researchers in Freud's Vienna were content to give brilliant diagnoses of illnesses and took little interest in finding cures. Neoclassical economics likewise displays little interest in intervening in "natural" processes. In contrast, whereas policy-oriented regional economics recognizes the importance of efficient markets, it also seeks to diagnose the causes of significant spatial disequilibria and to use regional analysis as a tool to diagnose malfunctioning of the economy as a whole. It then tries to find appropriate policies (cures) and to implement them in an efficient manner.

In contrast to biomedical research, however, regional economics is not able to perform, much less attempt to replicate, controlled experiments. For this reason, the comparative method is used in this volume to ascertain if there are certain empirical regularities that can be observed in the postwar period in different countries with respect to the evolution of regional economies, the nature of regional problems, the policies intended to deal with these problems, and the consequences of these policies.

Regional policy constitutes any and all conscious and deliberate actions on the part of government to alter the spatial distribution of economic and social phenomena, including population, income, government revenues, production of various goods and services, transport facilities, other social infrastructure, and even political power. Under this definition, many kinds of policy may be "regional" that are not usually so labeled: not only regional development policy but also transport policy, energy policy, trade policy, monetary policy, fiscal policy, communications policy, and science policy. It has been said, for example, that in the United States regional policy is called the Senate because all states have two senators and, consequently, the Senate expresses regional interests. Because each state has two senators, farm and rural interests have much more influence than in the more urban-oriented House of Representatives, whose members come from districts with roughly equal populations. From the time of Confederation in Canada to 1969, there was no Department of Regional Economic Expansion, but there was certainly a regional policy. In our view, however, no policy should be considered "regional," even if it has an impact on the distribution of economic and social phenomena in space, unless it is part of a formal effort to do so and unless that intention is clearly stated.

The nature of a nation's government structure can have important implicit differential regional development consequences. For example, France's long tradition of highly centralized administration has contributed greatly to the dominance of Paris, not only politically, but also in terms of education, culture, research facilities, higher order services.

and corporate headquarters. The same can of course be said about London. In contrast, federal states have greater pressures for regional equity, even if this is not a "natural" outcome of market forces. The Canadian government has provided a comparable level of public services in all provinces, and it has benefited relatively less developed provinces through systematic interregional transfer payments. In Australia, the Commonwealth Grants Commission endeavors to assure that the states have the capacity to provide similar standards of public service. Again, however, for present purposes, policies and programs are considered to be "regional" only when there is a clear intention and formal effort to make them regional in orientation.

Because this volume examines explicit policies intended to influence the intranational distribution of population and economic activity, or to change the nature of broad regional economies, we do not deal in any detail with "urban policies" whose objectives pertain only to individual cities. On the other hand, as pointed out, many nonspatial policies do have implicit differential regional consequences. In the United States, for example, defense expenditures have had little impact on some regions, but they have clearly contributed significantly to the recent growth of California and New England, and the space program has stimulated growth in the Southwest. In France, in the late 1970s, government subsidies to cover the deficits of the Paris public transportation system (not considered as part of regional policy) were five times the total amount of subsidies to firms that would decentralize from the Paris region (a main objective of regional policy). Before pondering too long on the irony of this situation, it should also be remarked that subsidies to the national railroad were also five times the decentralization subsidies. But the railroad subsidies primarily covered deficits in low-density provincial areas and therefore could be regarded as a net benefit for poorer regions. Detailed regional analyses should, insofar as possible, attempt to evaluate such unintended regional outcomes, but the complexity involved makes such undertakings frankly not feasible in the present context.

OBJECTIVES OF REGIONAL POLICY

Although the objectives of explicit regional policies vary from place to place and over time, they typically involve the pursuit of one or more of the following goals: reduction of regional disparities, whether for reasons of economic efficiency, political stability, or social justice; redistribution or change in growth patterns of population and economic activity in space; development of resource frontiers; and improvement in resource allocation by reducing unemployment and low-productivity employment and by promoting entrepreneurship and relatively rapidly growing sectors.

Regional development objectives often involve the issue of people-versus-place prosperity. *A priori* and *ex ante*, there is always an advantage in promoting employment creation where people live because the psychological and economic costs of migration are thus avoided and existing natural resources, capital equipment, and social infrastructure can then be utilized, instead of having to provide all these in another place. Of course, there may be cases in which the disadvantages of location, the costs of upgrading capital and skills in a particular place to make enterprises competitive, or the poverty of natural resources more than offset the *a priori* advantages of job creation where people live. But the advantages are highly visible, whereas the disadvantages are sometimes less so. This explains why regional development programs that focus on places are often undertaken, sometimes with enthusiastic popular support and why they seldom disappear altogether even when the support becomes less eager.

MAJOR THESES

A major thesis of this volume is that regional policies need to be viewed in the context of changing economic structures and changing determinants of location of economic activity. The increasing tendency to decompose various production processes into discrete components gives dominant enterprises—typified by the multinational corporation—ever greater flexibility with regard to the spatial location of these components. One need only remark the advent of the "world car." Potentially footloose activities have also increased in importance, especially in the case of scientifically oriented, high-technology firms for whom the transport costs of inputs and outputs are small in relation to the total value of their products. Account must also be taken of the vitality of many small and medium-sized enterprises, especially in high-technology sectors; of the growing significance of the services sectors, and especially producer services; of new computer and communications technologies; and of the increasing degree of economic sophistication on the part of public and private decision makers. Some of these phenomena may result in decentralization, but often relatively sophisticated activities are footloose only with respect to traditional local criteria, for example, the minimization of transportation costs. In fact, they often depend on the existence of a milieu; and location decisions are based on such considerations as the general educational level of the population, the degree of professional qualification, the dynamism of regional firms, the presence of universities and research centers, and the quantity and quality of producer services.

Another major thesis is that regional policies reflect the mutual interaction between the socioeconomic evolution of a nation and the prevailing economic and social philosophy of the time. For whatever reasons, there are definite swings in the ideological pendulum, and these swings are reflected in regional policies—or a lack thereof. Over time a nation may move from a laissez-faire attitude toward regional development, to relatively comprehensive regional planning, and then back again. At times, there may be an increase in regional policy activity in response to a worsening of socioeconomic conditions and a concomitant swing toward greater government interventionism. But this is not always the case. The rising prosperity of the 1960s highlighted structural difficulties that left certain groups and regions behind, which in turn led to unprecedented regional development policy efforts in numerous countries. Moreover, in periods of general economic stagnation, it may be difficult to implement focused regional policies because each region feels it is a special case, demands special treatment, but refuses to share the costs of development policies for other regions. Thus, although there is a relationship between prevailing socioeconomic attitudes and degree of regional policy effort, the relationship is too complex to be merely subsumed under fluctuations in general macroeconomic conditions.

Accordingly, regional policy reflects both what is happening within a national society and a national economy at any particular time and the prevailing economic and social philosophy of that time; and these interact with each other. With the passage of time, any one nation may move through virtually the entire spectrum from a laissez-faire attitude toward regional development to more or less complete *aménagement du territoire* or land use planning—and back again. Shifts in regional policy, however, do not take place in isolation. They are parts, and major parts, of the periodic—perhaps even cyclical—shifts in socioeconomic policy in general, and in the socioeconomic philosophy that lies behind it. Usually an upswing of activity under the general heading of "regional policy" is a response to a worsening of social and economic conditions in some manner or other and a consequent swing of the socioeconomic philosophy pendulum toward interventionism in general. Thus during the Great Depression, policy in the industrialized countries involved a sharp increase in interventionism, and the policies were distinctly regionalized because unemployment and poverty were concentrated in certain spaces. World War II brought more intervention, but a decline in overt regionalism, although the policies pursued brought reductions in regional disparities as a by-product. The postwar readjustment period brought a new wave of interventionism and regionalism, which prevailed until the 1970s. More recently there has been a retreat from both interventionism and regionalism, with the possible exception of a few developing countries that are committed to national development planning and still regard regional planning as the most effective way of doing it. Yet it is by no means clear that economic and social conditions in industrialized countries are improving.

Another major hypothesis to be tested by the case studies in this book is that the greater a role regional policy plays in national economic and social policy as a whole, the greater is the overlap among the following phenomena: regional disparities, measured in per capita income, unemployment, and general levels of social welfare; sharp contrasts in occupational structure and product mix; identification of "regions" with geographically and administratively delimited spaces that have political powers and responsibilities (provinces, states, districts, municipalities); and societies with differing religions, languages, and cultures. We shall see this thesis borne out with special clarity in the cases of Canada and Malaysia. It is also borne out, in the reverse sense, in Australia and the United States. France, Brazil, and the United Kingdom fall somewhere in between.

CONFLICTING CULTURE?

Robert C. Reich explains the swings of the economic policy pendulum in the United States in terms of two coexisting and conflicting cultures: One relates to government and politics and is concerned with social justice, participation, civil rights, social security and welfare; the other relates to business and economics and is concerned with productivity and growth, unemployment and inflation, savings and investment, and trade. Democrats and liberals, he maintains, lay claim to the first realm, Republicans and conservatives to the second. The two cultures have competed for ideological dominance, with sometimes one and sometimes the other predominating. The business culture prevailed in the 1880s and ushered in the era of the large corporation, but the failure to deal with civic responsibilities led to the Populist and Progressive countermovement, resulting in the Federal Trade Commission and laws governing hours of work and working conditions. During the 1920s, the business culture rebounded, but the Great Depression and the New Deal brought a new wave of interventionism. The civic culture took over again in the 1950s and 1960s but ended with the election of Ronald Reagan.

Whether or not this sort of analysis holds for other industrialized countries, or even for the United States itself, is a question we shall have to examine in the course of this book. But there can be no doubt that there are swings in the ideological pendulum, however caused; and there can also be no question that changes in regional policy are related to these swings. Because regional policy reflects the aspirations and ideas of social groups inhabiting particular territories as well as the ideological complexion of the nation as a whole, it represents a litmus test for detecting changes in a country's socioeconomic situation, as well as the responses of electorates and politicians to these changes.

NATURE OF THE STUDY

Comparative public policy studies frequently consist of collections of already published articles or of papers presented at conferences. In contrast, the authors of this volume met in 1986 to identify issues that were relevant to the countries represented here and to establish a common framework for their respective studies. They met again in the summer of 1987 at the Canadian Institute for Research on Regional Development, where they worked cooperatively to integrate their research efforts. Subsequent revisions were exchanged and criticized, and the final manuscript was prepared early in 1988.

The countries examined in this book include large, resource-rich, industrialized countries of relatively recent settlement (Australia, Canada, the United States), mature industrialized European nations (France, the United Kingdom), and a sample of newly developing countries that have opted for constructing national development plans by aggregating regional development plans (Brazil, Malaysia, Sri Lanka). They also represent both centralized and federal systems of government. All of the countries surveyed have had long experiences with regional development policies and have instituted fairly recent changes to their efforts. Some have intensified their efforts, others have attenuated them.

CANADA

A former Canadian prime minister observed that some countries have too much history but Canada has too much geography. Canada, with about 25,000,000 people, covers some 9,976,000 square kilometers.

Regional disparities and regional conflicts in Canada are great. Some areas of the country are highly developed and sophisticated, capable of competing with the most advanced urban areas in the world. Others are, by any measure, economically depressed. Canada is surely one of the most highly regionalized countries, and its economy is one of the most fragmented. Accordingly, the free market does not function well for all regions simultaneously, and policies applied uniformly throughout the country do not serve to eliminate the faults in market performance. Successive Canadian governments have recognized this fact.

Regional development, thus, enjoys priority status in Canada, and in government—regardless of which political party is in power. Former Canadian Prime Minister Pierre E. Trudeau, for example, claimed that the problem of regional disparities is as threatening to national unity as English–French relations.

Canada has witnessed, particularly since the 1960s, a variety of new policies, programs, and organizations aimed at promoting regional development. Recently, a major, reformed program of regional development policy was launched.

FRANCE

During the 1950s there was a growing perception in France that population and economic activity were becoming overconcentrated in the Paris region and that measures were needed both to slow the growth of Paris and to stimulate development in provincial areas. Following some tentative steps in this direction in the 1950s, the Gaullists implemented a series of major regional policy initiatives in the 1960s—the heyday of French regional development planning. In many respects, considerable progress was made in terms of achieving regional objectives. By the 1970s, for example, the rate of population growth of the Paris region was well below forecast levels, considerable industrial decentralization had been achieved, and many regions that had been experiencing net population outmigration for many years were now having net inmigration. The extent to which these phenomena were brought about by regional policy efforts, rather than by spontaneous market forces, may be debated, but in any case it seems clear that regional policies did play a positive role.

The period of national and international crisis that began in 1974 resulted in central government emphasis on market mechanisms and macroeconomic policies. National and regional planning, although not abandoned, were definitely relegated to secondary concerns. In 1981, the Socialists came to power and made administrative decentralization a major national objective. There was a concomitant revival of regional planning and promotion of regional and local development initiatives. However, the triumph of the center–right parties in 1986 brought about a return to reliance on free market forces and a deemphasis on national and regional planning.

It is evident that the nature and extent of regional development planning in France have depended on swings of the political pendulum. If history is any guide, there will be a revival of regional policy; and although it will differ in many ways from former attempts in this regard, there will still be much to learn from the failures and successes of the past.

GREAT BRITAIN

In many ways, Britain has led the way in putting in place regional development measures. The first effort to solve the country's regional problem was launched as far back as 1928, and since then, an extremely diverse variety of initiatives have been introduced. Some of these were discarded after only a few years, but others survived for a long time, some to this day.

Britain is a particularly interesting case for the study of regional development. Regionalism is pronounced, and there are important differences in the economic health of the regions. Added to this is the economic problems of the inner cities, which have of late received attention in political circles and in the media. The problems of the inner cities have also essentially been defined as a regional development problem.

Moreover, the two political parties that have dominated British politics over the past 50 years have fairly distinct political ideologies and hold widely divergent views on the role of government in the economy. This holds obvious implications for regional development policy. It has meant at times sudden and dramatic shifts in the policy and approach following a change of government.

UNITED STATES

In a loose sense, regional policies have, in varying degree, been a part of federal activism since the early years of the United States. This can be seen in such activities as infrastructure development ("internal improvements") intended to link far-flung frontiers to the national market; the encouragement of agricultural settlement in new territories; and regional approaches to river basin development, most notably in the case of the Tennessee Valley Authority. However, it was not until the mid-1950s that Congress recognized that special measures might be needed to overcome the problems of chronically depressed areas.

The apex of federal regional policy was reached in 1965, when a number of regional development agencies and programs were created, but during the 1970s, the climate of support for regional policies waned. During the 1980s, the United States virtually abandoned a national perspective on regional development policy issues.

In recent years, considerable national attention has been given to the need to enhance the competitiveness of the U.S. economy and to the related need for more rapid and efficient economic adaptability. These matters have typically been discussed in sectoral terms; but sectorally oriented proposals imply a national industrial policy, which, after much discussion, now tends to be regarded as an inappropriate means to enhance national competitiveness. Moreover, the industrial policy debate diverted attention from the more fundamental issues of regional development and decline, including the quality of government, the physical and social environment, information activities and networks, and, not least, human resource development. A more activist national government may well find it desirable to create institutional mechanisms that address regional policy issues within appropriate spatial contexts, while remaining consistent with the nation's federal system.

AUSTRALIA

The history of Australian regional development, policy, and planning is unique. Australians tend to think of "regions" as the six states. In sharp contrast to the history of other large countries of recent settlement, which was marked by moving frontiers, these "regions" all developed together in the nineteenth century, and they all developed in essentially the same way. Each state consists of a coastal city where the bulk of the population lives, and a thinly settled agriculture and mining hinterland where per capita incomes are about equal to the state average. Because of these similarities in timing and structure of development, Australia has never been plagued by large disparities in standards of living among states. Consequently, "regional policy" in the form of striving to reduce regional gaps has never played a major role in Australian politics.

Australian Labor party governments have shown more interest in regional policy than the various Liberal–National–Country party coalitions.

The Whitlam Labor government of 1972–1975, as part of its program of sweeping reform, endeavored to enlarge the role of the states and municipalities in economic and social development, mainly by providing greatly increased funds for this purpose. They set up regional authorities to help state and local governments spend their money. The main instrument of Labor government regional policy was the Department of Urban and Regional Development (DURD), which attacked its tasks with more missionary zeal than experience and skill. It established three growth poles, set up an Area Improvement Program to organize regional bodies with local representation, and provided funds to local governments through the Grants Commission. The coalition government of Malcolm Fraser quickly dismantled the regional development efforts that Whitlam had started. Social expenditures, including urban and regional development, were drastically reduced. DURD was scrapped and replaced by a Department of the Environment, Housing and Community Development with broader scope and less money. The growth centers were abandoned.

The return of Labor brought no explosion of interest in regional policy, no evident resumption of the urban and regional development programs of the Whitlam regime. They established 11 country centers to encourage local action development plans for small communities. The results thus far are not very impressive. The regions are too small for effective planning, and there is a lack of local initiative and entrepreneurship. Where larger regions are organized for development purposes, however, such as the Geelong Regional Commission, very impressive acceleration of development has occurred.

BRAZIL AND MALAYSIA

Brazil and Malaysia are both in the upper-income bracket among developing countries, both are rapidly growing, and both have a relatively long experience with formal regional development policy. Both still have frontiers, and resource frontier development has played a major role in regional policy. In Brazil in the early 1950s, drought relief in the impoverished northeast was a principal objective of SUDENE, the regional development authority for the northeast, and to that degree, reduction of regional disparities was an objective of regional policy. But in time, SUDENE's objective broadened to one of integrated development of the region, including ambitious programs of industrial development, rural-to-rural migration, education, health, transport, and urban renewal. Over the same period, regional development authorities were established to cover the entire country, and perhaps the most sophisticated of them all can be found in the country's richest state, São Paulo. Most of the regional development authorities, however, cover several states.

In the 1950s and early 1960s, resource frontier development was the main function of regional policy in Malaysia. But in May 1969, race riots between Malays and Chinese led to the introduction of a new economic policy (NEP), designed to reduce economic and social disparities between Malays and Chinese. The aims of the NEP became the principal objective of regional policy. Because the northeast states of Trengganu and Kelantan were both the poorest and the most purely Malay, there was special concern for the people of the northeast region. The policy, however, did not consist of transfers to those states from richer states, nor even of a concentration of development projects in those states. On the contrary, a major part of the solution of the problems of the northeast was seen to be emigration to other regions, both rural (as with the Pahang Tenggarra project) and urban (as with the Penang and Johore Baru projects and the plan to convert Kuantan into a growth pole). Indeed, the idea was to plan the entire urban structure and the entire aggregation of regions as an integrated system, an idea that, as things turned out, proved to be somewhat overambitious. In Malaysia as in Brazil, "regions" for policy and planning purposes were for the most part not states or any other political units; they started as especially created substate regions, and with the Fifth Plan (1985–1989), moved to regions as collections of states, as in Brazil.

Although mistakes have been made in the regional policies of Malaysia and Brazil, on the whole the policies have been well conceived, and they have made a fundamental contribution to the success with national development.

The chapters that follow show how each country adjusted its regional policies in response to changing socioeconomic circumstances. All of the countries surveyed launched ambitious regional development policies and programs in the 1960s, but by the early 1980s important cuts were being made in regional development programming in industrialized countries, and programs were being substantially modified in developing ones. Governments of all political persuasions instituted major modifications in regional programming. For example, in the early 1980s a new Conservative government in Britain curtailed regional development efforts as did a well-entrenched Liberal government in Canada.

Each study examines the past successes and shortcomings of regional policies in the respective countries reviewed and assesses new approaches undertaken in the 1980s. For each country, we pose four sets of questions.

1. What were the perceived problems that were expressed in regional terms and how were they formulated?
2. What were the political responses to these problems, within the various regions and at the center? What were the institutions, programs, and legislation that resulted? How did these fit into broader national policy? How did they relate to changes in government?
3. What were the underlying economic theories, political theories, and more general socioeconomic philosophies behind these policies?
4. What results were achieved? What lessons were learned?

Finally, although recognizing that regional policies are intimately tied to the political and economic histories of individual countries, there is a great deal to be learned generally from comparative analyses of regional development policies and programs. For example, the growth-center approach to regional development was widely applied in the 1960s and 1970s, but in the end, there was a great deal of disappointment with the results. In contrast to isolated case studies, the strengths and weaknesses of growth center theory and practice become much more evident in the light of comparative international analyses. Thus it is our intention to demonstrate that comparative analyses of regional development issues provide broader perspectives and more novel insights concerning actual and potential problems and opportunities than are likely to result from isolated studies of particular national experiences.

CHAPTER TWO

Regional Development Policy
The Canadian Experience

Canada joined other Western industrialized countries in the 1960s in declaring war on regional disparities, on poverty, and on a host of perceived public policy problems. By the early 1980s, it appeared that many political and policy actors became war weary and calls went out for governments to reduce the resources directed to fight such causes. There are now indications, however, that the Canadian government is preparing a new attack on regional disparities.

This chapter reviews past efforts, considers the various forces that have shaped Canadian regional development policies, and looks at recently announced efforts. An analysis of the forces shaping Canadian regional development must be carried out against the backdrop of several important features of Canadian politics.

First, the problem of regional development remains deeply rooted in Canada's economic and political forces. The center–periphery nature of Canada's economic structure has given rise to important differences in living standards and to different regional economic specializations. Although the Toronto region has been able to develop a highly sophisticated urban structure and a strong industrial base, some 1,200 miles east, most of the Atlantic region suffers from chronic unemployment, a weak urban structure, and a heavy reliance on natural resources. This situation, repeated in variations across the country, has led people in different regions to perceive their economic interests differently. Southern Ontario, for example, will tend to favor tariff protection, whereas the peripheral regions, particularly the western provinces, are much more likely to espouse free trade.

Canada's political system itself has also served to promote these differences. Canadian federalism has "institutionalized regionalism" with provincial governments becoming the channel through which regional interests have been articulated.[1] In *Public Money in the Private Sector*, Allan Tupper remarked that

> the Premiers have obviously mastered the rhetoric of regional alienation" and went on to suggest that debates about a Canadian industrial strategy are shaped at least in part by the "often conflicting goals of eleven interventionist governments.[2]

Provincial governments reject out of hand any notion that their respective economic circumstances are shaped by the market forces and by the geographically neutral policies of the federal government. In fact, provincial governments of the four Atlantic provinces, the four western provinces, and now Quebec, firmly believe that federal economic policies actually retard regional development and favor growth in southern Ontario.[3]

Certainly, the four Atlantic provinces regard regional development and a role for the federal government in ensuring balanced economic growth between the various regions as fundamental tenets of Canadian federalism. Former Premier of Newfoundland Brian Peckford, for one, recently warned that "Canada could not survive as a nation unless some tangible progress is made in alleviating regional disparities."[4] The importance of regional equity in economic policy making in Canada is such that it is now a part of the Canadian constitution. Indeed, in 1982, governments committed themselves through the Canada Act to "reducing disparities in opportunity."[5]

THE EARLY YEARS

Only after World War II did the federal government show greater concern for a regional balance in economic activity, perhaps because regional differences became much more apparent in these years. Shortly after the war, the federal Department of Reconstruction called a Dominion-Provincial Conference on Reconstruction. The federal government's submission revealed a total faith in Keynesian public works planning and in the need for federal control over fiscal policy. The federal government offered generous subsidies to provincial governments for planning and implementing public works, provided that the provinces agreed to place fully planned projects into a reserve or "shelf" to be implemented at a time to be designated by the federal government. Ottawa felt that this plan would enable it to mount a concerted attack on inflation and unemployment by directing projects to selected areas of the country. For a variety of reasons, including continuing prosperity, little came of Ottawa's plan.[6]

What brought the federal government to recognize regional economic imbalances was the fiscal weakness of the poorer provinces. In a very harsh manner, the Depression years had revealed this weakness. The Rowell–Sirois Commission had been established in 1937 to reexamine "the economic and financial basis of Confederation and . . . the distribution of legislative powers in the light of the economic and social developments of the last seventy years."[7] Essentially pessimistic about the capacity of governments to work together efficiently in joint activities, the commission had favored a clear delimitation of power. It had concluded that the Canadian fiscal system should enable every province to provide an acceptable standard of services, without having to impose a heavier-than-average tax burden. It had recommended a strengthening of the federal government's economic powers and a series of national grants to the poorer provinces so that they could offer public services broadly equivalent to those in the richer provinces.

Another royal commission was to come forward with suggestions about establishing special development plans. The Royal Commission on Canada's Economic Prospects (the Gordon Commission) reported in 1957 that "a bold and comprehensive and coordinated approach" was needed to resolve the underlying problems of the Atlantic region, which required special measures to improve its economic framework.[8] Those measures included a federally sponsored capital project commission to provide needed infrastructure facilities to encourage economic growth. The commission also called for measures to increase the rate of capital investment in the regions. In many ways the commission was breaking new ground in advocating special measures to involve the private sector in promoting development in slow-growth regions. Perhaps for this reason the commission remained cautious in its recommendations: "Special assistance put into effect to assist these areas might well adversely affect the welfare of industries already functioning in most established areas of Canada."[9]

As with the Rowell–Sirois Commission, the Gordon Commission's recommendations were to play an important role several years after being made public. The Gordon Commission was a creation of Louis St. Laurent's Liberal government and reported its findings in 1957. However, 1957 also saw a Progressive Conservative government elected in Ottawa. The new Diefenbaker government did not immediately embrace proposals inspired by a Liberal-appointed commission. The new government, however, was confronted by a recession and was quickly in search of innovative solutions. The recession once again underlined the persistence of regional imbalances. All regions felt the effect of the recession, but nowhere was it as severe as in the four Atlantic provinces. This helped convince the federal government that undirected financial transfers in the form of equalization payments were simply not sufficient to bring about structural changes in the slow-growth regions. Certain ministers in Ottawa were also pointing to what they viewed as unacceptable levels of poverty in numerous rural communities and arguing for special corrective measures.

The 1960 budget speech unveiled the first of many measures Ottawa has developed to combat regional disparities. The budget permitted firms to obtain double the normal rate of capital cost allowances on most of the assets they acquired to produce new products—if they located in designated regions (with high unemployment and slow economic growth).[10]

Shortly after this measure was introduced, Parliament passed the Agricultural Rehabilitation and Development Act (ARDA). It was an attempt to rebuild the depressed rural economy and represented Ottawa's first "regional" development program. ARDA began as a federal–provincial effort to stimulate agricultural development in order to increase income in rural areas. It aimed to increase small farmers' output and productivity by providing assistance for alternative use of marginal land, creating work opportunities in rural areas, developing water and soil resources, and setting up projects designed to benefit people engaged in natural resource industries other than agriculture, such as fisheries. Later, in 1966, the program was renamed the Agricultural and Rural Development Act (ARDA), and its objectives were adjusted. ARDA was expanded to include nonagricultural programs in rural areas, designed to absorb surplus labor from farming. Thus reducing rural poverty became ARDA's overriding objective.[11] Notwithstanding these adjustments, however, some Ottawa decision makers believed that ARDA still had one serious drawback: it lacked an appropriate geographical focus. It was, in the words of one federal official, "all over the Canadian map."

The Fund for Rural Economic Development (FRED), introduced in 1966, would deal with this concern.[12] The program could be applied only in designated regions, with widespread low incomes and major problems of economic adjustment. In the end, five regions were identified under FRED: the Interlake region of Manitoba, the Gaspé Peninsula in Quebec, the Mactaquac and northeastern regions of New Brunswick, and all of Prince Edward Island. Separate "comprehensive development plans" were then formulated for those five regions to develop infrastructure and industry.

The FRED plan for northeastern New Brunswick, for example, consisted of three elements: industrial development services, employment development activities, and industrial infrastructure. The first element was designed to lay the groundwork for industrial initiatives by providing essential research, technicians, and staff. It included the establishment of three regional industrial commissions that were set up to help residents promote the industrial potential of their areas. It also provided support for studies to identify and pursue specific development prospects and for the provision of management advisory services and training to improve both existing and proposed enterprises.[13]

A more direct stimulus to job creation was provided by the second component of the plan, which was responsible for developing public facilities and providing inducements to private enterprise. Under this heading, assistance was given to projects that were considered capable of creating long-term employment in the natural resources and tourism sectors, but that could not be carried out without some form of public assistance. The program also provided special incentives to selected business enterprises not eligible for assistance under existing programs. An interest-free forgivable loan of 50% of approved capital costs of up to $60,000 for new manufacturing or processing industries and up to 30% for modernizations or expansion was available. It was explicitly designed to encourage new entrepreneurs and further expansion of small existing businesses. A third component provided assistance to residents to relocate to selected centers that offered better employment opportunities.[14]

The federal government introduced in 1962 yet another development initiative—the Atlantic Development Board (ADB).[15] Unlike other regional development programs, this board would be active only in the four Atlantic provinces, as its name implied. Largely inspired by the Gordon Commission, the ADB was initially asked to define measures and initiatives for promoting economic growth and development in the Atlantic region. A planning staff was put together, mainly from within the federal public service. Considerable research was undertaken on the various sectors of the regional economy, and some consultations were held with planners at the provincial level.

Shortly after its creation, the board was given an Atlantic development fund to administer. By and large, the fund was employed to assist in the provision or improvement of the region's basic economic infrastructure. Over half of the fund, which totaled $186 million, was spent on highway construction and water and sewerage systems. Some money was spent on electrical generating and transmission facilities and in servicing new industrial parks at various locations throughout the region.

The fund did not provide direct assistance of any kind to private industry to locate new firms in the region. On this point, the ADB was criticized, notably by the Atlantic Provinces Economic Council, in a report on the Atlantic economy published in 1967. It was criticized also on other points. Some argued that ADB spending was uncoordinated, in that it was never part of a comprehensive plan gearing expenditures toward specific targets. Some said that spending was politically inspired and that in the end it simply became a tool of Jack Pickersgill, a powerful Liberal federal cabinet minister who represented a Newfoundland riding in the House of Commons. The ADB never did deliver a comprehensive regional development plan for the Atlantic provinces, despite its mandate to do so in 1963. There are a variety of reasons offered for this failure. Some observers suggest that the board was never given the political green light to deliver the plan, whereas others insist that the ADB was disbanded in 1969, either too early or precisely when it was on the verge of coming up with a comprehensive plan.[16]

The federal government introduced still other measures to promote regional development in the form of the Area Development Incentives Act (ADIA) and the Area Development Agency (ADA) within the Department of Industry.[17] Legislation establishing ADIA was passed in 1963. The central purpose behind these initiatives was to turn to the private sector to stimulate growth in economically depressed regions. This was to be done by enriching existing tax incentives and by introducing capital grants in designated areas.

Regions of high unemployment and slow growth were the target of these measures. Only regions reporting unemployment rates above a specified threshold level would become eligible. Manufacturing and processing firms were then invited to locate or expand operations in these regions. Three kinds of incentives were applied sequentially: accelerated capital cost allowances, a 3-year income-tax exemption, and higher capital cost allowances. In 1965, a program of cash grants was introduced over and above the capital cost allowances.

Assistance was provided automatically on a formula basis. It was applied in a nondiscretionary manner to areas chosen solely on the basis of unemployment levels, and Ottawa quickly discovered that the program had limited potential as a development tool. Virtually no opportunity existed to relate assistance to development planning. In addition, because of the program's regional formula, the areas eligible for assistance did not include main population or industrial centers within slow-growth regions, where new manufacturing initiatives could be expected to have a better chance of success.

Throughout the 1960s, the federal government also sought to develop human resources. It set up manpower training plans as well as mobility schemes. The Technical and Vocational Training Assistance Act (TVTA) called for agreements to be signed with each province for technical training of youths or for adult retraining.[18] Essentially, the agreements enabled provincial governments to construct training and vocational schools as well as to develop new manpower training and upgrading courses.

The federal government followed with another manpower development initiative—the Occupational Training Act (OTA).[19] This act included both manpower training and mobility measures designed to deal with the country's structural unemployment. The federal government also sponsored other manpower mobility initiatives through such special development plans as FRED.

This brief outline of regional development initiatives by the federal government during the 1960s suggests that Ottawa was prepared to intervene directly to stimulate growth in lagging regions. Up until 1957, regional economic disparities had only been analyzed by royal commissions and had received little attention in terms of concrete federal initiatives. Within 10 years, Ottawa had moved in a very dramatic fashion away from its cautious, conservative, and frugal approach to economic policy to a preoccupation with slow-growth regions. It stacked one development initiative upon another in the belief that these would correct the country's substantial regional disparities.

THE TRUDEAU LEGACY

Throughout the 1968 election campaign, which saw the election of the first Trudeau government, Trudeau himself stressed time and again the importance of regional development to national unity. He went so far as to suggest that the problem of regional development was as threatening to national unity as the language issue and English–French relations.[20] In fact, he saw the two as somewhat interwoven, in that regions which were predominantly francophone were also economically underdeveloped.

Once elected, he moved quickly to establish a new department with specific responsibilities for regional development—the Department of Regional Economic Expansion (DREE). The new department was able to build from several programs first introduced by the Diefenbaker government and then continued or expanded in the Pearson era. The two most important, it will be recalled, were ARDA (Agricultural and Rural Development Act) and FRED (Fund for Rural Economic Development). These were complemented by a number of other initiatives, including the At-

lantic Development Board and incentive schemes to attract the private
sector to especially designated regions of the country.

It was clear early on that the Trudeau government had ambitious
intentions for regional development. It would attempt to accomplish
more, considerably more, than what had been done to date. Politically,
the Trudeau government had made regional development and language
policies central to its goal of giving Canadians a "just society." Economically, it was possible to stress regional development because in the
late 1960s, the national economy was buoyant, the federal treasury was,
relatively speaking, burgeoning, and the trend in policy development
was in the direction of explicit redistributive priorities. The first DREE
minister, Jean Marchand, summed up the situation by pointing out that
"because things are boiling over in central Canada, monetary conditions
have to be tightened in order to head off inflation. The restraint may be
felt here [Atlantic Canada] even though, far from the economy boiling
over, there is persistent and severe unemployment."[21]

Because of these economic circumstances and because of its high
priority status, funding for regional development initiatives "was never
a problem in DREE's early years."[22] DREE integrated the various regional development programs administered by several departments and
agencies and introduced two new major ones.

Underpinning the very purpose of these two new programs was the
"growth pole" concept. Inspired by the works of French economist
François Perroux, the growth pole concept was one that would see
growth concentrated around certain focal points. Perroux suggested that
if efforts were made to strengthen these focal points, a process of self-
sustaining economic growth would be set in motion.[23]

Marchand and senior DREE officials embraced this concept and
came forward with a "special areas" program and one for "regional
industrial incentives." The two programs shared the same objective—to
encourage manufacturing and processing industries in selected communities from slow-growth regions having growth potential.[24]

Specifically, the following would take place. Industrial centers with
the potential for attracting manufacturing and processing firms would
be identified. A special area agreement with the relevant provincial government would then be signed. This would provide for the construction
of the required infrastructure, such as roads, water and sewer systems,
and schools, thus laying the framework within which industrial growth
could occur. The thinking here was that the industrial framework and
the physical infrastructure in slow-growth regions were as unresponsive
and stagnant as the state of industrial activity.

With the required infrastructure in place, the regional industrial incentives program, through cash grants, would then be able to attract new manufacturing industry to the seleted centers. The cash grants would lower the cost of setting up production. The intent was to compensate the investor for locating in economically weak regions through a grant sufficiently large that the new production facility would generate the same return on investment that it would have had, had the firm located in southern Ontario without the grant.

The special areas program, as noted, was delivered through federal–provincial agreements. A great variety of projects were sponsored, including highways, water systems, industrial parks, tourist attractions, servicing of industrial land, sewer systems, and school. Funding arrangements were also varied, ranging from federal financing of 50% of the cost of certain projects, plus a loan for part or all of the remainder. In the case of highway construction, Ottawa paid up to 100% of the cost.[25]

The second Marchand program, one that remained important throughout the life of DREE was a regional incentives program (RDIA). This provided grants to companies calculated on the basis of new jobs created in a designated region and on capital cost of the new or expanded plant. Later, a loan guarantee program was added to the regional incentives scheme.

For both programs, Marchand staked out a policy position from which he never deviated. He insisted that DREE's existence was tied to the notion of regional equity in national economic development. He singled out eastern Quebec and the four Atlantic provinces as the regions requiring special recognition. He repeatedly suggested that if DREE were to spend less than 80% of its budget east of Trois-Rivières, then the department would be failing in its purpose.[26]

Only a few years after the two programs were introduced, however, DREE came under persistent attack on at least one program—the special areas program. Provincial governments in particular argued that the program was highly discriminatory in that it favored certain communities over others. More important, the provinces were highly critical of DREE's approach to federal–provincial relations. Ottawa, provincial governments insisted, had adopted a "take-it-or-leave it" approach to federal–provincial relations in the area of regional development that made close federal–provincial cooperation impossible.[27] There was, for example, no opting-out provision, with the result that provincial governments refusing to go along with federal initiatives were in fact foregoing federal funds.

There was also no convincing evidence that the two programs had contributed in any significant fashion to the reduction of regional disparities after 3 or 4 years of operation. Though the time lapse was short, Atlantic Canadians in particular grew impatient and renewed calls for more effective measures to "ensure" that the region would catch up economically to the rest of the country. They pointed to standard indicators of economic well-being, such as unemployment and per capita income, which had widened among the different regions.

With the aid of hindsight, we now know that too high expectations had been pinned on the growth pole concept, a concept that still remains to this day incomplete. Benjamin Higgins, in *Growth and Change,* put it succinctly when he stated that "perhaps never in the history of economic thought has so much government activity taken place and so much money been invested on the foundation of so confused a concept as the growth pole became in the late 1960s and early 1970s."[28] In any event, because virtually every politician wanted a growth pole designation for his riding, the constant pushing and pulling for designation became very difficult to manage politically.

A major policy review of regional development programming was launched inside DREE in 1972. In a federal election of that year, the Trudeau government barely clung to power, returned in a weak minority position in the House, and suffered particularly heavy losses in western Canada.

Trudeau immediately launched a series of measures to recapture public support. In the area of regional development, he moved Marchand out of DREE and replaced him with another powerful minister, Don Jamieson, of Newfoundland. Trudeau also requested that DREE be involved in the preparation of the Western Opportunities Conference that had been called shortly after the 1972 election.

Jamieson pressed on with DREE's major policy review. Its conclusions were twofold: First, that the special areas program had too narrow a focus and did not lend itself to new and imaginative ways of pursuing development opportunities; and second, that federal regional development programming had to be pursued in close harmony with provincial governments.[29]

It was this policy review that gave rise to the General Development Agreements (GDAs) and to the decentralization of DREE. As has been explained elsewhere, GDAs were broad enabling documents that permitted the federal government and individual provincial governments to sponsor a variety of projects under individually negotiated subsidiary agreements.[30] These subsidiary agreements could be provincewide in scope, concentrate solely on a specific subprovincial area, an economic sector, or even a single industry.

Provincial governments applauded the GDAs and the kind of

federal–provincial cooperation that they entailed. From a provincial perspective, the GDAs had numerous attractive features. It meant new discretionary spending in a high profile field—economic development. It had the provincial governments actually delivering the project, so that they were viewed as the benefactors. By and large, the provinces came forward with proposals, and the federal government responded.

The GDA approach was not without its problems and critics, however. In Ottawa, the GDA system was criticized for being little other than enabling documents. Senior officials in economic departments, including Finance and Treasury Board, were puzzled by the hodgepodge approach of the GDAs. They had hoped that the GDAs would "harden" over time and evolve into strategic documents or at the very least into guides to preferences or priorities for sponsoring initiatives. Thus viewed from Ottawa, the GDAs represented little more than a new source of funding for provincial governments to tap for whatever development initiative they desired, whether or not it corresponded to a coherent strategy.

The scope and type of activities sponsored by the GDAs is mind boggling. Virtually every economic sector was covered by the GDAs. In Newfoundland, the GDA sponsored initiatives in tourism, forestry, recreation, fisheries, highways, special projects for Labrador, ocean research, special projects for St. John's, mineral development, industrial development, rural development, agriculture, and federal–provincial planning. Nova Scotia's GDA supported mineral development, special projects for the Halifax–Dartmouth area, the Strait of Canso and Cape Breton, agriculture, industrial development, forestry, tourism, energy, dry dock development, and special measures for Sydney Steel Corporation and for Michelin Tires.[31]

The Quebec GDA led to some 15 subsidiary agreements, which in turn gave rise to numerous projects: establishment of newsprint mills, including one in Amos; industrial studies; mineral research and exploration; construction of a number of industrial parks, including one near Mirabel airport; highway construction; and new tourism facilities.

Ontario signed several subsidiary agreements. One was designed to strengthen the urban system of northern Ontario by providing for new industrial parks and new water and sewer systems in Parry Sounds, Timmins, Sudbury, and North Bay. A forestry subsidiary agreement promoted projects to improve forest management, accelerate reforestation, and construct new forest access roads. Community and rural resource development became the subject of another subsidiary agreement: the Upper Ottawa Valley and the Kirkland Lake areas benefited from industrial land development studies, geoscientific surveys, and hardwood forest renewal schemes. A $180-million subsidiary agreement for strengthening the competitive position of the province's pulp and paper industry was also signed.

The western provinces set up a number of subsidiary agreements with DREE. Manitoba's concerned the development of the province's northlands, its industrial sector, agriculture, tourism, water development and drought proofing, and the development of the Winnipeg core area. Saskatchewan signed agreements for the northland, for the development of a major tourist attraction in the Qu'Appelle Valley, for water development and drought proofing, and for long-term development of its forest industry. Alberta signed six subsidiary agreements with DREE. They involved the processing of nutritive products; attempts to improve incomes, living standards, and community facilities in northern Alberta; and further development of the northern transportation system. In British Columbia, the GDA gave rise to numerous initiatives, in highway construction, support of the northeast coal industry, industrial development, agriculture and rural development, tourism, forest management, and development of the Ridley Island port facility.

In 1979, the federal government signed new 5-year GDAs with the Northwest Territories and Yukon. DREE's activity began there in 1977–1978 with the introduction of special, if modest, ARDA-type programs to assist people of native ancestry to start commercial ventures. DREE's expenditures in the Northwest Territories were $800,000 for the period 1978–1979. The GDAs earmarked relatively modest amounts for community economic development in the Northwest Territories and for renewable resource development projects and tourism in Yukon.

The list of GDA projects goes on and on. Over 130 subsidiary agreements were signed between 1974 and 1982, with a total financial commitment of close to $6 billion.

There is little doubt that the strength of the GDA system was in its flexibility. One senior DREE official remarked that the problem of regional economic disparity "is economic and not constitutional." "Jurisdictional lines," he went on, "ought to be blurred so that appropriate, viable and coordinated measures to stimulate economic development [could] be brought forward."[32] The GDAs certainly did this.

Provincial governments grew particularly fond of the GDAs. They applauded their flexibility and the kind of cooperation that they promoted. They had strong reasons to do so. An opportunity presented itself in Halifax with the possible development of a world-class dry dock facility. DREE and the province simply got together and signed an agreement, and the project went ahead. No program limits existed to restrict their activities. Similarly, Quebec felt that a series of recreational parks would help its tourist industry. DREE agreed, and an agreement was signed involving $76 million of public funds. Ontario, wanting to diversify and stabilize the economics of single-industry communities, turned to DREE and signed a $20-million agreement to put a series of infrastructure projects in place.

Shortly after the introduction of the GDAs, it became clear that the relations between Ottawa and the provinces had been reversed. Unlike the situation under Marchand and Kent, when Ottawa had presented projects in a "take-it-or-leave it" fashion, provincial governments were now proposing initiatives, and the federal government was reacting. Admittedly, poorer provinces, contributing only 20% of the cost, were never in a position to adopt a cavalier posture vis à vis the federal government. Nevertheless, even they were in an enviable bargaining position, preparing initiatives to which the federal government would respond. If DREE refused to support a particular proposal, the province simply came back with another. Though the GDA system also allowed the federal government to make proposals, this did not occur often.[33]

Another attractive feature of the GDA approach for the less-developed provinces was the cost-sharing formula. With Ottawa contributing 80 to 90% of the cost, virtually any kind of economic initiative became viable. In many ways, Ottawa acted like the Treasury Board—it reviewed proposals from provincial governments, accepting some and rejecting others.

The one recurring criticism leveled at GDAs by less-developed provinces was that DREE had spread its efforts too thinly and had moved away from its firm commitment to the Atlantic provinces. If one compared DREE spending with the pattern established by Marchand and Kent, then this criticism had some validity. By 1977–1978, DREE was spending 39% of its resources in the Atlantic provinces, 31% in Quebec, 5% in Ontario, and 21% in the western provinces. In 1970–1971, the breakdown had greatly favored the Atlantic provinces, which received over 50% of DREE funds, with Quebec following at 23%; Ontario received less than 5%, and the western provinces about 16%.[34]

Criticism of the GDAs was heard frequently in Ottawa. Many thought that provincial DREE officials had become too imbued with local attitudes. They were simply echoing provincial governments' priorities and were unable to bring a national, or even interprovincial, perspective to their work. How else could one explain the "hodgepodge" of projects DREE was supporting? From an Ottawa view, not one of the GDAs pointed to an overall development strategy. They supported rural development if a provincial government favored it, or tourism projects, or highways construction. Simply put, no one could discern a central and coherent purpose in any of the GDA strategies.

Viewed from Ottawa, provincial DREE and provincial government officials employed the concept of developmental opportunities to justify whatever project they wanted approved. Building from a region's strength was not evident in the proposals put forward. Over 50% of DREE's expenditures in the Atlantic provinces went for the provision of infrastructure facilities, in particular, highway construction. This was hardly the kind of spending that Treasury officials had expected to see in DREE's pursuit of development opportunities or in its mandate to build on the strength of regional economic circumstances.

The Newfoundland GDA combined a sectoral with a spatial approach—with no apparent link between the two. That is, it supported development initiatives for key economic sectors of the province and then went on to support special "regional" development packages for selected areas of the province. It supported projects in forestry, including forest protection and the construction of access roads. It did the same for industrial development, with substantial funds committed to the construction of an industrial park and new highways linking the park to a community and to another highway. The GDA gave rise also to a rural development agreement that, among other things, provided administrative grants to development and regional councils. A subsidiary agreement for Labrador covered street improvement in certain towns, an auxiliary sewage collection system, a student dormitory for a vocational school, and a new industrial park.

GDA-sponsored initiatives in one province could be in direct conflict or competition with another in a neighboring province. Eugene Whelan, former minister of agriculture, put it this way:

> When I was . . . in New Brunswick, one thing they [farm organizations] were raising Cain about was the fact that DREE was setting up another operation in another [province] of the Maritimes to produce cabbages . . . when they already had a surplus of cabbages which they could not get rid of.[35]

It is also important to bear in mind that by the late 1970s, economic circumstances had changed considerably from when DREE was first established. In fact, by then there were a number of factors at work that were having a profound impact on the future direction of regional policy. *Stagflation* had crept into our economic vocabulary, describing the difficult position of having at the same time both inflationary pressure and slow or no growth. An international recession had struck. Canada's

industrial structure was found wanting, with some of its major components no longer capable of competing internationally. There was increasing talk about the need for government intervention to assist in the
industrial restructuring of Canada's industrial heartland of southern
Ontario and southern Quebec. The country's textile industry was in
some difficulty, as were the automotive industry and heavy appliance
sector. Thus, in some ways the regional problem had spread from eastern Quebec and the four Atlantic provinces into regions that had traditionally led the nation in economic performance. Partly as a result of this
but also because of the countrywide application of the GDA approach,
DREE's budget was no longer concentrated in eastern Quebec and the
Atlantic region. Montreal, for example, became a designated region under DREE's regional incentives program.

At the political level in Ottawa, it was fast becoming obvious that
cabinet ministers and government members of Parliament were less
than enthusiastic about the GDA approach. Essentially, they regarded it
as an instrument substantially financed with federal funds but clearly
favoring the political profile of provincial governments. Even Pierre De
Bané, the new minister of DREE appointed in 1980, suggested publicly
that

> [he] would be surprised if 10 percent of Canadians are aware that
> DREE grants to business account for only 20 percent of the depart-
> ment's budget, the rest going to the provinces.[36]

These forces led the federal government to launch a second major
review of its regional development policy. This review revealed that the
regional balance in the national economy was changing and that now
both problems and opportunities existed in all regions. The opportunities were thought to lie in the anticipated economic benefits stem-
ming from "megaprojects" that were primarily energy related. The Atlantic provinces, for instance, were expected to benefit from a number of
megaprojects associated with offshore resources. To deal with this development, the review recommended that regional economic development concerns should be central to public policy planning at the federal
level. A key element of the review was federal–provincial relations. On
this point, the review stressed the importance of close federal cooperation but stated that "joint implementation of economic development
programming [i.e., DREE's GDA approach] may not always be desirable."[37] Direct federal delivery of regional development initiatives
should be preferred in a number of situations.

Shortly after the policy review was completed in early 1982, the
then-prime minister, Pierre Trudeau, unveiled a major reorganization of

the federal government. DREE would be disbanded, the GDAs would be replaced by a new and simpler set of federal–provincial agreements, a new central agency charged with the responsibility of ensuring that regional development concerns would be central to decision making in Ottawa was to be established, and a regional fund would be set up. DREE, the prime minister explained, had not been able to launch a sustained effort at promoting regional development. As a simple line department, it had been incapable of directing the departments to contribute to Ottawa's overall regional development policy. A new central agency, the Ministry of State for Regional and Economic Development (MSERD), would now be able to ensure a "governmentwide" focus on regional development, thus strengthening Ottawa's commitment to regional development, and a new line department, the Department of Regional Industrial Expansion (DRIE), would deliver regional and industrial development programs.[38]

The Cabinet established MSERD by adding regional policy and coordination to the functions of the existing Ministry of State for Economic Development. That ministry had been set up in late 1978 to coordinate and direct economic development policy and to manage the economic policy "expenditure envelope." The envelope system integrated into a single process the separate functions of setting priorities, establishing spending limits, and making specific expenditure decisions. Within the envelope system, thus, MSERD was to advise deputy ministers and ministers on Ottawa's economic development budget and recommend allocation of funds between programs.

In addition, MSERD was to see that "regional concerns are elevated to a priority position in all economic decision-making by Cabinet."[39] Because of this added responsibility, the new ministry had to decentralize part of its operations. Offices comprising 8 to 12 person years were established in every province. These offices were directed by a senior executive, called the federal economic development coordinator (FEDC), who

> advises Cabinet, co-ordinates the activities of the federal government in the region, promotes co-operation with the provincial government, labour, business and other economic development groups, ensures that information about government policy is available in the field, and works with other federal departments.[40]

The ministry would, whenever appropriate, also appoint special project directors in the region "to cut red tape on mega projects and avoid undue delay in project planning, approval and completion."[41]

The FEDC, however, would direct activities in his region, keeping federal officials in the field informed of the activities and decisions of the Cabinet Committee on Economic and Regional Development. He would also coordinate the federal presence in the regions and "serve as the chairman of a committee of economic development departments in the region."[42]

Through this committee and from his own staff work, the FEDC would propose an economic development plan for his province. In turn, this plan would be the basis for federal–provincial negotiations for economic development and also assist in making federal departments and agencies more sensitive to regional circumstances.

The importance of having all federal departments play a more active role in regional development was stressed by the prime minister and MSERD's minister, Senator Bud Olson. While announcing the appointment of the FEDC for Prince Edward Island, for example, Senator Olson declared that the Cabinet Committee on Economic and Regional Development had "launched a process of review of all existing economic development programmes to determine if they can be further directed toward regional objectives."[43]

Largely because of the expected role of the FEDC, the new ministry was described by Ottawa as a "decentralized central agency." It would provide the full Cabinet with regional information developed by federal sectoral departments in the regions or by on-site research and analysis with MSERD. Thus, the information would not, as with DREE, be based almost solely on federal–provincial discussions under the various GDAs.

The agency would, however, remain largely Ottawa based. The head office would increase its allocation of person years (originally established in 1978 at more than 100) by almost 200, and the new regional offices received 100—producing a head office to regional staff ratio of 2 to 1, considerably higher than DREE's ratio of 3 to 7. The rationale for a substantial increase in person years was built around the need for ensuring that the "regional dimension" was incorporated in the federal government's decision-making process. To do this, MSERD required an enhanced information system on regional issues. A new position, that of associate secretary or associate deputy minister, was set up. Around it the regional information network would be built, including the regional offices. Moreover, approval was given for the Ottawa office to establish a major projects branch to facilitate governmentwide approaches to the development and management of the various major projects.

Nearly 2 years later, the MSERD legislation was finally amended to incorporate the regional responsibility that was added to MSERD's mandate. The legislation was no more explicit on objectives than was the old

DREE legislation; it said nothing about goals. It was not clear whether regional balance in economic growth or the reduction of regional disparities was to be paramount. MSERD's concern, the new legislation stated, was the "expansion of the economy through the development of productive enterprise in *every* region of Canada."[44]

New "Economic and Regional Development Agreements" (ERDAs) would replace GDAs so as to clear the way for the federal government to deliver specific initiatives directly. In practically every other aspect, however, they would resemble the GDAs. In fact, the legal format of the ERDAs and the federal-provincial coordinating mechanism at the officials level are virtually identical to the GDAs.

A regional development fund was also established. The purpose of the fund was to support special regional and economic development efforts and would be funded by "money freed up as the existing GDAs expire."[45] In other words, it involved no new funding but was simply a continuation of the funding level established for the various GDAs.

The new Department of Regional Industrial Expansion was formed through the amalgamation of the regional programs of DREE with the industry, small business, and tourism components of the Department of Industry, Trade and Commerce (IT&C).

The integration of DREE and IT&C, it was hoped, would capture the most positive characteristics of both DREE's decentralized and regionally sensitive organization and IT&C centralization and ability to gather industrial intelligence and conduct relations with industry and government. In short, DRIE would not be as decentralized as DREE or as centralized as IT&C.

DRIE was to set up provincial and subprovincial offices to deliver its programs. These offices have become the new department's principal contact point for DRIE clients applying for assistance under the department's programs. Unlike as with DREE, however, they have little say in the formulation of policy or programs. These functions, along with the gathering of industrial intelligence, have become the responsibility of new sectoral branches in DRIE's Ottawa office. DRIE's Ottawa-region staff ratio has been set at 6 : 4, compared with DREE's 3 : 7.[46]

Nevertheless, compared to other federal departments and agencies, DRIE is highly decentralized and "regionally sensitive." It was designed to represent the "leading edge" in Ottawa's new economic development orientation and the model on which other departments are encouraged to pattern themselves. The new department is expected to integrate regional and sectoral interests, be highly visible in the regions, and emphasize efficient program delivery.

The first DRIE minister was Ed Lumley, who rose in the House of Commons on 27 June 1983 to explain Ottawa's new industrial and regional development program. Lumley cautioned that "combatting regional disparities is difficult even in good economic times. . . . It is much more difficult in a period when, because of a worldwide downturn [Canada's] traditional industries are suffering from soft markets, stiff international competition, rapid technological change and rising protectionism from the countries that make up our market." A new program to meet these circumstances would have to be one that he could "clearly recommend to the business community, to the Canadian public and to Members of Parliament."[47] DRIE, Lumley reported, had come up with such a program. It was a

> regionally sensitized, multifaceted programme of industrial assistance in all parts of Canada. . . . This is not a programme available only in certain *designated* regions. Whatever riding any Member of this House represents, his or her constituents will be eligible for assistance.[48]

The program could accommodate a variety of needs, including investment in infrastructure, industrial diversification, the establishment of new plants, and the launching of new product lines.

An important distinguishing characteristics of the new Industrial and Regional Development Program (IRDP) was the "development index."[49] The index established the needs of individual regions, as far down as a single census district. All are arranged in four tiers of need. The first, for the most developed 50% of the population, covers districts with a need for industrial restructuring. In this tier, financial assistance is available for up to 25% of the cost of modernization and expansion. At the other end of the spectrum is the fourth tier, which includes the 5% of the population living in areas of greatest need (based on level of employment, personal income, and provincial fiscal capacity). In this tier, financial assistance is available for up to 60% of the cost of establishing new plants.

The program can provide financial assistance to both business and nonprofit organizations through cash grants, contributions, repayable contributions, participation loans, and loan guarantees. This assistance is available for the various elements of "product or company cycle": economic analysis studies; innovation (including product development); plant establishment, modernization or expansion; marketing (including exact development measures); and restructuring.

A REVIEW OF THE TRUDEAU LEGACY

After 15 years in power and after Trudeau having pledged that regional development would enjoy high priority status, few in Canada would argue that the efforts were successful. Standard economic indicators, such as earned per capita income and employment rates, showed no progress in reducing regional disparities.

A comprehensive evaluation of the regional development efforts during the Trudeau years is not possible. Regional development expenditures have not been large enough for us to be able to assess their impact in relation to other economic forces, such as interest rates, the value of the Canadian dollar, and even other federal expenditures, such as transfer payments to provincial governments and individuals.

There is another major stumbling block in evaluating the success of DREE. Its objectives were not very clear, and its policy framework kept changing. At one point, the growth-pole concept held sway. Then DREE sought to tie its efforts to the idea of development opportunities. This in turn was followed by an attempt to assess initiatives in terms of their relevance to a region's natural economic strength. Toward the end, senior DREE officials frequently spoke about local or community development concepts. Even when a particular theory was in vogue, it did not prevent the department from sponsoring a variety of initiatives that did not readily fit in with that theory.

With the introduction of the General Development Agreements (GDAs), however, came an all-embracing and unexceptionable theoretical framework, essentially nonselective and hardly a guide for action. The department had, in the words of a DREE economist, "ten policies—one for each province."[50] Viewed from the regions, DREE funds represented a "B" budget fund for provincial governments, from which they would seek funding for new economic development. Provincial governments came forward with proposals, and, if these proved unacceptable, they simply came back with a new set. The result is that DREE funded a variety of projects, not always mutually supportive.

The goals and objectives of the GDAs were extremely broad and of little benefit even as a checklist against which to assess proposed projects. New Brunswick's GDA did not, for example, prevent DREE from providing assistance for the construction of a marina for local pleasure-boat owners, for highway construction, and for the establishment of a community college. Such a variety of theoretical and policy frameworks makes it impossible to evaluate the effect of DREE expenditures. Even evaluating the impact of individual GDAs is very difficult, if at all possible.

The frequent changes of policy and organizational direction posed yet another difficulty. Before a thorough assessment of one approach could be initiated, a new one would take its place. Insufficient time had elapsed to determine the effect of a particular program on a given sector.

With a new policy announced, officials had little interest in assessing a program that was now history.

New policies were introduced for a number of reasons, not simply because existing ones were no longer effective. In fact, federal–provincial competition appears to have been largely responsible for at least two of the three major policy reviews. In 1973, the federal government sought to establish closer links with provincial governments by introducing the GDAs. By 1981, Ottawa concluded that it was not getting the credit to which it was entitled and decided to scrap these agreements. Because the principal issue behind the two last policy reviews was federal–provincial tension, it may well be more appropriate to assess them from this perspective rather than from one of regional development. Certainly, the 1973 policy review placed the provinces in a favored position in shaping new regional development initiatives. The 1982 review appears to have made it much more difficult for the provinces to do so, with the federal government now having the option of delivering certain projects directly.

The poorer provinces meanwhile continued to hurl a series of charges at the federal government for not doing enough for regional development. Worse, they insist, whatever funding is made available for regional development is invariably pulled and pushed outside of slow-growth regions to the more economically prosperous regions.

There is one regional development program that has been evaluated by numerous government officials, outside consultants, and critics—the Regional Development Industrial Incentives Act (RDIA). The fact that it was a continuing, self-contained program, supporting easily identifiable projects, probably explains why it was so often evaluated. It took up only 20% of DREE's budget, compared with about 80 percent for the GDAs. The evaluations led to a variety of conclusions, both favorable and unfavorable.

The Economic Council of Canada found that the incrementality of projects under RDIA was between 25 and 59% and that of jobs between 35 and 68%. An investment project is considered incremental if the firm, without assistance, would not have undertaken the project or would have undertaken it outside the designated region. The lower rates, 25 and 35%, represent, according to the council, a very conservative estimate of DREE's success. On the whole, the council found the program beneficial, with a benefit-to-costs ratio of between 3 and 19 to 1. The council concluded:

> The subsidies . . . seem successful enough to be a paying proposition. The value of the jobs created appears to outweigh the inefficiency involved in locating production inappropriately.[51]

David Springate found that regional incentives grants had relatively little influence on the investment decisions of large firms. He concluded that the grants produced few changes in timing, size, or technology of the project.[52] Carleton Dudley suggested that the grants were not sufficiently generous to offset the added operating cost of locating in slow-growth regions. He estimated the potential of grants for reducing the operating cost of a firm to be between 1 and 5% of sales, substantially less than the added cost of operating in designated regions, estimated to be between 5 and 20%.[53]

Some studies of RDIA have attempted to identify various characteristics associated with the type and degree of incrementality. According to LeGoffe and Rosenfield, incrementality tended to be higher when the projects involved small, new products; equipment had been modernized; an element of high risk and high profitability existed; and foreign competition was high. Incrementality tended to be lower for larger projects undertaken by firms that had experience with similar projects; projects that were necessary for the normal continuation of a firm's operations; and projects showing a high profit/investment ratio.[54]

However, incrementality is a controversial issue. The lack of consensus about it may well stem from the difficulty of measuring it reliably. Dan Usher explained the difficulty:

> Normally one is taxed or subsidized for doing something regardless of whether one would do it or not in the absence of the tax or subsidy. It is as though the family allowances were restricted to children who would not have been conceived, in its absence, or Crow's Nest Pass rates restricted to grain that would not have been grown if freight rates were higher.[55]

Others have suggested that the RDIA program had a built-in capital bias that ran counter to its objective of job creation. A RDIA grant, it was pointed out, lowered the cost of capital by a greater percentage than it lowered the costs of labor. Firms were encouraged, in other words, to emphasize new plants and equipment rather than new jobs. Robert Woodward concluded: DREE fails to achieve the greatest number of new jobs and incurs a higher cost per new job created, by continuing with the subsidies that are inconsistent with their goals.[56]

Several important considerations have been largely overlooked in evaluations of the regional incentives program. The first DREE minister, Jean Marchand, warned that regional development programs, such as special-areas and regional incentives, must have a limited geographical application, or their value would be severely diluted. By the time that DREE was disbanded, the regional incentives program had been extended to include all four Atlantic provinces; all of Quebec; northern Ontario south to and including Parry Sound, Nipissing, Renfrew, and Pembroke; all of Manitoba and Saskatchewan; northern Alberta; northern British Columbia; and the territories. All in all, the program covered 93% of Canada's land mass and over 50% of the population.

Clearer objectives would have focused the program. Its objectives kept evolving or changing, more to justify new area designations than as a result of changing economic circumstances. In the early years its principal aim was the promotion of new employment opportunities in slow-growth regions, notably Atlantic Canada and eastern Quebec. In 1971, and again in 1977, Montreal was designated under DREE's regional incentives program to encourage rapid-growth manufacturing industries.

The criteria for area designation were particularly loose and ill defined. All that was required to designate a new area was an order-in-council or a decision from the federal Cabinet.

TRANSFER PAYMENTS

It is hardly possible in Canada to review regional development efforts without considering federal transfer payments to the provinces and individuals. In 1957, two decades after the Rowell–Sirois Commission recommended that grants be made available to the poorer provinces, the federal government set up its fiscal equalization program. It was intended to reduce disparities between regions, to achieve a national standard in public services, and at the same time to equalize provincial government revenues. Ottawa thus undertook to ensure that all provinces would have revenues sufficient to offer an acceptable level of public services. Payments under the equalization schemes were and are unconditional, and eligible provinces need not spend the resources on economic development. The payments help poorer provinces pro vide services but do not necessaily assist them in integrating their economies more successfully into the national economy and in supporting regional growth from within.[57]

This limitation does not in any way minimize the importance of the equalization payments, which constitute regular commitments on the part of Ottawa to equalizing the fiscal capacities of all provincial governments. In turn, provincial governments in slow-growth regions can provide a level of public services roughly comparable to those available elsewhere. The payments also offer financial stability to provincial governments so that a competent public service can be retained and some degree of forward-looking and long-range planning can be undertaken. In itself, however, the equalization program does not earmark special funding to put in place measures to stimulate self-sustaining economic growth.

The equalization scheme and other federal transfer payments in the health and social services field have served to close the gap with the national average on a number of fronts in the provision of public services. For example, over the past 25 years, the Atlantic provinces moved considerably closer to the national average in health and education expenditures. Newfoundland, for example, now has a per capita education expenditure level within 7 percentage points of the national average. In the health field, its per capita spending moved from 46% of the national average to 81% in the same period. When the provincial hospital bed capacity per capita is measured, one finds that the most disparate province was within 15 percentage points of the national average in 1981, compared with 26 percentage points in 1961.[58]

Federal transfer payments have not only increased the capacity of provincial governments to provide a better level of services to their residents; there is also some evidence to suggest that they have enabled individual Canadians in traditional have-not regions to acquire basic household necessities. Regional disparities in this respect are now virtually nonexistent, whereas they were extremely wide some 20 years ago. For example, again with 100 representing the national average, Newfoundland moved from 38.3% in 1961 to 97.1% for the indicator "households with refrigerator" in 1981. Under the heading "households with telephone," Prince Edward Island moved from 64% in 1961 to 94% in 1981. Ontario, meanwhile, declined from 109 in 1961 to 100.6 in 1981. For the heading, "households with exclusive use of installed bath facilities," New Brunswick saw its position move from 78.8% in 1961 to 99.6% of the national average in 1981. Ontario's position, on the other hand, went from 112.8% to 110.6%.[59]

THE MULRONEY COMMITMENT

During the 1984 election campaign, Brian Mulroney outlined a number of specific regional development measures that a Progressive Conservative government would implement. DRIE, he revealed, would be given a "specific legislative mandate to promote the least developed regions" and "every department will be required to submit to the Standing Committee of Parliament on Economic and Regional Development annual assessments of the effect of departmental policies on specific regions."[60] DRIE would also be given a wide range of new policy instruments. For instance, in addition to incentive grants, DRIE would be able to offer tax incentives. In the case of the four Atlantic provinces, efforts would be made to improve the economic infrastructure of the region. Such efforts would include facilities for transportation and communications, as well as training programs, improved market research, and other similar measures. Commitments were also made to put in place measures designed to assist communities suffering from chronic unemployment and very little economic activity.

By the time the Mulroney government assumed office, seven ERDA agreements had already been signed. The new government did not attempt to change or to urge the provinces to change the substance of these agreements. In fact, it moved quickly to sign ERDAs with the three remaining provinces—namely Ontario, British Columbia, and Quebec. The three new ERDAs follow the administrative format and program approach of the seven signed earlier. The new Mulroney government also inherited a fully implemented Industrial and Regional Development Program (IRDP).

In line with its election pledge to promote the least developed regions, the Mulroney government unveiled some adjustments to IRDP in November 1984. The new DRIE minister, Sinclair Stevens, pointed out that the adjustments were designed in part to "ensure that support is provided in areas of the country where it is most needed."[61] Important restrictions were applied to Tier 1 regions, or the most developed areas of the country. For instance, "modernization" and "expansion" projects are no longer eligible for assistance in these regions.

Shortly after the Mulroney government assumed power, the press reported that it was adopting and would continue to pursue at least during the first months of its mandate a "Mother Hubbard" approach. That is, the Conservatives would maintain that the previous Liberal government had left things much worse than they had anticipated and that very little funding was left to undertake new initiatives.

In the area of regional development policy and programs, the Mother Hubbard analogy is apt: As in the nursery rhyme, the new government found "the cupboard was bare."

The Mulroney government inherited no organization, no pool of expertise on regional development issues. DREE's personnel had been dispersed throughout the government when the department was disbanded. Moreover, any hopes that regional development would be awarded added priority with the establishment of MSERD were dashed when former Prime Minister Turner during his brief 2-month stay in power did away with that ministry to streamline government operations.

With respect to any established level of funding for regional devel-

opment purposes, the most that can be said is that it is unclear what
levels actually existed when the new government was sworn in. Virtually nothing was said about the regional fund after it was first established. Trudeau has declared that the fund would reach $200 million by
1984–1985. It is impossible to determine if in fact it did ever reach that
level or, for that matter, even if the fund still exists. The Mulroney
government was thus left to define a new regional development policy
with very little to build upon in terms of any central expertise or capacity
to assist in the definition process, in terms of government structure, or
of existing policies or programs and funding. It can be argued that the
Trudeau government came full circle on regional development. It began
with ambitious goals and programs and ended with virtually no programs and certainly no policy.

THE MULRONEY SOLUTION:
AGENCIES FOR REGIONAL DEVELOPMENT

By 1986, the government concluded that mere adjustments to DRIE
programs would not suffice. For one thing, regions such as Atlantic
Canada were becoming increasingly critical of DRIE, which, they insisted, was an industry department primarily concerned with sectoral,
rather than regional, issues. For another, it was also evident that the
economic recovery taking hold was largely concentrated in central Canada. It was becoming obvious that the premise underpinning the policy
shift that saw the doing away of DREE and the establishment of DRIE
was false. Resource-based megaprojects did not transform the economy
of Atlantic Canada. That of southern Ontario and southern Quebec was
demonstrating remarkable resilience and not the "unprecedented soft-
ness" that had been predicted earlier.

In response to these developments, the prime minister embarked
on a multistop tour of Atlantic Canada where he met with provincial
premiers and community leaders. The premier of New Brunswick urged
Mr. Mulroney to establish a new economic development agency that
would be specifically concerned with Atlantic Canada.[62] Shortly after
his visit, the prime minister unveiled his government's plans to establish
the Atlantic Canada Opportunities Agency (ACOA).

The agency, the prime minister explained, would only be established after Atlantic Canadians had been given an opportunity to voice
their views on its mandate, policies, and programs. A university professor from Atlantic Canada was asked to "consult with a cross-section
of Atlantic Canadians and report to the prime minister on the establishment of ACOA."[63]

Several months later, in June 1987, the prime minister announced the details of the agency. There would be a federal commitment of $1.05 billion over 5 years in new money for regional development for Atlantic Canada.[64] Effective decision making would be decentralized to the region with the head of the agency holding the highest rank available in the Canadian Public Service. The agency's head office was to be located in the region—in Moncton, New Brunswick—rather than in Ottawa. The head of the agency in turn would report directly to a Cabinet minister and not through another permanent official. The work of the agency, it was explained, would be guided by an advisory board made up of prominent Atlantic Canadians.

The agency would play a dual role—one of advocacy to ensure that national economic policies are adjusted to correspond to the economic circumstances of Atlantic Canada and the other to put in place programs designed to assist entrepreneurs or would-be entrepreneurs to launch new businesses in the region. The agency also assumed full responsibility for the ERDAs. In addition, most of the DRIE programs including IRDP were transfered to the new agency. It was made clear, however, that the agency had the mandate to define new programs for Atlantic Canada. It was also made clear that the programs would have few built-in restrictions, so as to allow maximum flexibility to the decision makers in the region. The agency's efforts were to be on developing an entrepreneurial spirit among Atlantic Canadians and rely less and less on attempts to lure outside investors to the region.

It appears that the Atlantic agency paved the way for similar agencies in other regions of the country. Two months after ACOA was unveiled, the prime minister announced a new economic development agency to assist in the industrial diversification of western Canada. The goal of the Western Diversification Office (WDO) is to help move the western economy away from the volatile resource and agriculture sectors. The prime minister released a background paper on opportunities for diversification in the west at the same time he announced the establishment of the agency. Funding for the WDO was set at $1.2 billion.[65] The western agency was patterned directly on ACOA, the one difference was that the WDO agency has no advisory body.

At about the same time the WDO was established, the prime minister also announced still new measures for promoting development, this time in Canada's north and unveiled special "regional development" measures for northern Ontario, including the establishment of a new "office" for northern Ontario and a special development fund. The northern Ontario scheme will cost $100 million over 5 years. Key features of the program include $40 million in direct loans and grants and $60 million in loan guarantees "for small and medium-sized business from the region." A Northern Ontario Advisory Board was also set up to guide program implementation.[66] Specific initiatives directly involving the private sector, it was announced, would be put in place "as soon as possible."

Shortly after announcing the establishment of the WDO, the prime minister declared that DRIE would be "replaced" by a new department, the Department of Industry, Science and Technology (DIST), which would be concerned with growth prospects in the "high tech" sector. The department will have offices in "all" regions (i.e., provinces) and will try to promote growth in traditional slow growth regions.

NATIONAL EFFICIENCY VERSUS EQUALITY: THE DEBATE UNDERPINNING CANADA'S REGIONAL DEVELOPMENT EFFORTS

From the early years right down to the most recent developments in Canadian regional development policy, the debate over efficiency versus equality has resulted in policy revision after policy revision and in new approaches to the issue that have been introduced in quick succession over the past 25 years.

During the 1960s, the central purpose of Canada's regional development policy was clear—to alleviate regional disparities, as measured by per capita income and unemployment rates. With growing government deficits, regional development planners, particularly those in Ottawa, began in the late 1970s to define regional development essentially as synonymous with economic development but at the regional level. Thus the purpose behind a regional development policy was to permit each region of Canada to achieve its full economic development potential, much in the same way that national economic policies are designed to achieve Canada's full economic development potential.

Regional economic development policy was then described as constituting a "no-cost" policy. There could well be some short-run inefficiencies in resource allocation but over time, regions would become economically self-sustaining. DREE, by and large, was initially at least responsible for this "no-cost" myth by producing countless reports pointing to vast untapped economic potential in the lagging regions. Former DREE minister Marcel Lessard explained: "[DREE is not] a welfare agency . . . our primary objective . . . is to help each region of Canada nurture . . . those areas and prospects with the best potential for development."[67]

By the early 1980s, a new policy shift was unveiled. The recession hit Canada's industrial heartland particularly hard. The policymakers in Ottawa concluded that it made little sense to employ limited government resources in an attempt to promote economic development in all regions when the country's highly developed regions were themselves reeling from massive job loss and no growth. Canada's regional development efforts were effectively terminated.

By the mid-1980s, with the country's strong economic performance largely concentrated in the more developed regions of the country, the call for new regional development efforts earmarked for the traditionally slow-growth regions (in particular, Atlantic Canada) was increasingly being heard. How could the federal government stand idly by, the argument was heard time and gain, and see high unemployment and no growth in Atlantic Canada while central Canada's economy was buoyant? In short, the efficiency versus equality debate was again raging in full force.

It is important to stress that this debate in Canada has been institutionalized. Four of the 10 provincial premiers in the federation are from Atlantic Canada. First ministers conferences that bring together the Canadian prime minister and the 10 provincial premiers are now regular events in Canada. These conferences are held before television cameras and provide a highly visible forum for provincial premiers to defend the interests of their provincial constituents and to be seen doing so. Atlantic premiers invariably pin the blame on their regions' underdevelopment on federal government policies and programs. They consistently argue that these policies favor the more populous central provinces of Ontario and Quebec. They also consistently remind the prime minister, other premiers, and the national television audience what former Prime Minister Trudeau has said about regional disparities being as threatening to national unity as is the English–French conflict. It was largely in response to these arguments and to improving economic circumstances that led the Mulroney government to establish regional development agencies.

NOTES

[1]Allan Tupper, *Public Money in the Private Sector* (Kingston: Institute of Intergovernmental Relations, Queen's University, 1982), pp. 41, 49.
[2]Ibid., p. 41.
[3]Ibid., Chapter 4.
[4]Government of Newfoundland, *Discussion Paper on Major Bilateral Issues: Canada-Newfoundland*, p. 4.

[5]Canada, *The Canadian Constitution 1981—A Resolution Adopted by the Parliament of Canada*, December 1981 (Publications Canada, 1981).

[6]Based on a presentation by Benjamin Higgins at the Canadian Institute for Research on Regional Development, Moncton, New Brunswick, in November 1984. Professor Higgins was employed by the federal government to work on the reconstruction conference.

[7]Canada, *Report of the Royal Commission on Dominion-Provincial Relations*, 1940, pp. 269–276.

[8]Canada, *Report of the Royal Commission on Canada's Economic Prospects*, 1957, p. 404.

[9]Ibid.

[10]See Anthony Careless, *Initiative and Response: The Adaptation of Canadian Federalism to Regional Economic Development* (Montreal: McGill-Queen's University Press, 1977), pp. 39–88.

[11]Ibid., pp. 71–99.

[12]See, among others, Thomas N. Brewis, "Regional Development in Canada in Historical Perspective," in N. H. Lithwick (Ed.), *Regional Economic Policy: The Canadian Experience* (Toronto: McGraw-Hill Ryerson, 1978), pp. 215–219.

[13]Canada, Department of Regional Economic Expansion, *Annual Report 1969–1970*, pp. 12–16.

[14]Ibid.

[15]Frank Walton, "Canada's Atlantic Region: Recent Policy for Economic Development," in *The Canadian Journal of Regional Science*, Vol. 1, No. 2 (Autumn 1978), pp. 35–52.

[16]See Careless, *Initiative and Response*, pp. 113–116.

[17]Ibid., pp. 91–108.

[18]Ibid., Chapter 4.

[19]Ibid., Chapters 2 and 3.

[20]See, for example, Walton, "Canada's Atlantic Region, p. 44.

[21]Canada, Department of Regional Economic Expansion, *Atlantic Conference '68—A New Policy for Regional Development*, 29 October 1968, mimeo, p. 7.

[22]See Donald J. Savoie, *Regional Economic Development: Canada's Search for Solutions* (Toronto: University of Toronto Press, 1986).

[23]François Perroux, *L'Economie du XXe siècle* (Paris: Presses universitaires de Paris, 1959), p. 179.

[24]See, among many others, J. P. Françis and M. G. Pillai, "Regional 'Economic Disparities,' Regional Development Policies in Canada," in *Regional Poverty and Change* (Ottawa: Canadian Council on Rural Development, 1973), pp. 136–137.

[25]See Savoie, *Regional Economic Development*, Chapter 4.

[26]"The more you extend it," he insisted, "the more you weaken it—special areas programs. We have to stick to our guns." See Canada, House of Commons, Standing Committee on Regional Development, *Minutes of Proceedings*, 1970, p. 2:62.

[27]Careless, *Initiative and Response*.

[28]Benjamin Higgins, "From Growth Poles to Systems of Interactions in Space," in *Growth and Change*, Vol. 14, No. 4, p. 5.

[29]See Donald J. Savoie, *Federal-Provincial Collaboration: The Canada-New Brunswick General Development Agreement* (Montreal: McGill-Queen's University Press, 1981).

[30]Ibid.

[31]Ibid. See also Savoie, *Regional Economic Development*, Chapter 5.

[32]See Savoie, *Regional Economic Development*, Chapter 2.

[33]Ibid.

[34]Ibid., pp. 107–166.

[35]Canada, Proceedings of the Senate Standing Committee on Agriculture, Minutes of Proceedings (Ottawa, 1977), pp. 11–19.

[36]"Provinces Must Fit Programmes to Ottawa's—DeBané says," *Globe and Mail* (Toronto), 13 August 1981, p. 1.

[37]See Canada, Department of Finance, *Economic Development for Canada in the 1980s* (Ottawa: Department of Finance, 1981), p. 11.

[38]Canada, Office of the Prime Minister, *Release—Reorganization for Economic Development*, 12 January 1982.

[39]Ibid.

[40]Ibid.

[41]Ibid.

[42]Canada, Ministry of State for Economic and Regional Development, *Contacts in Federal Economic and Regional Development Departments*, mimeo, January 1974.

[43]Canada, Ministry of State for Economic and Development, Notes for an Address by the Honourable Bud Olson, Minister of State for Economic Development—A FEDC for PEI (undated).

[44]Canada, The House of Commons, Bill C-152, An Act Respecting the Organization of the Government of Canada and Matters Related to or Incidental Thereto—As passed by the House of Commons, 25 October 1983, Schedule 11, Section 35, 22.

[45]Quoted in Donald Savoie, *Regional Economic Development* (Toronto: University of Toronto Press, 1986), p. 86.

[46]See Savoie, *Regional Economic Development*, p. 80.

[47]Canada, DRIE, Spending Notes—The Honourable Ed Lumley to the House of Commons on the Industrial and Regional Development Program, 27 June 1983, 1, 2.

[48]Ibid.

[49]Ibid.

[50]Quoted in Savoie, *Regional Economic Development*, p. 118.

[51]Economic Council of Canada, *Living Together* (Ottawa: Minister of Supply and Services, 1977), Chapter 8.

[52]David Springate, "The Effect of the Canadian Government's Attempt to Influence the Investment Decisions of Private Businessmen by Means of the Regional Development Incentives Act," Ph.D. thesis, Harvard University, 1972.

[53]Carleton Dudley, "Summary of a Theoretical Financial Analysis of the Long-Term Subsidy Value of the Regional Development Incentives Program in Canada 1969–1972," University of Ottawa, Department of Geography, April 1974.

[54]J. P. LeGoff, "Les subventions à l'investissement: Leur potentiel de relocalisation," *l'Actualité économique*, July 1977.

[55]Dan Usher, "Some Questions about the Regional Development Incentives Act," in N. H. Lithwick, *Regional Economic Policy: The Canadian Experience* (Toronto: McGraw-Hill Ryerson Ltd., 1978), p. 286.

[56]R. Woodward, "The Effectiveness of DREE's New Location Subsidies," *Canadian Public Policy*, Vol. 1, No. 2, pp. 217–230.

[57]Savoie, *Regional Economic Development*, Chapter 9.

[58]Ibid., p. 117.

[59]The analysis is based on data obtained from Statistics Canada.

[60]Statement by Hon. Brian Mulroney at Halifax, Nova Scotia, 2 August 1984.

[61]Ottawa, Department of Regional Industrial Expansion, *Adjustments to Industrial and Regional Development Program—News Release*, 9 November 1984.

[62]See, New Brunswick, Notes for Premier Hatfield for presentation to the Atlantic Focus Conference, undated.

[63]Canada, Office of the Prime Minister, Release, Appointment of Donald J. Savoie to consult Atlantic Canadians on the establishment of an economic development agency for the region, 23 October 1986.

[64] Canada, Office of the Prime Minister, Release, Atlantic Canada Opportunities Agency Announced, 6 June 1987.

[65]Canada, Office of the Prime Minister, Notes for the Right Honourable Brian Mulroney, The Western Diversification Office, 4 August 1987. See also "1.2 B planned for agency to help West, sources say," *The Ottawa Citizen*, August 4, 1987, p. 7.

[66]"North Ontario given boost in federal plan," *Toronto Star*, July 14, 1987, p. 8.

[67]Canada, Proceedings of the Standing Senate Committee on National Finances (21 February 1981), issue no. 3, P. 3A:7 and 3A:8.

CHAPTER THREE

Regional Change and Regional Development Planning in Postwar France

THE EARLY YEARS

France's efforts with respect to comprehensive regional development planning (*aménagement du territoire*) evolved during the postwar years primarily as a response to what was widely perceived to be an overconcentration of population and economic activity in the Paris region and a concomitant neglect of the provinces. This disequilibrium was particularly emphasized by Gravier in a dramatic and influential book that contrasted Paris with the remaining "French desert."[1] Between 1880 and 1936, the Paris region absorbed 3.3. million immigrants from the provinces; the capital tripled in size, whereas the rest of France experienced an absolute decline in population. Between 1896 and 1936, industrial employment in France as a whole increased by 3%, but it rose by 45% in the Paris region. Traditional administrative centralization in Paris was strongly reinforced by the railway system, which, beginning in the 1830s, was constructed in a politically motivated pattern that radiated from the Parisian hub so that efficient relations could be maintained between the ministries and provincial prefectures. The lack of direct transportation linkages between provincial cities provided a strong inducement for further concentration of government, business headquarters, higher education, and financial institutions in Paris.[2] Between 1881 and 1975, the proportion of France's total population accounted for by the Paris region increased from 5% to 19%.[3]

The term *aménagement du territoire* was first used in 1949, when an office for *Aménagement du Territoire* was created within the Ministry of

Construction. The notion that policy interventions were necessary to bring about a "better distribution" of population and economic activity was consistent with the national system of indicative planning that evolved as a response to reconstruction needs following the war. The indicative plans implemented between 1946 and 1963 were undeniably successful. The French Gross National Product (GNP) rapidly surpassed its prewar level, and the attitudes and calculations of economic agents became increasingly based on the assumption that the economy would continue to expand and modernize.[4] However, although the need for regional development planning was widely acknowledged in principle, concrete achievements in this regard remained quite limited. During the 1950s, the central government encouraged local "expansion committees" and created a system of subsidies and tax concessions intended to induce firms to shift plants away from Paris or to open new ones in less developed areas. Restrictions were also placed on the location or expansion of factories in the Paris region. Despite some successes, these measures were not sufficiently strong to bring about the desired degree of decentralization and particularly not beyond a distance of 200 kilometers from Paris. Some regional plans were prepared, but they were largely descriptive, proposing vague goals and giving little attention either to means or to priorities. Moreover, there was no incentive to give these documents more precision, so long as they were virtually ignored in the national planning process.

When the Gaullists came to power, regional development policy was strengthened. However, before new regional programs were formulated and implemented, it was necessary to at least begin a reform of France's traditional administrative structure. Regional planning required a geographic scope broader than that afforded by the 90 (now 95) departments into which the nation was divided. In addition, each Paris ministry had organized its technical services on a different geographic basis, so that a reform was needed in order to harmonize their various activities spatially. In 1960 France was divided into 20 program regions, plus the region of Paris. (At present, there are 22 regions). Many of the "new" regions took names that recalled their medieval past, for example, Brittany, Languedoc, Provence, Alsace, Lorraine, Normandy (Upper and Lower), Burgundy, and the Franche-Comté. The prefect of the principal department in each region was designated the regional prefect and was given responsibility for coordinating regional economic programs. Regional administrative conferences were given responsibility for planning and implementing the parts of the national plan with regional implications. Their membership included the regional departmental prefects, as well as civil servants from the various national tech-

FIGURE 1. Regions, regional capitals, and departments of France.

nical services. In 1965, regional economic development committees were instituted to provide a consultative mechanism concerning the economic and social implications of the national plan in the respective regions. Their membership included both local elected officials and representatives from relevant socio-occupational groups. The Fourth Plan (1961–1965) included an initial attempt at quantifying regional objectives in a manner that would permit a nationalization of the regional plans. The procedure involved the elaboration of a catalogue of the public investment programs forecast at the regional level by some ministries for the years of the plan's application. However, the programs did not imply actual budget commitments. Beginning in 1965, this process was considerably extended, so that since then it has been possible to have information on the financial effort devoted to regional planning objectives, by region, as well as valuable data concerning the social and economic evolution of each region.

DÉLÉGATION À L'AMÉNAGEMENT DU TERRITOIRE ET À L'ACTION RÉGIONALE (DATAR)

In 1963, several bodies were established to bring greater spatial coherence to regional development planning at the national level. By far the most significant was the Délégation à l'Aménagement du Territoire et à l'Action Régionale (DATAR) because of the immediate operational responsibilities it was given with respect to the regional orientation of the national plan. Over time, DATAR has been attached to various ministries, but essentially it has been a relatively small and flexible interministerial body concerned with the promotion of regional development planning. In this regard, it has been less an administrative agency in the traditional sense than one geared to the coordination, guidance, and stimulation of government actions so that regional development issues are taken into account at various levels of government and in the national plans. A number of development funds have been subject to DATAR's influence, but until recently the most important has been the Special Fund for Regional Development Planning (FIAT). It has been used primarily to finance infrastructure projects that have not been specifically included in ministerial budgets but that have been deemed to be necessary for the application of regional policies. Although FIAT'S projects are planned and initiated by DATAR, they have always been designed to be taken over eventually by the relevant technical ministries. It has been estimated that during the 1970s, two-thirds of total FIAT resources were devoted to regions with a high priority for regional development projects. One-third was spent on large projects outside of priority regions; these included the industrial–port complex of Fos, near Marseille, provincial new towns, nuclear power plants, and high-technology complexes. Total FIAT outlays were multiplied by an estimated five times when account is taken of induced public and private expenditures. In 1984, the FIAT was allocated 856 million francs, and in 1985, 907 million francs.[5]

To facilitate DATAR's continuous process of adaptation to changing regional development issues, the agency's head has relied on a core staff that is few in number—recently some 40 persons—but highly qualified and representative of the entire spectrum of French public services. DATAR has maintained close links with central government agencies, and it has frequently organized interministerial work groups in order to promote its development objectives. In the regions, DATAR's correspondents have been the regional prefects—who since 1982 have been called Commissioners of the Republic—as well as locally elected officials, whose role has increased considerably since the initiation of administrative decentralization reforms in 1982 and 1983. Unlike the various ministries, DATAR has not had a formal network of "external services," but it has nonetheless subsidized public, private, and mixed entities that have served to implement its objectives at the regional and local levels in such matters as industrial and tourism development, rural renovation, metropolitan planning, and industrial conversion. Since 1969, DATAR has also maintained a network of information offices in Western Europe, Japan, and the United States to promote international investment in France, and particularly investments that can make a contribution to regional development policy objectives.

THE FIFTH PLAN: 1966–1970

The Fifth Plan represented a major breakthrough in the incorporation of regional objectives into the national planning process, and for the first time the regions were directly associated in the preparation of the plan. As in the Fourth Plan, a distinction was made between policies that would accompany the spontaneous development of the stronger regions and those that would attempt to induce development in the weaker ones. Among the eight broad policy measures were proposals to modernize agriculture and rural areas, to assist particularly vulnerable old industrial areas, to develop transport and communications networks, and to initiate a water policy. However, the principal new policies involved the industrialization of the west and the implementation of an urban development policy based on the concept of an urban hierarchy. The 10 regions of the west were to receive between 35% and 40% of new national industrial employment created between 1966 and 1970. Emphasis was placed on light industry and related services because of their labor-intensive nature and their relative freedom from transport and energy cost limitations. Urban policy accorded priority to the provision of "high-level" facilities for culture, research, higher education, medical care, government, and communications in nine large provincial urban complexes: Lille-Roubaix-Tourcoing, Nancy-Metz-Thionville, Strasbourg, Lyon-St. Etienne, Grenoble, Marseille-Aix, Toulouse, Bordeaux, and Nantes-St. Nazaire. The growth of these regional metropolises was intended both to counterbalance the "excessive" growth of the Paris region (which, however, was not to be deprived of its vital national and international roles) and to provide, by 1985, regional social and economic leadership, relatively free from dependence on Paris. In keeping with the hierarchical diffusion of innovation model popular at the time, the Fifth Plan also called for investments in "regional relay centers" that would be linked to the regional metropolises by rapid transport and communications, thus enabling the former to transmit the influence of the metropolises to their outlying hinterlands. Finally, provision was made for the development of new towns in the vicinity of Paris, as well as near such larger provincial cities as Rouen, Lille, and Lyon.

THE SIXTH PLAN: 1971–1975

The preparation of the Sixth Plan was marked by a relative emphasis on sectoral policies as contrasted with regional concerns, despite the fact that the technical and administrative means for the regionalization of the plan had been greatly improved. The immediate cause was fear of international competition as a result of Common Market trade liberalization. Indeed, the very principle of voluntaristic regional development planning was increasingly questioned by many leading industrialists and government officials, who argued that France's competitiveness depended on free market forces that alone could bring about higher productivity and lower costs. This implied limiting national planning in general, and, in the spatial domain, a concentration of investments in already-industrialized regions so that scale and external economies could be better realized.[6]

Despite these problems, the Sixth Plan, as finally elaborated, came out favoring the pursuit of regional development policy, even if the propositions presented in this regard were relatively sparse in comparison with those in the Fifth Plan. Unprecedented priority was given to environmental and quality-of-life issues, and numerous concrete measures were in fact implemented to realize the plan's objectives. Industrial decentralization, particularly in favor of the west, continued to be promoted. Decentralization of private decision-making centers, higher order service activities, and public investments were also encouraged. In urban policy, the Sixth Plan called for the promotion of medium-sized cities, those in the 20,000 to 200,000 population range. Between 1962 and 1968, cities in this group experienced population growth nearly equal to that in cities of over 200,000 population and the Paris region combined. It was felt that medium-sized cities offered an attractive life-style, that they provided locations for small industrial plants that provided employment opportunities for local rural populations, and that they served as relay points for innovative diffusion from regional metropolises. Although the plan merely suggested that policies for medium-sized cities should be entertained, DATAR followed up by organizing a system of "development contracts" between the national government and local elected officials, primarily in cities with between 20,000 and 100,000 inhabitants. The national government assumed about one-third of the total outlays, the rest being paid by the cities concerned. For the most part, the projects consisted of parking lots, green spaces, pedestrian streets, cultural facilities, and similar undertakings to enhance the quality of life, but they had relatively little to do with employment creation or regional development.

THE "GOLDEN AGE": AN APPRAISAL

A "golden age" is usually only recognized as such after the fact. If French regional development policy could be said to have had a golden age it was during the decade after the creation of DATAR in 1963. In contrast to the subsequent period of "crisis," the 30 years following World War II were characterized by sustained economic growth. In many respects the regional policies that emerged during this time can be viewed as an effort to redistribute the fruits of growth in a more spatially equitable manner, though efficiency objectives were also present, such as in the desire to reduce external diseconomies of agglomeration in Paris. Public opinion polls in the 1960s indicated that decentralization policies had wide public support among Parisians as well as provincial residents. In many respects, considerable progress was achieved by the mid-1970s in terms of major regional objectives. It should be pointed out, however, that many of these regional outcomes may well have occurred spontaneously, though perhaps not to the same extent, without explicit regional policies and programs. For examples, demographic and industrial decentralization were evident in numerous other industrial countries, no matter the degree to which regional policies were adopted. Moreover, French industrial decentralization, although quantitatively impressive, was often a mixed blessing for the receiving communities.

If the first wave of industrial decentralization, in the 1950s, largely favored regions near Paris, gradually more distant areas were also brought into this process. Meanwhile, contrary to all expectations, the growth of the Paris agglomeration was slowing; instead of the 9 million inhabitants forecast for 1968, the census of that year recorded only 8.25 million, and the number of outmigrants from Paris became nearly as numerous as the number of inmigrants. Between 1954 and 1962, the regions of the west and southwest lost 400,000 employed persons, but between 1962 and 1968 they gained 200,000, despite an acceleration of the exodus out of agriculture. The 1975 census confirmed this reversal of past trends. There was net outmigration from Paris and the regions of the west and southwest, which accounted for only 21% of new French industrial employment between 1954 and 1962, accounted for 53% between 1962 and 1968, and for 64% between 1968 and 1975. By 1975, Brittany, the Loire Region, and Poitou-Charentes traditionally sources of heavy outmigration, now registered net inmigration. The regional metropolises were growing more rapidly than Paris, and small and medium-sized cities were growing still faster. Migration was no longer uniquely in the direction countryside-small city-large city; there were also important streams of return migrants to rural areas and small towns.[7] The coefficient of correlation between French regional per capita income and regional net migration between 1954 and 1962 was 0.87. Throughout much of the 1960s interregional migration patterns continued to conform to neoclassical economic logic, with urban polarization, reinforcement of large industrial zones, and rural outmigration. However, the corresponding coefficient between per capita income and regional net migration between 1968 and 1975 was −0.57.[8]

On the other hand, of the 3,500 industrial decentralization operations undertaken between 1950 and 1975, only one-fifth of the establishments concerned became provincial in terms of headquarters location, and these typically were small firms. By 1971, 45% of all industrial employees working outside of Paris worked for firms based in the Paris region. Thus, even though the Paris region was losing manufacturing activities, it was maintaining its clear preeminence with respect to headquarters, functions, and the provision of higher order services.[9] Moreover, although Paris-based firms created 500,000 industrial jobs in the provinces between 1950 and 1975 (about half of all such employment created nationally during this period), they tended to be in the low-wage, relatively unskilled category, in keeping with the routine manufacturing of standardized products in the mature phase of the product cycle. Indeed, evidence indicates that industrial decentralization was less a consequence of regional policy than of a spontaneous movement away from the increasingly scarce and expensive labor of Paris in favor of "the privileged reservoir of unskilled labor: women, rural residents, immigrants, and the young."[10] A 1975 survey of 788 decentralization operations showed that only 30 were influenced by government subsidy programs, and that most of the plants went to areas that did not qualify for subsidies.[11]

Among the large projects that DATAR promoted outside the priority development regions, those involving industrial–port zones were particularly inspired by, or at least consistent with, the theory of growth poles formulated by French regional economists in the 1950s and 1960s. During the postwar years, the steel and petrochemical sectors played a major role in the growth of numerous industrialized nations. Because of the frequent need to import vast quantities of minerals and oil, these sectors were increasingly located in port complexes. Prior to 1974, three major industrial–port complexes were accorded priority development in France: Le Havre, on the Seine estuary; Calais-Dunkirk, in the north; and Fos, which was intended by DATAR to become "the economic pole of southern Europe." With the exception of Le Havre, which has benefited from greater diversification as well as its proximity to the Paris region, these massive efforts have had disappointing results. The Calais-Dunkirk complex, which was intended to be a catalyst for the industrial conversion of the north, has in fact experienced high rates of unemployment owing to the decline of the steel industry. In 1969, it was estimated that as many as 500,000 persons would be attracted to the pole of Fos, but by 1982 the actual number was only 60,000. As of 1980, the average amount of private investment alone needed to generate a new job in Fos was 1 million francs, and each new job indirectly induced only one other job in the region.[12] Part of the difficulty arose because of uncontrollable international variables, and part because of the centralized, top-down management style favored by the government and DATAR in the 1960s—an approach that hindered cooperation and resource mobilization at the local level. However, a large part was also due to overoptimism in terms of the growth pole approach to regional development. "The concept of diffusing regional development from a few spatial growth poles that attract industry and generate multiple induced effects, because of the growth of one or two generative industrial sectors, needs to be re-evaluated in light of experience with industrial-port zones. The integration of such poles with a socio-economic hinterland that already possesses a significant size and diversification seems to be an essential condition for real development."[13]

In urban policy, DATAR's centralized, top-down style had at least superficial parallels with the designation of regional metropolises in the context of the spatial hierarchical diffusion of innovation model. However, by 1974, urban development policy had become so lacking in focus that it would be difficult to speak of there having been any coordinated or consistent approach at all. In addition to the nine original regional metropolises, four others—Rennes, Clermont-Ferrand, Nice, and Dijon—were added in 1970. Other urban development efforts were made on behalf of the new towns near Paris and certain provincial cities; a group of "relay cities" on the periphery of the Paris Basin (Reims, Troyes, Orléans, Tours, Le Mans, Caen, Le Havre, Rouen, Amiens); medium-sized cities in the 20,000–200,000 population range; and finally even small towns in the 5,000–20,000 population range. With the onset of the crisis, DATAR's centralized orientation toward urban development was to give way to greater emphasis on the support of locally inspired actions, eventually to the point where a "policy" of too many policies, prior to 1974, seemed to evolve into a situation lacking any guiding principles concerning the role of the urban system in regional economic development.

REGIONAL DEVELOPMENT PLANNING AND THE "CRISIS"

Beginning in 1974, French regional development issues and policies were fundamentally altered as a result of a series of national and international difficulties that the French collectively subsume under the term *the crisis*. This period was characterized by a dramatic increase of petroleum prices, the disintegration of the international monetary system, a lowered rate of economic growth, massive unemployment, tight government budgets, and a reexamination of the desirability of the nature of modern growth. At the same time, French industry was experiencing increasing international competition from low-wage countries, as well as from its progressive integration into the European Common Market. French agriculture, although on balance benefiting from the Common Market, nevertheless was also required to adapt itself to a new policy environment. With mounting inflation and unemployment, the French system of indicative planning lost much of its credibility. President Valéry Giscard d'Estaing largely abandoned his predecessor's grand industrial policies—based on sectoral plans and a few large firms that were supposed to protect the many small and medium-sized producers that supplied and bought from them—in favor of greater reliance on market mechanisms and macroeconomic policies. In 1978, Giscard d'Estaing revived grand industrial policy, but the large firms that were promoted were no longer to dominate all parts of all markets. Instead they were supposed to develop expertise in particular market niches, expertise that would enable them to be competitive in those segments of world markets. Although this policy reduced France's trade deficit, it did not prevent inflation or a gradual increase in the rate of unemployment.

Because all regions were adversely affected by the crisis, each region demanded special treatment, without, however, wishing to pay the costs of assisting the others. Lacking a "surplus" from growth to redistribute, the means of regional development policy were concentrated in the most affected areas. This approach, which was largely justified on grounds of "national solidarity," had negative consequences. Given the difficulties of measuring precisely the various degrees of regional distress, the definition of zones to be assisted was often based more on the interplay of national and local political considerations than on objective criteria.[14]

THE SEVENTH PLAN: 1976-1980

The Seventh Plan was the last to be implemented before the Socialists came to power in 1981. (An Eighth Plan was being prepared for the 1981–1985 period, but it was scrapped by the Socialists in favor of a reformulated plan for 1984–1988, based on quite different perspectives.) It reflected the general evolution of the time toward economic liberalism and against impediments that planning might imply for the free functioning of the marketplace. Nevertheless, the regions were given an opportunity to make known the public investment priorities that they wished to have incorporated in the plan. There was remarkable agreement that social projects that would enhance the quality of life (health, education, recreation, etc.) should be given precedence over projects having a more economic orientation. For the most part, the plan itself contained little that was novel with respect to regional development objectives. It essentially called for efforts to help rural areas experiencing heavy outmigration and for means to rationalize urban growth patterns. The plan set forth 25 national priority action programs (PAPs) that the central government intended to assist financially. Only a few of these were specifically spatial in nature—for example, the improvement of transportation networks in the west, the southwest, and the central Massif, the improvement of navigation possibilities on the Rhone and Saone rivers, and the enhancement of rural areas. The national PAPs were complemented by regional and local PAPs involving joint funding by national and regional authorities. The funds designated for regional PAPs amounted to 5.5 billion francs, compared with 50 billion francs for the national PAPs and 199 billion francs for the entire plan.[15] Perhaps the most original regional planning aspect of the Seventh Plan was the policy of contracts for small rural regions (*contrats de pays*), which were used to maintain and encourage the socioeconomic development of small towns (5,000 to 20,000 inhabitants) and their rural environs. Regional public authorities, with subsidies and loans from the central government, were entrusted with carrying out this policy, as that of the previously implemented policy for medium-sized cities. Some 300 contracts were approved for these small towns, which, although accounting for only 10% of the national population, have nonetheless been growing more rapidly than any other size category of cities.[16]

DATAR ON THE DEFENSIVE

By the end of the 1970s there was mounting criticism of DATAR and the entire regional development planning process, which seemed to many critics to be more a means for responding after the fact to effects of market forces than a means for formulating and implementing novel undertakings. This argument was specifically raised by Aydalot with respect to the shifts in emphasis over time in urban development policy from the regional metropolises to medium-sized cities and then to small towns and rural areas.[17] Aydalot also argued that whereas the primary formal justification for industrial decentralization policy was the economic development of lagging regions, in fact this policy primarily benefited Paris. The industrial decentralization effort was not at all directed against Paris. None other than J. Monod, the head of DATAR during its golden age, expressed the reason for decentralization in a speech given at Chateauroux on 26 July 1972:

> To the extent that Paris will be freed of the services and jobs that are neither necessary nor useful to it, it will be technically possible to create the material conditions for giving Paris the maximum opportunity to increase its international financial role. The spatial division of labor, the inequality of opportunity in the regions, and the assignment of subordinate functions to the provinces are not unexpected by-products of a policy conceived according to other objectives, but rather the result—wholly accepted if not wished—of a policy patiently carried out for 25 years.[18]

As in other countries with industrial decentralization policies, the relevant subsidies were not given to urban or regional authorities but directly to business firms, and, in the case of France, primarily to large firms. It has been observed that French industrial policy in general has primarily benefited the state, its bureaucracy, and a few large corporations. The government has become one of industry's best customers, and in some markets its position approaches monopsony. One study found that only five large firms received 50% of all government subsidies for industry, including those for sectors, research and development, exports, and regional development. Another indicated that three public enterprises received nearly one-third of all subsidies and that nine firms (some public, some private) received over half. A survey of small and medium-sized firms, designed to evaluate the extent to which government funds for big business trickled down to their level, found that most subsidies flowed only as far as the subsidiaries of the large recipients. Small, independent firms lacked knowledge of government programs as well as clout with the bureaucrats. In addition, they are dependent on the speed with which they can obtain aid; to receive assistance far in the future is barely preferable to no aid at all.[19] In regional policy, DATAR was often accused of favoring large firms rather than undertaking the risks frequently associated with aiding small and medium-sized enterprises. In 1976, for example, three projects involving the automobile industry absorbed 30% of DATAR's outlays; and the amount of aid per job created was 25,000 francs, as compared with only 8,200 francs for 543 other assisted projects. Similarly, in 1976 subsidies for the north and Lorraine alone amounted to 39% of DATAR's industrial assistance.[20] The degree of support for these old industrial areas was criticized for being an excessively defensive effort to maintain past structures—a dependence on textiles, coal, and steel—or to neutralize the consequences of decline, while at the same time diverting funds from genuine regional development functions. Moreover, even on grounds of social justice it seemed questionable to devote so much aid to the north and Lorraine, when other regions that were also experiencing high unemployment rates could not generate the publicity given in the media to the problems of militant strikers in a relatively few large firms in the old industrial regions. It was clear that solutions for the latter would eventually have to involve the creation of new economic activities or outmigration, yet regional policy was not following these orientations. As Guichard argued,

> The problem of these regions is to find new directions and not be victimized by their symbols. In the long run, their human resources and their location at the heart of Europe's economic 'golden triangle' will be significant advantages. The duty of the State is to avoid transforming them into assisted regions, reinforcing thereby their negative image.[21]

By the end of the Seventh Plan period the links between national and regional planning had become very tenuous. In 1977, one DATAR official was quoted as saying that there were in fact no operational links between DATAR and the national plan.[22] The lack of progress with respect to the regionalization of the plan was also apparent in the Seventh Plan, though in any case this process could be viewed as a rather feeble substitute for genuine decentralization of decision-making authority. The regions were merely consulted about matters that local and regional elected officials would have decided for themselves in less centralized nations. The stage was set for the reform-minded Socialists to make decentralization a major objective when they came to power.

NEW ORIENTATIONS IN THE FRENCH REGIONAL ECONOMY

Before examining the innovations in regional development policy made in the Ninth Plan, it is first necessary to consider in more detail the nature and significance of dynamic demographic and economic phenomena that have necessitated fundamental revisions of the conventional wisdom that inspired the grand regional planning orientations of the precrisis period. In particular, spontaneous processes have compelled a fresh appreciation of the development possibilities represented by small and medium-sized enterprises (SMEs) and regions that have not depended on heavy industry. The section that follows discusses recent interregional migration patterns in the light of changing residential preferences, often conditional on noneconomic motives. Then the new dynamism of SMEs will be considered and related to the increasing importance of technological change and of the tertiary sector—and particularly producer services—for regional development.

INTERREGIONAL MIGRATION

By the late 1960s it had already become fashionable for residents of Paris and large provincial cities to forsake central city apartments for free-standing homes in the suburbs. Young urban professionals in particular began to exhibit an unprecedented anti-Paris snobbism, and many came to perceive that life in the warm south or near the sea or mountains could be more agreeable than that in Paris. Thus it became "almost more chic to say that you live and work in Annecy or Avignon than in Montparnasse—a strange reversal."[23] Between 1975 and 1982, Paris and its immediate suburbs lost 220,000 inhabitants. In contrast, rural communes, which accounted for 27% of the national population in

1975, recently accounted for 35% of all new construction.[24] Population in the Ile-de-France—excluding Paris and the ring of immediately adjacent departments—and in the western and southern portions of the Paris Basin increased at twice the national average annual growth rate, which was 0.43% between 1975 and 1982. The Rhone-Alps region, which contains Lyon and Grenoble, also grew more rapidly than the nation as a whole during this period. The traditionally lagging regions of the west experienced population growth and, taken as a whole, net inmigration. However, among all French regions, by far the most rapid growth took place in the two located on the Mediterranean Sea: Languedoc-Roussillon and Provence-Alps-Riviera. Despite an excess of deaths over births, this area grew at over three times the national rate because of very high net inmigration. This phenomenon was rather paradoxical in view of the fact that the Mediterranean regions were experiencing critical problems in the viticultural and agricultural sectors, high unemployment rates, and considerable restructuring within the industrial sector.[25]

Population decline between 1975 and 1982 was typical in a long but relatively low-density band of settlement extending from the Pyrenees in the southwest through the Massif Central to the Ardennes in the northeast. However, recent net inmigration has tended to offset much of the population deficit resulting from an excess of deaths over births; and much of this area has benefited from increasing family tourism and from the establishment of second homes used for leisure and vacation purposes. In contrast, the major old industrial region extending across northern France from Upper Normandy to Lorraine was experiencing heavy net outmigration. The number of departments in this northern fringe that had net outmigration increased from 10 during the 1968–1975 period to 16 between 1975–1982, and the outmigrants tended to be the younger and better educated members of the labor force.[26]

It should be stressed that the general movement of population from the north and northeast toward the regions of the south and southwest cannot be explained by differences in regional incomes, which remain higher to the east of a line from Caen, in Normandy, to Marseille, in the southeast. Rather, recent migration patterns seem more related to cultural processes than to economic variables.[27] People have been moving away from urban–industrial areas that have been losing their traditional environments and life-styles in favor of places that have retained their regional character. Similarly, changing social values have made it fashionable to remain close to one's traditional provincial roots, which has led to reduced outmigration from less industrial regions. Moreover, rural areas are less and less dependent on agriculture, and the diffusion

of transportation and communications has considerably reduced the disadvantages of rural locations with respect to the mobility of goods,
persons, ideas, and techniques. In contrast to large, congested urban
regions, the most dynamic environments—which nonetheless include
the Paris region—tend to associate cities that have a relatively high
quality of life with a rural milieu that has not been "ruined" by industrialization. The correlation between net migration and change in employment in the 22 regions was higher from 1975–1982 than from 1968–
1975, but evidence suggests that the direction of causation runs more
from migration to employment than in the opposite direction. Moreover, this process has favored regions that, although not characterized
by remarkably high growth rates, nevertheless have attributes that accord with widespread aspirations concerning quality of life and quality
of the environment.

SMALL AND MEDIUM-SIZED ENTERPRISES AND ENDOGENOUS DEVELOPMENT

Since the beginning of the crisis, large oligopolistic firms have on
balance laid off industrial workers. Meanwhile, for the first time since
the beginning of French industrialization, SMEs have been coming to
the fore and increasing their share of industrial employment. Moreover,
the regions that have displayed the greatest economic vitality in recent
years have been those where large oligopolies have been the least in
evidence and where the proportion of small and medium-sized firms
has been relatively high.[28] In comparison with firms in the old industrial
regions, those in the regions of the south and west have less need to
undertake radical technical adaptations, which limits the need to substitute capital for labor. Although the south and west are relatively specialized in industries that face increasing competition from low-wage
developing countries, their products tend to be protected by the specialized demand of French consumers as well as French utilizing industries. Moreover, labor in the SMEs of the south and west is less costly
than that in old industrial regions, and the workers are less organized
and less militant. In view of the extension of transportation and communications and the absence of urban–industrial congestion, firms have
been able to reap the benefits of the labor market at the same time that
white-collar and technical employees have been able to realize their
aspirations with respect to quality-of-life considerations.[29]

The resurgence of SMEs since the beginning of the crisis, after over
a century of continuous concentration of employment in large firms, is

one of the more remarkable attributes of the contemporary French economy. Data on the evolution of employment by size of establishment are presented in Table 1. The figures represent most paid employment, but do not include workers in agriculture, public administration, and public enterprises. During the 1969–1973 period employment grew by 300,000 to 400,000 workers per year, with the greatest increases being accounted for by large establishments, that is, those with 200 or more employees. With the onset of the crisis, total employment remained relatively stable over time. However, this aggregate stability masked major differences by size of establishment. Between 1974 and 1980, employment in large establishments declined by 557,000 workers, but it rose by 705,000 in the other two categories; small establishments alone accounted for an increase of 555,000 workers, a 16% gain. If one examines only the evolution of manufacturing employment, in view of the fact that service establishments are often small, similar results are obtained.

The data in Table 2 indicate that manufacturing employment declined in medium-sized and large establishments between 1974 and 1980. In contrast, whereas employment in small establishments declined between 1969 and 1973, it increased in the 1974–1980 period. The overall employment change patterns shown in Table 2 were also characteristic of most industrial sectors.

Other studies indicate that the proportion of French workers accounted for by firms with fewer than 50 employees increased from 43.1% in 1976 to 49.1% in 1983. The number of SMEs created between 1981 and 1983 averaged 68,000 per year; the corresponding figures for 1984 and 1985 were 73,000 and over 103,000, respectively, or a 20% increase over the last 2 years.[30]

The increase in importance of SMEs can be explained in part by factors associated with the crisis, which changed the industrial de-

Table 1. Change in Employment (Thousands) by Size of Establishment: 1969–1973 and 1974–1980

Size of establishment	Absolute change (thousands)		Percentage change	
	1969–1973	1974–1980	1969–1973	1974–1980
Small (1–19 employees)	+166	+555	+5	+16
Medium (20–199 employees)	+712	+150	+17	+3
Large (200 or more employees)	+863	−557	+22	−12
Total	+1,741	+148	+15	+1

Source. Xavier Greffe, *Territoires en France* (Paris: Economica, 1984), p. 56.

Table 2. Change in Employment (Thousands) in Manufacturing,
by Size of Establishment: 1969–1973 and 1974–1980

Size of establishment	1969–1973	1974–1980
Small (1–19 employees)	−104	+37
Medium (20–199 employees)	+154	−156
Large (200 or more employees)	+585	−495

Source. Xavier Greffe, Territoires en France (Paris: Econmica, 1984), p. 57.

centralization strategy pursued by large firms. These factors included increased transport costs caused by the energy crisis, the closing of some mass consumption markets, a diminution of interregional wage differences, and a decrease in the real value of government decentralization subsidies. The efforts made by large firms in order to adapt to the changing economic environment resulted in plant closings, increased automation, and the exportation of some activities. The consequent rise in unemployment was particularly marked among relatively low-skilled workers in local labor markets that experienced growth during the years of industrial decentralization. Survey evidence indicated that over 70% of the blue-collar workers were in the unskilled category in only 29% of the nondecentralized plants of large firms: However, this was the case in 59% of the decentralized plants of large firms and in 43% of local SMEs.[31] Similarly, Aydalot estimated that the ratio of unskilled to skilled workers was 1.05 in Paris, 1.44 in communes with between 50,000 and 100,000 inhabitants, 1.89 in communes with between 5,000 and 10,000 inhabitants, and 2.03 in rural communes. In terms of regions, the proportion of unskilled workers was 17% in the Paris region, 27% in the north, 33% in the southwest, 44% in the southeast, and 56% in the Paris Basin.[32]

Local areas where unemployment was especially severe typically lacked the decision-making capacity and human resources capable of initiating new local development projects. But it was precisely this dilemma that gave a strong impetus, both in the regional economic literature and in local practice, to find possibilities for the development of local entrepreneurship. Thus, Aydalot has argued that in place of an imported but tenuous regional economic dynamism, to which whole regions had become accustomed, it is now necessary to substitute an endogenous dynamism, which alone can bring about genuine development.[33] In terms of theory this implies a movement away from the top-down center–periphery analyses that fairly accurately described spatial economic processes during the 1950–1975 period, in favor of the analysis of "regional production processes" that take into account the interrelated technical, social, organizational, and spatial aspects of production. Furthermore, efforts in this regard, which have begun only relatively recently, need to take account of the fact that since the onset of the crisis, the phenomena that have been primarily responsible for generating development have been service firms in technologically advanced sectors and small, locally created industrial firms.

LOCAL DYNAMISM AND TECHNOLOGICAL CHANGE

In France, as elsewhere, virtually all regions attach considerable importance to high-technology activities in seeking solutions to their economic problems. In this regard they may take solace from a recent report prepared by the Organization for Economic Cooperation and Development on French national innovation policy, which finds that there may be an inherent conflict between the organization of French research and the new patterns of economic growth.[34] The traditional system, which emphasizes elite education and top-down, state-led, large-scale programs, may no longer be consistent with the stimulation of development and employment. It is increasingly clear that technology contributes to economic development through a bottom-up process in which small SME formation, entrepreneurial activities, diffusion of new technologies, and a large pool of skilled human resources are the critical factors. In regional terms, this implies a spatial decentralization of funding from the central government, so as to promote the growth of competitive markets that implement the diffusion of innovation. Innovation policies should not be bureaucratized at the regional level but should rather be targeted directly at SMEs. The report further suggests that generic technologies should be diffused throughout the industrial fabric and that the ability of the Agency for the Valorization of Research to support local initiatives should be strengthened.

It is noteworthy that the growth pole orientation that characterized much of French industrial development policy in the years prior to the crisis has had parallels with respect to research activities. The California model, and Silicon Valley in particular, has represented an example for emulation with respect to the polarization of advanced technology firms that were "footloose" in terms of traditional industrial location criteria. In this regard, the French Riviera appeared to be an especially promising region. IBM established a major research laboratory at La Gaude, a village near Nice, not only because of its proximity to an international airport but also because of its proximity to sun, sea, and mountain amenities as well as a university capable of providing researchers and engineers.[35] After Texas Instruments located in the same area, the French government decided to create, near Nice, a "city of science," Sophia Antipolis, that would concentrate a variety of research activities. In keeping with the Silicon Valley model, it was expected that numerous small-scale initiatives would be induced by the presence of a few large high-technology enterprises. Although some large French and foreign firms were attracted to the Sophia Antipolis complex, they tended to set up research centers, but only a very few manufacturing plants.[36] Moreover, the research activities of the complex had little relevance to existing local manufacturing firms, so the diffusion effects on local growth were minimal.[37] In view of the fact that the relationship between research and manufacturing is far less close in France than in Japan and the United States, Pottier concludes that France "must avoid relying on the mirage of local development initiated by the creation of research complexes, despite the fact that this is a fashionable notion," and instead emphasize decentralized research centers linked to dominant regional activities.[38]

The positive role that technological change can play in restructuring local economies has been receiving increasing attention in France. Perrin's analysis of how new structures emerged from older ones in the Alès Basin, some 60 miles north of Marseille, has received particular attention.[39] Perrin argues that local systems do not just incorporate technological progress but also produce it and that local dynamism tends to reinforce itself. During the 1950s the Alès Basin was a medium-sized industrial area characterized by the extraction and processing of natural resources. Between 1954 and 1980, employment in the area's coal mines declined from 15,000 to 1,200 workers. Meanwhile, thousands of jobs were also lost in such other traditional sectors as textiles, forestry, food processing, and construction materials. Yet contrary to what might have been expected, this isolated old industrial region experienced a remarkable rejuvenation by incorporating technological progress in a series of development phases. First, large local engineering and chemical plants that had been established before 1960 continued to develop technologically more sophisticated products and to improve workers skills. From 1960 to 1970, branch plants in the textile and electrical equipments sectors were located in the area. In keeping with the nature of French industrial decentralization during this period, the relevant activities involved mass production using low-skill labor. Beginning in the mid-1970s, the area attracted more externally controlled branch plants—at first in the electrical equipment sector and later in numerous other sectors—that utilized new technologies and relatively skilled labor. Then, from 1978 on, numerous SMEs were created; these

high-technology, high-skilled local undertakings have been largely export oriented. Meanwhile, there has been rapid growth of employment
in induced local producer-service firms, whose existence has in turn
made the area still more attractive for small and medium-sized industrial
enterprises. Today the economic structure of the Alès Basin is diversified and modern, with strong endogenous interindustry linkages.

The restructuring of the Alès economy was initiated and sustained
by two phenomena that have been generally characteristic of successful
French medium-sized local systems since the crisis: the introduction of
new technologies and the emergence of concerted local development
initiatives. The breakthroughs in terms of technological advance occurred in 1975, when skilled labor was created by a major new electrical
equipment plant, and between 1978 and 1982, when 16 local firms were
formed. The presence of numerous local decision-making centers in
Alès has reduced external dependence and enhanced internal integration and dynamism, particularly through spontaneous formal and infor-
mal collective planning mechanisms that address development issues. A
strong technical and general education system guarantees a supply of
skilled males and females who are adaptable to new technologies. Moreover, the labor market is open and flexible because it is not dominated
by one or a few large firms. The restoration of mining sites and the
provision of urban amenities has been undertaken to provide a high
quality of life. In addition, an agency assists entrepreneurs by introducing them to business associations, finding appropriate plant sites, helping them to obtain financial assistance, and by helping to relocate employees coming from outside the area. The restructuring of Alès and
similar experiences in other French communities suggest that the study
of local economic dynamism should not be limited merely to industrial
sectors, tertiary activities, exports, or other particular economic variables
but should rather treat this process in broad socioeconomic terms, as a
vital ecosystem that can acquire the capacity to innovate.[40]

It should be pointed out that emphasis on local development potentials does not imply an autonomous, development-from-below strategy.
Local systems are not incapable of dealing with the consequences of the
global technological revolution or the new international division of labor. Local dynamism based on SMEs can involve both a high degree of
endogenous decision-making control and extensive networks of external
contacts.

The French regional economics literature frequently advises regions
and communities not to bet their economic futures on interventions by
large external industrial enterprises. The nature of industrial decentralization that typified the pre-1975 period—branch plants, routine produc-

tion, low-skill labor—and the fact that large industrial firms have cut back employment during the crisis years lend considerable credence to this view. Nevertheless, some large industrial firms have initiated programs to support local development by establishing linkages with numerous innovative SMEs. Such programs have provided logistical support in terms of research centers, provision of land, and financial assistance, typically through loans rather than capital participation.[41] Rhône-Poulenc, for example, made an inventory of small high-technology firms to identify promising enterprises that had not been able to take advantage of their patent rights or had not been able to market their products. Some hundred small firms received contracts as a result. Similarly, Pechiney Ugine Kuhlman established a program of cooperation with regional SMEs seeking to ameliorate their cash flow by selling technologies abroad. The program involves common international marketing and contracting, as well as the direct association of small firms in large-scale projects where PUK needs their complementary activities.[42]

An emphasis on fostering local development potentials also does not imply that the central government should simply leave individual communities and regions to their own devices, especially in matters of technological innovation and adaptation. Numerous government institutions and authorities have in fact been created to promote local initiatives in one manner or another, but they have been slow to change their traditional modes of operation and to be unresponsive to the specific needs of persons attempting to initiate small scale projects.[43] For example, public regional research centers have tended to work through the intermediary of chambers of commerce instead of working directly with SMEs. Because such centers have acted more as providers of general information than as partners seeking specific solutions to a firm's specific needs, they have not been genuine catalysts for technological progress.[44] To be more effective they need to identify the specific technological requirements of SMEs and then express them in scientific terms for research institutions. Conversely, they should also be aware of technological information that may be valuable to firms even though the latter have not specifically solicited aid. In sum, regional research centers need to provide an active interface between firms and research institutions.[45]

Finally, the important role that banks and other financial institutions have in local development is evident. The experience of other countries indicates that it is vital to have the financial means to support not only the commercialization of products but also the different phases of technological innovation processes. In France the lack of risk capital in this regard remains a significant impediment to local economic dynamism.

THE ROLE OF THE TERTIARY SECTOR

Growth-pole theory and economic base theory both have regarded industrial expansion as the major factor in regional economic development. Within these contexts the tertiary sector has been essentially treated as a residual resulting from industrial development and population growth and therefore not in need of policy measures in its own right. In recent years, however, increasing attention has been given to the developmental role of the tertiary sector in general and producer services in particular. The growing importance of tertiary activities is not a phenomenon that opposes goods and services but rather involves a combination of the two. Goods manufacturing involves increasing amounts of nonmaterial inputs as firms devote more of their resources to research and development, engineering, distribution, marketing, management, and planning. Goods manufacturing is also associated with tertiary employment in related sectors. For example, considerable employment in tertiary activities is linked to auto production: auto sales and repair, transportation, driver training, car rentals, insurance, and tourism agencies. In 1980, the French auto industry employed 500,000 persons (many of whom were in internal producer services occupations), but employment in linked tertiary sectors was about twice as great.[46] More generally, the growth of producer services in France has proceeded rapidly since the 1960s; employment in this regard rose from 4.8% of total tertiary employment in 1962 to 8.1% in 1980.[47]

Valeyre's analysis of the spatial dynamics of tertiary jobs linked to French manufacturing from the beginning of the century to 1975 showed how the growth of employment in producer services within and external to firms has been related in increases in the division of labor. Internal and external producer services have a similar spatial distribution.[48] The Paris region has a very high concentration of employment in such activities. In contrast, the situation is relatively unfavorable in the west, the Massif Central, and Franche-Comté, whereas the southeast occupies a middle position. In 1975 the Paris region accounted for 22% of total French employment, but the region's share of producer services was 41% and reached 55% in technical engineering services and data processing, 61% in advertising, and 61% in marketing research. As a consequence of spatial concentration, provincial manufacturing firms often must turn to national producer service firms, usually Parisian, for such high-level services as research, advertising, marketing, and management consulting. The demand for highly specialized external producer services is particularly high among large multiplant manufacturing firms. Such services have tended to locate near the decision-making centers of the most important large enterprises, which are much more geographically concentrated than are small and medium-sized firms. The latter have relatively little effective demand for external producer services, with the exception of accountants and bankers. Moreover, because producer-service firms are oriented toward the needs of large firms, they often are not very responsive to the needs of small firms. Thus even dense concentrations of SMEs have not sufficed to attract producer services. It should be emphasized, however, that these findings only concern the period up to 1975 because of a lack of more recent comparable data. The industrial restructuring and diffusion of transportation and communications that have taken place since then have the potential to transform information networks and industrial organization, which in turn could reverse the long-run tendency toward geographic concentration of production in favor of a more balanced development among the different regions.

Planque has argued that the revolution in transportation and communications facilities, the diffusion of data-processing capabilities, and the diseconomies of large urban agglomerations have already in fact combined to create a solid basis for a decentralization of population and economic activity that is qualitatively superior to the industrial decentralization of the pre-1975 years.[49] However, in view of the persistence of spatial inequalities and the limited extent of decentralization to date, Cunha and Racine maintain that any expectation of dynamic processes that will automatically reduce regional inequalities is premature.[50] In particular, although the decentralization of producer services is neither technically nor economically insurmountable, their growth in peripheral areas is not likely to occur spontaneously. External relationships of industrial firms already are more a matter of industry–tertiary linkages than of industry–industry linkages, and this is likely to reinforce the advantages of major urban centers that already possess most of the sophisticated producer services. Thus, although the potential for decentralization is present, it is not likely to occur in significant degree without public policy measures that reinforce the endogenous potentials of peripheral regions. Monneyer similarly points out that producer service activities are dependent on their markets, but even more so on the quality of the skills locally available to them; therefore their expansion in a region presupposes the existence of a highly educated and creative work force.[51] The regions that are particularly privileged with respect to the quality of the labor force are those in the southern third of the country, as well as the Ile-de-France and, to a somewhat lesser extent, Alsace. Higher order services and research and development are, however, still heavily concentrated in the Ile-de-France. In 1982, for example, it accounted for 46.9% of national research and development employment. Rhone-Alps accounted for 9.6% and Provence-Alps-Riviera for 7.6%; no other regions had as much as 4%.[52]

THE STATE OF THE REGIONS IN THE 1980s:
A SYNTHETIC SUMMARY

The symbols shown in Table 3, which was made by the Working Group on Regional Disparities for the Commissariat Général du Plan during the preparation of the Ninth Plan, represent a synthesis of cur-

Table 3. *Relative Degree of Economic and Social Problems in French Regions in the 1980s*

	Level of economic development	Employment change since 1974	Labor market situation in 1982	Level of social development
Alsace	+	+	+ +	+ +
Aquitaine	=	+	=	+ +
Auvergne	=	+	+	=
Lower Normandy	−	+	=	−
Burgundy	=	=	+	=
Brittany	−	−	=	=
Center	+	+	+	=
Champagne-Ardennes	+	−	=	−
Corsica	−	=	=	=
Franche-Comté	=	−	+	−
Upper Normandy	+	−	−	−
Ile-de-France	+ +	−	+ +	+ +
Languedoc-Roussillon	−	+ +	−	+
Limousin	−	=	+ +	=
Lorraine	=	−	=	−
Midi-Pyrenees	−	+	=	+
North-Pas-de-Calais	−	−	−	−
Loire Region	=	+	−	=
Picardy	=	=	−	−
Poitou-Charentes	−	+	−	=
Provence-Alps-Riviera	+	+	−	+ +
Rhone-Alps	+	−	+	+ +

Note. The symbol − indicates maximum difficulty, and the symbol + + indicates minimum difficulty. These symbols represent a position in relation to other regions and should not be interpreted quantitatively. The symbol = does not necessarily imply a value equal to the national average but only a middle position among the regions. The symbols in Column 2 do not necessarily imply absolute increases or decreases in employment but rather reflect trends in employment change.

Source. Commissariat Général du Plan, *Rapport du Groupe de Travail Disparités Spatiales* (Paris: La Documentation Française, 1984), p. 97.

rent economic and social tendencies in the 22 regions. Given the context of the post-1974 period, none of the regions is in a wholly satisfactory situation. Nevertheless, there are clear differences in the acuteness and extent of regional problems. Two groups can be readily identified. The first includes the relatively strong regions and the second those that are confronted by severe social and economic difficulties. The remaining regions are in an intermediate category; the existence of marked problems in certain domains does not threaten the entire regional economy.

The group of strong regions includes Ile-de-France, Rhone-Alps, Alsace, and Provence-Alps-Riviera. Although employment in manufacturing and in lower order services has been declining in the Ile-de-France, the labor market situation has been less adversely affected than that in the nation as a whole. Higher order service activities have been growing rapidly and the unemployment rate is relatively low. Per capita income is by far the highest in France, and the region ranks highest in terms of most social indicators. Rhone-Alps has many of the same advantages as Ile-de-France, though in lesser degree. The decline in manufacturing employment that it has experienced since 1974 has been more severe than the corresponding decline in Ile-de-France, but its overall unemployment rate nonetheless remains relatively low. The Alsation economy, which benefits from proximity to West Germany, has been even stronger than that of Rhone-Alps. Provence-Alps-Riviera is the least industrialized of the strong regions. Although it ranks eighth among all regions in per capita regional product, it ranks sixth in per capita income because of transfer payments to the elderly and the unemployed. Despite steady employment growth, the unemployment rate has remained relatively high because of continuing heavy inmigration. Provence-Alps-Riviera is clearly among the top four regions in terms of most indicators of health and education attainment.

The principal group of regions with severe and mutually reinforcing social and economic difficulties is located in the old industrial area stretching from the English Channel to the Swiss border. This group includes North-Pas-de-Calais, Picardy, Upper Normandy, Champagne-Ardennes, Lorraine, and Franche-Comté. The textile and coal sectors were already in difficulty during the period of strong growth prior to 1974, but since then there has been a steep decline in overall industrial employment in the north and Lorraine and general stagnation in the other regions in this group. Relatively large numbers of young persons in the total population and lack of employment opportunities have resulted in high unemployment, primarily in the northern zone, and accelerated outmigration, principally from the eastern areas. The relatively high per capita incomes found in the old industrial areas are not likely to persist without considerable industrial restructuring; the standard of living in the once-prosperous north has already become significantly inferior to that in the rest of the country as a result of many years of adverse structural problems. The combination of employment decline, large numbers of young persons entering the labor force, low levels of educational attainment, and inferior social infrastructure cause the departure of the better educated and more highly motivated elements of the population, as well as to preclude the initiation of new activities with new technologies and promising growth prospects.

In addition to the old industrial regions, the essentially rural regions of Limousin and Corsica are also experiencing acute difficulties. In both regions there is a relatively high proportion of older persons and a relatively low proportion of persons in the professional and managerial categories. In Limousin, and to a lesser extent Corsica, the unemployment rate is low because of an inactive labor market: There are few jobs but also few young persons seeking employment.

The remaining regions, those in an intermediate situation, are found in the west and the south. Although this is not a homogeneous group, the importance of agriculture is relatively great, and per capita regional product and income tend to be lower than the national average. However, most of these regions have been experiencing relatively rapid total employment growth, often in SMEs. One exception is Burgundy; its economy is dominated by large firms and employment change there has been comparable to that in the nation as a whole. Another exception is Brittany, where, although industrial employment has held up well, total employment growth has been limited by a large exodus from the relatively large agricultural sector. The southwestern regions of Aquitaine, Midi-Pyrenees, and Languedoc-Roussillon all rank high in terms of indicators of health, education, and social infrastructure. This is particularly the case for Aquitaine, whose overall level of social development is comparable to that of Provence-Alps-Riviera. And among all French regions, only Languedoc-Roussillon has experienced growth in industrial employment since 1974.

Finally, a shift–share analysis was made during the preparation of the Ninth Plan in order to identify the residual, or "competitiveness," component of employment change in each region.[53] This is the part of the rate of employment change that cannot be explained by either the national effect (assuming each regional sector would have experienced the national rate of change in that sector) or by the structure of regional employment. The study covered 40 sectors and compared the 1968–1975 period with 1975–1981. Between these two periods there was a pronounced increase in the relative importance of the competitiveness effect, suggesting a relative increase in the importance of endogenous factors in regional development. Languedoc-Roussillon had by far the greatest positive value for the competitiveness component of both total and industrial employment change, followed by a group of regions, including the other five southwestern regions, the Loire Region, Lower Normandy, and Alsace. In contrast, industry appeared to be repelled by the nature of the old industrial regions in the distressed northern arc.

DECENTRALIZATION AND THE NINTH PLAN: 1984–1988

In 1981, François Mitterand, the new Socialist president, declared that "to become what it is [*pour se faire*] France had need for strong and centralized power; today it needs decentralization of power in order not to become undone [*pour ne pas se défaire*]."[54] Decentralization, the *"grande affaire"* of the Socialists, was given an unprecedented legal basis by a law passed on 2 March 1982; by 1985, 20 laws and more than 180 decrees had been promulgated to define and organize the new division of competencies, powers, and means between the central government and regional and local authorities.[55] Before 1982, the regional budgets were for all intents and purposes controlled by regional prefects, who were appointed by the national government. Regional councils deliberated but could neither legislate nor execute economic policies and programs. The reform provided for the election of regional councils by direct universal suffrage and essentially transferred the powers of the regional prefect to the presidents of the regional councils. Under decentralized indicative planning, regional plans are to be established side by side with the national plan, and major responsibilities for economic policy are delegated to the regions. Regions can now intervene on behalf of companies in difficulty, and they can decide which firms to subsidize in order to create new employment. In effect, however, these interventions are limited to SMEs. In cases where assisted investment projects have significant national consequences—for example, when major projects of large firms affect opportunities in more than one region—the responsibility for industrial policy decisions is at the national rather than the regional level.

Although the regional councils were consulted during the preparation of the Ninth Plan, their influence on its principal orientations was marginal. Because the decentralization reforms were phased in only gradually over a number of years, the regions were still operating under the old, largely centralized system of planning. Nevertheless, in 1983 and 1984 the regions were invited to define their priorities, which, after

modification at the national level, became embodied in a system of national–regional planning contracts.

NATIONAL–REGIONAL PLANNING CONTRACTS

At the heart of regional development planning in the Ninth Plan are
contracts concluded between the central government and the regions.
These contracts define concrete actions that the central government and
the regions jointly commit themselves to undertake during the period of
application of the plan. The emphasis given to the contractual nature of
this effort reflects the intent of the Socialists to transform the central
government's traditional authoritarianism in dealing with the regions.

The first stage of the contracting process for the Ninth Plan involved
the formulation of regional plans after consultations among elected officials and advisory groups representing various social and economic interests. Then the central government reviewed the regional plans to
identify regional objectives that coincided with the goals of the national
plan, in this case the 12 priority execution programs that represented the
major orientations of the Ninth Plan. After a period of negotiation, the
contracts as finally adopted were signed by the presidents of the regional councils and the regional prefects, representing the national government. For the first time in history of the regionalization of the plan, the
central government and the regions went beyond merely drawing up a
catalogue of intentions and establishing very global financial "enve-
lopes." Rather, the partners agreed upon specific programs with assured levels of financing. Another important difference from past regional development planning was a shift in emphasis in the regional
plans away from infrastructure projects in favor of more support for
directly productive activities and of efforts to deal with employment
problems.

As the data in Table 4 indicate, the central government committed
38.9 billion francs to financing planning contracts with the regions,
which themselves agreed to expenditures of 25.9 billion francs. The
outlays of the regions represent a significant part of their total budgets—
between 30% and 60%, depending on the region. In addition to the
funds shown in Table 4 (which are about 18 times the industrial subsidies of DATAR from 1974 to 1980), an approximately equivalent
amount of investments would be made in the regions through the budgets of departments, communes, and chambers of commerce. Ile-de-
France was the only region to contribute more than the central government, but its massive demographic and economic resources give it un-

Table 4. Funds (in Millions of Francs) Committed to National–Regional Planning Contracts for the Period of the Ninth Plan: 1984–1988

Region	Central government funds	Regional funds
Alsace	1,100	700
Aquitaine	1,470	930
Auvergne	775	450
Burgundy	851	601
Brittany	1,804	814
Center	860	610
Champagne-Ardennes	850	445
Corsica	1,100	300
Franche-Comté	847	550
Ile-de-France	7,137	8,465
Languedoc-Roussillon	1,381	776
Limousin	757	308
Lorraine	2,979	942
Midi-Pyrenees	1,433	787
North-Pas-de-Calais	3,950	2,450
Lower Normandy	770	450
Upper Normandy	865	523
Loire Region	1,180	883
Picardy	1,776	851
Poitou-Charentes	1,250	630
Provence-Alps-Riviera	2,796	1,897
Rhone-Alps	2,980	1,520
Total	38,911	25,882

Source. Délégation à l'Aménagement du Territoire et à l'Action Régionale, *Rapport d'activité 1984–1985* (Paris: DATAR, 1986), p. 11.

usual financial means. In the other regions, the ratio of central government-to-region contributions was on average 1.8 to 1.0. In terms of total contract funds per capita, the average amount was 1,180 francs, ranging from 651 francs for the center to 1,628 francs for the north, which, along with Lorraine (1,465 francs) benefited from special industrial restructuring efforts.[56]

The distribution of the 8.7 billion francs that the central government devoted in 1985 to national–regional planning contracts provides at least a rough indication of the priorities accorded to various activities. Transportation received 32.2%; agriculture, 17.7%; tourism and the environment, 16.3%; health and related social projects, 12.6%; education, 9.8%; research and industrial modernization, 7.4%; and cultural development, 3.6%.[57]

Although the Ninth Plan as a whole was not taken very seriously

after a change of government and economic policies in 1984, the national–regional planning contract initiative nevertheless appeared to be
successful in many respects. The national press, in particular, strongly
approved of this evolution in inductive planning. The regions had the
rare experience of at least a similitude of "negotiation" with Paris, and
Paris was clever enough to tell each region that its planned projects were
"the best," thereby creating an illusion of "getting more than the others."[58] In fact, the regional planning process did result in considerable
political unanimity and greater regional cohesion. In many cases it affirmed a regional identity previously ignored or even denied, and it
helped to develop, at the regional level, greater planning expertise and
an enlarged capacity for negotiation.[59] Guillaume argues that the planning contracts have revealed a desire to break with tradition and promote the future through advanced technology, rather than prolonging
the past. The contracts

> have created an environment in which decentralized initiative is
> flourishing. They emphasize helping others to help themselves.
> Each region has developed its own set of institutions for delivering
> such help. Some cooperate with private enterprise through local
> chambers of commerce; others have developed special associations
> of private enterprises; still others have created local committees to
> support growth.[60]

On the negative side, although the plans formulated by the regions
contained many project proposals, it is difficult to discern in them any
clear regional development strategy.[61] This lack was also reflected in the
planning contracts, which involved a large number of sectors and sometimes an excessive dilution of funds spread thinly over multiple projects.
In a sense it could be said that the contracts represent a substitute for
genuine regional plans. Moreover, the actual content of the contracts
was heavily influenced by the central government; for fear of "losing
money," the regions frequently agreed to share in financing projects
that were not among their own priorities. Thus, in many domains, the
supposedly regionalized contracts call for the same actions. This was
particularly evident in cultural matters, where Paris imposed an identical policy on each region. For the regions, the contracts represent a
"freezing" of a large part of their total resources according to objectives
established in the national plan. In many cases this involves considerable additional efforts, sometimes outside of any previous experience, as
in higher education. In contrast, funds provided by the central government are for the most part those that would have been made in the
regions even in the absence of planning contracts.[62] Finally, the regional

plans emphasized actions directed toward the "environment" for promoting productive activities (research, education, technology transfer) to the detriment of traditional infrastructure.[63] But, as was shown previously, the central government's 1985 budget for planning contracts devoted about one-third of the total to transportation infrastructure, and another 17.7% to agriculture, which is not even one of the Ninth Plan's own 12 priority execution programs.

Although decentralization initiatives seem to be flourishing at the regional and local levels, it is still evident that the centralizing traditions of Colbert die hard in France. If the contractual process survives its apprenticeship,

> It will be, in particular, necessary—and difficult—to make all the partners understand that decentralized planning does not stop at the signature of national–regional planning contracts or at their implementation.[64]

INDUSTRIAL POLICY

When the Left came to power in 1981, it proceeded to implement numerous policies that it had advocated during its years in opposition. The government budget for 1982 entailed a 27% increase in spending over 1981. Minimum wages and social benefits were increased sharply, the workweek was reduced to 39 hours, and a fifth week was added to annual vacation leaves. During the summer of 1981 alone, 55,000 new jobs were added in the public sector. An unprecedented program of nationalization was undertaken, following which public enterprises employed 750,000 workers, produced 25% of industrial output, and accounted for more than half of production in highly concentrated, capital-intensive sectors with large research expenditures and a high propensity to export. Efforts were made to reverse the decline in manufacturing employment, to rescue industries in trouble, and to reduce the share of imports in domestic consumption. The government also attempted to intervene in vertical streams of production (it became popular in the regional economics literature to analyze these *filières*) in order to promote a tightly knit industrial fabric. It was held that no niche is viable on its own; it depends on the viability of vertically linked activities, upstream and downstream.[65]

By 1984 it was clear that the Left was failing to achieve its own economic objectives. Public enterprises were drowning in red ink, manufacturing employment declined, and productive investment stagnated. The French share of world markets fell from 10% in 1980 to 8.5% in 1984, whereas imports increased. Little was achieved with respect to the "reconquest" of domestic markets or the buttressing of whole vertical production streams. Major redirections of industrial policy initiated in 1983 were confirmed in 1984 with the resignation of Pierre Mauroy as prime minister and his replacement by Laurent Fabius. Modernization replaced employment as the goal. The importance of the home market and the need to occupy all stages of each *filière* were no longer mentioned. Public enterprises had to become profitable even if they laid off workers, and private companies had to become more competitive because the economy would be open to increasing foreign competition. "Speeches by members of the government became full of references to modernization, innovation, entrepreneurial spirit, and even profit. References to economic and social inequalities, worker participation, and full employment were no longer heard. The microeconomic austerity practiced in the public sector was thus extended. The sectoral plans were slowed down or abandoned."[66] Nevertheless, the government did not abandon all of its activism. In particular, it reinforced its regional policies. To cope with the decline of traditional industries in old industrial regions, it introduced a new policy of *pôles de conversion* (industrial restructuring poles). In addition, the promotion of research was one area in which the government continued to pursue its original strategy, which has recently been complemented by local efforts to create "*technopôles.*"

PÔLES DE CONVERSION

In 1984, the government designated 15 *pôles de conversion*, zones that would benefit from new programs or enhanced funding under existing programs because the areas were particularly adversely affected by industrial transformations. The industries concerned were principally the declining steel, mining, and shipbuilding sectors but also included the less "traditional" auto and telecommunications sectors, which were experiencing strong international competition. The designated zones were located in nine regions, but most attention was focused on the north and Lorraine.

The special measures for the *pôles de conversion* were both economic and social in nature. The first programs involved 1.6 billion francs for public works programs that would provide immediate employment. These were followed by programs concerning research, education, business expansion, and further infrastructure development. In 1984 and 1985, 4.5 billion francs were budgeted to assist projects that would create employment in public and private enterprises. A special fund for

Lorraine received 500 million francs, and other diverse activities received 305 million francs.[67] The costs of social measures taken in the name of "national solidarity" could not be established beforehand, but they were estimated to be nearly equal to the value of new investment in the steel industry.[68] The social measures often involved special payments for early retirement and voluntary "quits." In 1984, the government increased payments to laid-off workers in the steel, coal mining, and shipbuilding sectors to 70% of their base pay for 2 years. Because these payments were associated with the concept of regional revitalization, they were termed "leaves for retraining" (*congés de conversion*). The government also instructed public enterprises to take the consequences of their cutbacks into account, particularly by creating "restructuring companies" (*sociétés de conversion*) that were supposed to seek out and encourage replacement activities in *pôles de conversion*. In addition, a number of large private firms created similar companies.[69]

Despite the efforts made on behalf of the *pôles de conversion*, in retrospect it appears that they mainly served to cushion the effects of market forces rather than to reverse regional decline. In part this was due to the continuing weak condition of the French economy, but there were also some specific factors that hindered restructuring. For example, despite subsidies and government pressures, many potential replacement industries—including public enterprises—simply refused to locate in *pôles de conversion*, and some that did were themselves declining sectors. Moreover, local firms and elites frequently lobbied against the entry of new industry, placing labor market and local power considerations above regional development objectives.[70] In the north and Lorraine, efforts by the restructuring companies did result in the creation or preservation of some 10,000 jobs,[71] but overall these groups have had only a marginal impact on regional restructuring. In particular, they have had little effect in stimulating the development of SMEs, which was supposed to be one of their principal objectives.[72]

TECHNOPÔLES

In recent years, local public authorities in most regions have created "science parks" intended to attract high-technology activities. These projects, which have come to be known as *technopôles*, attempt to promote technology transfer and cross-fertilization among research centers, higher education, and industry. They should not be equated with the *pôles technologiques* that DATAR has been encouraging for some years. The latter term refers to technical–industrial *filières* that government research policy has tried to reinforce, upstream and downstream, through the activities of regional centers for innovation and technology transfer, of which more than 100 are in existence. The economic consequences of a *pôle technologique* are likely to be widely diffused regionally and even interregionally. In contrast, a *technopôle* implies a relatively high degree of concentration of spatial outcomes.

Although it lacks any official science park, Paris and its southern suburbs clearly represent the foremost *technopôle* in France. There, "within a few kilometers of one another, are found universities, *grandes écoles*, research institutes, industrial laboratories, and firms specialized in high technology. If there is a French equivalent to Silicon Valley this is it."[73] At the second rank are Lyon, Toulouse, and Grenoble, each of which has, in its own way, simultaneously developed education–research–production complexes. In contrast, isolated technopôles are rather rare. The most prominent is Sophia Antipolis (mentioned earlier), to which may be added Atalanta, a Breton *technopôle* consisting of high-technology activities grouped around the National Center for Telecommunications Studies, which was decentralized from Paris in 1971. Most other *technopôles* are still only in the project stage, though Metz 2000, in Lorraine, recently was selected, after considerable local efforts, as the site for France's first teleport. Given that Metz 2000 also has the School for Advanced Electrical Studies, it may well have a bright future as a communications center. For the mayor, in any case, these developments promise "to preserve my city and my region from a third shipwreck, after those of steel and the automobile."[74] But certainly not all of the *technopôle* initiatives—which often absorb large amounts of local resources—will succeed. Put in the context of increasing international, as well as national, competition, for every few "star" cases, "there are hundreds of science and technology parks in OECD nations struggling to 'make it.' Many can be expected to renounce their original objective and turn into hybrid industrial developments as holding costs dictate that other functions must be admitted. Others will fail entirely."[75]

Even the successful *technopôles* do not account for enough employment to expect that they themselves could, in the short term, significantly reduce France's high rate of unemployment—about 12% in 1987. Nor have they—Paris aside—induced the industrial spread effects that one associates with Boston's Route 128 or Silicon Valley, though these continue to influence the expectations of many *technopôle* developers.[76] On the other hand, spatial concentration of high-technology activities does appear to be efficient in view of the external economies of agglomeration that are realized. At the same time, however, the greater ease of long-distance communications means that there may well be more interactions among *technopôles* than between *technopôles* and their respective hinterlands. To the extent that this will be the case, the provincial *technopôles* may well play an increasing role in the long run in promoting more "balanced" development vis-à-vis Paris, but they may also produce development that is more spatially "unbalanced" at the regional level.

WITHER FRENCH REGIONAL DEVELOPMENT PLANNING?

In 1986 the parties of the center–right returned to the government under a free market banner, and by 1987 they had brought about sweeping privatization and deregulation. Part of the strategy of the new minister of industry was "to forbid his subordinates to include interventionist proposals in their reports to him,"[77] though he would try to help SMEs and to promote enterprise zones throughout France. The noninterventionist stance was reflected in the status accorded to DATAR, which was criticized for being too large and bureaucratic, for having too many different kinds of assistance funds, which tended to compartmentalize its activities, and for having lost flexibility by committing too many of its resources to national–regional planning contracts. In real terms, DATAR's budget for intervention in regional development planning fell by 53% between 1980 and 1986. Moreover, for all practical purposes DATAR was excluded from playing its essential, activist interministerial role on behalf of regional development policies.[78] With decentralization, many government agencies, banks, and public enterprises began to deploy their own respective strategies at the local and regional levels, diffusing various types of development formulas and assistance in an attempt both to create and to satisfy local and regional demands. This remarkable phenomenon tended to deprive DATAR of its unique entrepreneurial role with respect to local initiative and regional development projects.[79] By 1987, DATAR had been stripped of its functions with respect to human resources development and medium and long-term development planning and evaluation. Rural planning was also slated for transfer to the Ministry of Agriculture. The principal functions that remained were coordination of French and Common Market regional policies, attraction of foreign capital to declining industrial areas, attraction of multinational European headquarters to Paris, and coordination of certain large infrastructure projects, notably *autoroutes* (express highways).

In April 1987, Prime Minister Chirac announced a new plan that will add, at a cost of 70 billion francs, 2,730 kilometers of *autoroutes* to the

5,700 already realized. At the time, he stated that this decision clearly showed the importance that his government attached to regional development planning, "which has not gone out of style, but rather is needed again in the perspective of the creation of a large, single European market in 1993."[80] He further pointed out that the mission of regional development planning should be "to open the regions to one another as well as to the European Community, to create the conditions for economic development as balanced as possible, and to promote the adaptation and development of certain sensitive territories: rural zones and regions most adversely affected by the crisis."[81] Nevertheless, it was not clear how the *autoroutes* policy was supposed to improve the development of France's regions or the nation's international competitiveness. One observer thought that the policy would have the merit of placing France in the center of Europe, so that the British could more easily go to Spain and the Belgians to Italy.[82] This seems to indicate that the new regional development policy primarily represents a rather expensive gift from France to its neighbors.

It would be ironic if French decentralization efforts were to result in a dismantling of French regional development planning. It has been argued that "decentralization is, by all evidence, a process whose effects will be seen in the long run. One should not be too preoccupied with transitory phases and temporary problems. It is in the long run that one should examine the efficiency of the decentralization process."[83] Be that as it may, it is already clear that decentralization should not be viewed as a substitute for regional development policy. As the national–regional planning contract process has shown, the central government is still reticent concerning the transfer of real power to the regions, which in turn often do not have the resources and competence to undertake development planning in terms of well-considered goals and strategies. The regions also have tended to favor already-growing sectors and localities at the expense of lagging areas, thereby threatening to produce, at the intraregional level, the imbalances that regional policy has sought to ameliorate at the interregional level. Given this state of affairs, it would be premature to expect that decentralization will assure adequate regional development planning. This further suggests a continuing need for DATAR but a reformed DATAR that would concentrate on regional development projects with multiregional implications and coordinate the new decentralized regional planning with national objectives—a vital function in a France that is still far from being or becoming a federal state.

Finally, despite the many criticisms that have been made concerning the past performance of DATAR, and regional development planning in general, it is worth recalling that progress has been made with respect to key long-term objectives. There has been a slow but steady reduction in interregional inequalities. Including Ile-de-France, the regional per capita income index (France = 100) ranged from 79 to 144 in 1962; by 1985 the corresponding values were 89 to 131. Without Ile-de-France, the 1962 range was from 79 to 100, and the 1985 range was from 89 to 100.[84] The industrialization of the Paris Basin and the west, much criticized from a qualitative point of view, has in fact held up relatively well during the crisis. And the development of the regional metropolises and some other comparable cities has profoundly modified the Paris–French desert image. France today is a nation of cities, not a nation of one city, Paris. The new provincial urbanites, it has been argued, have chosen equilibrium "among professional success, family, and leisure, the three central values of the French today. In Paris, one desperately pursues the three and in the end sacrifices two. The success of the large provincial cities is to have reconciled all three values."[85]

It could be argued that these phenomena might well have occurred in any case, but it seems fair to conclude that regional development planning has played a positive role in promoting and orchestrating the process of change. It also has contributed to the alleviation of numerous local problems, even if it has not been able to, and cannot be expected to, reverse the fortunes of large, old industrial areas that resist fundamental restructuring. One should not claim too much for French regional planning or its possibilities for changing the outcomes of the marketplace. But neither should one be too pessimistic about the possibilities that do exist for making a positive difference, whether by accelerating or sustaining spontaneous development, or by correcting, however modestly and after the fact, some of the less desirable consequences of structural change.

NOTES

[1]Jean-François Gravier, *Paris et le Désert Français* (Paris: Flammarion, 1947).

[2]Joseph Lajugie, Pierre Delfaud, and Claude Lacour, *Espace Régional et Aménagement du Territoire,* seconde édition (Paris: Dalloz, 1985), pp. 72–74.

[3]Jean Watin-Augouard, *La France* (Paris: Ellipses, 1986), p. 45.

[4]Henri Aujac, "An Introduction to French Industrial Policy," in William James Adams and Christian Stoffaes, eds., *French Industrial Policy* (Washington, DC: The Brookings Institution, 1986), p. 14.

[5]Jean-Paul Laborie, Jean-François Langumier, and Priscilla de Roo, *La Politique Française d'Aménagement du Territoire de 1950 à 1985* (Paris: La Documentation Française, 1985), pp. 24–26.

6Lajugie *et al.*, *Espace Régional et Aménagement du Territoire*, pp. 288–91, 909.

7Ibid., pp. 439–440.

8Philippe Aydalot, "Crise économique, crise de l'espace, crise de la pensée spatiale," in Bernard Planque, ed., *Le Développement Décentralisé* (Paris: Presses Universitaires de France, 1983), p. 92.

9Olivier Guichard, *Propositions pour l'Aménagement du Territoire* (Paris: La Documentation Française, 1986), p. 10.

10Philippe Aydalot, "L'aménagement du territoire en France: une tentative de bilan," *L'Espace Géographique*, Vol. 7, No. 4 (October 1978), p. 251.

11Ibid.

12Laborie *et al.*, *La Politique Française*, p. 18.

13Ibid., p. 96.

14Guichard, *Propositions pour l'Aménagement du Territoire*, pp. 11–12.

15Lajugie *et al.*, *Espace Régional et Aménagement du Territoire*, p. 321.

16Laborie *et al.*, *La Politique Française*, p. 35.

17Philippe Aydalot, *Une Evaluation Critique de l'Aménagement du Territoire*, Dossier du Centre Economie, Espace, Environnement, Université de Paris I, December 1980, pp. 17–18.

18Ibid., p. 15.

19Aujac, "An Introduction to French Industrial Policy," pp. 32–35.

20Aydalot, *Une Evaluation Critique*, p. 19.

21Guichard, *Propositions pour l'Aménagement du Territoire*, p. 19.

22Saul Estrin and Peter Holmes, *French Planning in Theory and Practice* (London: George Allen & Unwin, 1983), p. 114.

23John Ardagh, *France in the 1980s* (New York: Penguin Books, 1982), p. 126.

24Philippe Aydalot, "Questions for Regional Economy," *Tijdschrift voor Economische en Sociale Geografie*, Vol. 75, No. 1 (1984), p. 6.

25Jean Bouchet, "Mouvements démographiques et évolutions du territoire: éléments de problématique," *Revue d'Economie Régionale et Urbaine*, No. 5 (1983), pp. 669–692.

26Ibid.

27Philippe Aydalot, *Note sur les Migrations Interrégionales en France: 1975–1982*, Dossier no. 40 du Centre Economie, Espace, Environnement, Université de Paris I, June 1984; Philippe Aydalot, *Economie Régionale et Urbaine* (Paris: Economica, 1985), pp. 174–175; Claude Pottier, "Facteurs de rééquilibrage spatial de l'emploi industriel, les régions françaises face à la crise," in Philippe Aydalot, ed., *Crise et Espace* (Paris: Economica, 1984), pp. 122–139; Commissariat Général du Plan, *Rapport du Groupe de Travail Disparités Spatiales* (Paris: La Documentation Française, 1984), pp. 14–19.

28Philippe Aydalot, "Prise en compte des facteurs spatiaux et urbains dans la politique de développement," *Revue d'Economie Régionale et Urbaine*, No. 2 (1985), pp. 167–180.

29Pottier, "Facteurs de Rééquilibrage Spatial."

30Jean Gatel and Solange Passaris, "Le développement local: des territoires, des hommes, des initiatives, le partenariat," *Revue d'Economie Régionale et Urbaine*, No. 1 (1986), pp. 167–180.

31Jean-Claude Perrin, "Economie spatiale et mésoanalyse," in J.-H. Paelinck and A. Sallez, eds., *Espace et Localisation* (Paris: Economica, 1983), pp. 201–230.

32Philippe Aydalot, "La division spatiale du travail," in J.-H. Paelinck and A. Sallez, eds., *Espace et Localisation* (Paris: Economica, 1983), pp. 183–185.

33Aydalot, "Crise économique, crise de l'espace, crise de la pensée spatiale," pp. 101, 104.

34*OECD Observer*, No. 140 (May 1986), pp. 9–13.

35Philippe Aydalot, "A la recherche des nouveaux dynamismes spatiaux," in Philippe Aydalot, ed., *Crise et Espace* (Paris: Economica, 1984), p. 52.

[36]Claude Pottier, "The Adaptation of Regional Industrial Structures to Technical Changes," *Papers of the Regional Science Association*, Vol. 58 (1985), pp. 60–72.

[37]J. Philippe, "Les services aux entreprises et la politique de développement régional," in Antoine Bailly and Denis Maillat, eds., *Le Secteur Tertiaire en Question* (Paris: Anthropos, 1986).

[38]Pottier, "The Adaptation of Regional Industrial Structures," p. 71.

[39]Jean-Claude Perrin, "La reconversion du bassin industriel d'Alès: contribution à une théorie de la dynamique locale," *Revue d'Economie Régionale et Urbaine*, No. 2 (1984), pp. 237–256.

[40]Ibid., p. 253.

[41]Gatel and Passaris, "Le développement local."

[42]Xavier Greffe, *Territoires en France* (Paris: Economica, 1984), pp. 63–64.

[43]Gatel and Passaris, "Le développement local."

[44]Philippe, "Les services aux entreprises."

[45]Denis Maillat, "Les conditions d'une stratégie de développement par le bas: le cas de la région horlogère Suisse," *Revue d'Economie Régionale et Urbaine*, No. 2 (1984), pp. 257–273.

[46]Bailly and Maillat, *Le Secteur Tertiaire en Question*, p. 30.

[47]Ibid., p. 43.

[48]Antoine Valeyre, "La dynamique spatiale des emplois de service liés à la production industrielle," *Revue d'Economie Régionale et Urbaine*, No. 4 (1985), pp. 703–725.

[49]Bernard Planque, *Innovation et Développement Régional* (Paris: Economica, 1982).

[50]Antonio Cunha and Jean-Bernard Racine, "Le rôle des services aux entreprises dans une société post-industrielle," *Revue d'Economie Régionale et Urbaine*, No. 5 (1984), pp. 731–756.

[51]Marie-Christine Monnoyer, "Evolution du marché des services aux entreprises et formulation de stratégies de développement pour les activités de services: implications régionales," *Revue d'Economie Régionale et Urbaine*, No. 5 (1984), pp. 777–791.

[52]Commissariat Général du Plan, *Développement Décentralisé et Equilibre du Territoire*, Vol. 5 of Annexes au Rapport de la Commission Nationale de Planification (Paris: La Documentation Française, 1982), pp. 24, 33.

[53]Commissariat Général du Plan, *Rapport du Groupe de Travail Disparités Spatiales*, op. cit., pp. 65–74, 134–37. See also Michel Hannoun and Georges Sicherman, "Résorption des disparitiés régionales et nouveaux clivages," *Economie et Statistiques*, No. 153 (March 1983), pp. 59–74; and Sylvie Mabile and Hubert Jayet, "La redistribution géographique des emplois entre 1975 et 1982," *Economie et Statistiques*, No. 182 (November 1985), pp. 23–35.

[54]Quoted in Pierre-Henri Derycke, "Les enjeux financiers de la décentralisation," *Revue d'Economie Politique*, Vol. 95, No. 5 (September-October 1985), p. 675.

[55]Ibid.

[56]Lajugie *et al.*, *Espace Régional et Aménagement du Territoire*, pp. 356, 362.

[57]Délégation à l'Aménagement du Territoire et à l'Action Régionale, *Rapport d'Activité 1984–1985* (Paris: DATAR, 1986), p. 13.

[58]Jean-François Bazin, "Prospectives—les contrats de Plan en Bourgogne," *Revue d'Economie Régionale et Urbaine*, No. 3 (1986), p. 378.

[59]"L'avenir de la région," *Cahiers Français*, No. 220 (March-April 1985), Supplement no. 6, p. 4.

[60]Henri Guillaume, "Implications of the New Indicative Planning," in William J. Adams and Christian Stoffaës, eds. *French Industrial Policy* (Washington, DC: The Brookings Institution, 1986), p. 125.

[61]Laborie et al., La Politique Française, p. 118.

[62]Bazin, "Prospectives—les contrats de plan en Bourgogne," pp. 379–380.

[63]Laborie et al., La Politique Française, p. 118.

[64]Lajugie et al., Espace Régional et Aménagement du Territoire, p. 363.

[65]Christian Stoffaës, "Postsript," in William J. Adams and Christian Stoffaës, (eds.), French Industrial Policy (Washington, DC: Brookings Institution, 1986), pp. 198–210.

[66]Ibid., pp. 206–207.

[67]Délégation à l'Aménagement du Territoire et à l'Action Régionale, Rapport d'Activité 1984–1985, pp. 15–23.

[68]Sharon Zukin, "Markets and Politics in France's Declining Regions," Journal of Policy Analysis and Management, Vol. 5, No. 1 (1985), p. 46.

[69]Laborie et al., La Politique Française, pp. 97–98.

[70]Zukin, "Markets and Politics in France's Declining Regions," pp. 40–57.

[71]Délégation à l'Aménagement du Territoire et à l'Action Régionale, Rapport d'Activité 1984–1985, p. 22.

[72]Yves Janvier, "Développement local et groupes industriels: qu'attendre des sociétés de reconversion," Espaces Prospectifs, No. 4 (January 1986), pp. 1–26.

[73]Michel Savy, "Technopôles et aménagement: l'expérience française," Revue d'Economie Régionale et Urbaine, No. 1 (1986), p. 50.

[74]Marie-Anne Lescourret, "Les beaux jours des technopôles," L'Express, 26 September, 1986, p. 40.

[75]David Wadley, Restructuring the Regions (Paris: Organisation for Economic Co-operation and Development, 1986), p. 106.

[76]François Gillet, "La Z.I.R.S.T. de Meylan, Espaces Prospectifs, No. 1 (June 1985), pp. 125–151; Yves Janvier, "Economie et pratiques territoriales de développement: les rôles des technopôles?," Ibid., pp. 91–124.

[77]François Guillaumet, "A French Official Wants to Stop Ministering to Industry," Wall Street Journal, 27 August, 1986, p. 13.

[78]Guichard, Propositions pour l'Aménagement du Territoire, pp. 56–57.

[79]Serge Wachter, "L'Aménagement du territoire et son institutionnalisation: des réseaux centraux et locaux," Revue d'Economie Régionale et Urbaine, No. 3 (1985), pp. 559–575.

[80]Alain Faujas, "Le gouvernement programme la construction de 2730 kilomètres de voies autoroutières," Le Monde, 15 April 1987, p. 31.

[81]Ibid.

[82]Alain Faujas, "L'Europe par le bitume," Le Monde, 15 April 1987, p. 31.

[83]Derycke, "Les enjeux financiers de la décentralisation," p. 681.

[84]The 1962 index values are from Commissariat Général du Plan, Rapport du Groupe de Travail Disparités Spatiales, p. 127; the 1985 index values are from Air Inter, Franceco (1986), p. 21.

[85]Anne Beaujour and Geneviève Lamoureux, "12 villes pour vivre mieux," L'Express, 26 September, 1986, p. 38.

CHAPTER FOUR

The Evolution of Regional Policy in Great Britain

Successive British governments have sought to narrow regional disparities in employment and income for some 50 years. The efforts have varied greatly both in scope and intensity during this period. G. C. Cameron has compared the history of regional policy in the United Kingdom to

> that of a man with a grumbling appendix. Every now and again he feels acute pain and is forced to take a batch of medicines. Although his condition improves, he is never quite sure which of the medicines, singly or in combination with others, actually did the trick. However, at least he can forget about his discomfort and can turn his attention to other more pressing affairs. Then, sadly, his pain returns. This time, he changes the dosage and hastily adds a few new medicines to his treatment. The new combination seems to work and once again he feels confident that the problem has been solved. Sadly, disillusionment is just around the corner.[1]

Others have made similar observations about regional development efforts in Britain.

Although both of the major political parties in Great Britain have at one time or another and with varying degree of enthusiasm been committed to put measures in place to reduce regional disparities, the regional problem in Britain is very widespread and, in many ways, is somewhat more complex than in other countries. In Britain, for example, attempts to promote regional development, particularly of late, have been inextricably bound up with the concept of town and land use planning and urban economic development. That is, the regional problem goes beyond a concern for underdeveloped areas and includes issues of urban decay, congestion, and sprawl in parts of Britain, especially in the midlands, the southeast, and London. Thus, the issue of regional development has been seen by many as involving not one, but two problems.

Gavin McCrone goes further, suggesting that Britain's regional problem can in fact take many forms but that

> three major types may be distinguished. First, there are the agricultural regions which, untouched by industrialization, cannot provide their population with living standards comparable to the rest of the country. The second type . . . is one which is industrialized, but whose industry is either stagnant or in decline. . . . A third type is a congested region, whose further development entails high social costs and disproportionate public investment in various types of infrastructures.[2]

In part, the differences among regions and the various forms of the perceived problem, combined with their visibility, accounts for the numerous shifts in focus of regional policy over the years. This chapter reviews these shifts, seeks to identify some of the forces that have shaped British regional policy, and briefly reports on the success of the policy.

THE EARLY YEARS: DEFINING TARGETS AND DESIGNING WEAPONS

The depression years revealed, in a very harsh fashion, the regional imbalance in the British economy. The effects of the depression were not uniform. Whereas the unemployment rate in London and the southeast rose to 15% by the early 1930s, elsewhere, it was even more alarming, rising to more than 30% percent in Wales, for example, and in some areas and towns as high as 70, 80, and even 90%. By 1934 unemployment in the traditionally more prosperous regions began to fall to relatively acceptable levels. However, in Wales, the north, and Scotland it remained high.[3]

To be sure, Britain had seen regional problems before. They had, however, never been as severe and had essentially been limited to the declining rural areas. Accordingly, no specific regional development initiatives were introduced until the late 1920s.

The first British regional policy was announced in 1928. Although today it would hardly be described as visionary, at the time it was seen as innovative and far reaching. The Industrial Transference Board was designed to retrain the labor force and upgrade their skills, as well as to encourage their movement to expanding areas and industries.[4] Grants and loans were available to assist those who had to relocate in order to find employment elsewhere in the country.

By the early 1930s, the government saw that its labor policy, however innovative, could not by itself deal adequately with the problem and consequently commissioned a series of studies on specific areas. On the basis of these studies, the Special Areas Act was passed, which designated four areas—South Wales, northeast England, Clydeside–North Lanarkshire, and West Cumberland—for special development efforts (see Fig. 2). Commissioners were appointed to define measures to promote the rehabilitation of these areas.[5]

Initially, at least, expectations of success were high. They were,

FIGURE 2. The prewar special areas.

however, short lived. For one thing, urban areas within the designated special areas were not eligible for assistance. Thus, towns that potentially at least could have provided the basis for new development were excluded. But there were other, even more important, restrictions. It was not possible under the scheme, for example, to support proposals that could qualify for other types of government grants nor could funding be provided to a profit-making enterprise.[6]

The government recognized the inherent problems with this approach and in 1936, together with the Bank of England, assisted in the establishment of the Special Areas Reconstruction Association (SARA) by which loan capital was provided for small businesses in the designated areas. But again, the measure was too restrictive to have any kind of major and lasting influence, although revisions were introduced to the scheme from time to time, either to expand the program to make larger firms eligible or to inject additional monies.[7]

Other new measures were introduced in 1937 through amendments to the special areas legislation. For instance, provisions were made for the establishment of trading estates. These estates, operated by non-profit making companies, provided some services and factory space to firms, with rents charged on a recover-cost basis. At the same time, some tax incentives were also granted to firms operating in the designated areas. These, then, essentially, are the form British efforts at promoting regional development took in the interwar years. D. W. Parsons correctly states that "taken together," these efforts "in comparison with other industrialized countries at this time, present a unique approach to industrial planning and employment policies."[8]

Some of the government measures taken during this period only became visible after the war. Largely on the basis of a critical report from Sir Malcolm Stewart, commissioner for northeast England, the government established a royal commission to "inquire into the causes which have influenced the present distribution of industrial population . . . and to report what remedial measures, if any, should be taken in the national interest."[9] In his third annual report, Sir Malcolm had expressed deep concern that the battle for development in depressed areas was not being won and that further development of high-growth areas, such as London, should be controlled. Certainly, the experience of the depression years fed speculation on the effects of long-term market forces on the general dispersal of the population. Along with others, Sir Malcolm had been troubled by the massive geographic shifts in the population, and he came forward with a series of suggestions to deal with the situation.

The government responded by setting up a Royal Commission on the Distribution of Industry and Population (the Barlow Commission). In its final report in 1940, the commission concluded that there was, indeed, cause for concern. It recommended "national action" to deal with the situation and identified several measures to be taken, ranging from the establishment of a new central authority to specific initiatives to decentralize both industry and population. But as Parsons writes, the Commission did not present its report at the "most propitious time." By 1940, he explains, the Commission's *"raison d'être* was . . . seemingly as redundant as the promises extracted by Chamberlain from Herr Hitler."[10] Clearly, the problem of unemployment that was in any event being temporarily resolved through rearmament, was being shunted aside for a more urgent task. But the report was to have a strong influence in shaping regional development efforts for some time to come; some of its recommendations were only introduced in the 1960s. Indeed, the Barlow report, together with another government-sponsored report, the Beveridge Report on Employment Policy, combined with the espousal of Keynesian economic principles, were to form the basis for Britain's postwar policy on full employment and the regional dispersion of industry and population.

POSTWAR EFFORTS: 1945–1951: A POLITICAL COMMITMENT TO REGIONAL DEVELOPMENT

Gavin McCrone has written that

> the foundation of British regional policy from 1945 to 1960 was the Distribution of Industry Act of 1945. The Act was supplemented by the Distribution of Industry Act of 1950 and some important changes were introduced in the Distribution of Industry (Industrial Finance) Act of 1958, but the basic character of the 1945 Act remained unchanged during the period.[11]

To be sure, the Barlow report had an important influence in shaping postwar regional development efforts and, more specifically, the setting up of the Distribution of Industry Act, but there were also other forces at play. There is no doubt that Britain wanted to avoid a return to the prewar situation of depressed areas, and the political will to prevent this from happening was strong.[12]

Even during the war years, the notion of maintaining regional balance in economic activity and population distribution was part of the general economic policy debate. The coalition government contributed to the debate in a direct and visible fashion. It released in 1944 a white paper on employment policy that not only called for full employment but also outlined measures designed to deal with acute structural unemployment in certain regions. These included worker retraining programs and steps to influence the location of industries. The general approach, however, essentially remained one of focusing development efforts on selected areas.

Thus, the Distribution of Industry Act replaced the prewar legislation on special areas. The Board of Trade took over the responsibilities of the prewar Special Areas Commission. In many ways, the powers granted to the board were similar to those which had been assigned to the commission. The board, among other things, made loans, made provision for basic public services, and gave grants to assist specific development initiatives. The one important difference was that no provision was included in the new legislation to put in place any kind of tax incentives to promote regional development.

This is not to suggest, however, that Britain's postwar regional development policy was less ambitious than its prewar efforts had been. Quite the opposite. As Gavin McCrone argues, the "emphasis a government puts on its regional policy is at least as important to securing success as the measures themselves"[13] and the immediate postwar British Labour government did place considerable emphasis on its regional policy. Expenditure levels under the Distribution of Industry Acts, if nothing else, confirm this. Over £30 million were spent by the Labour government under the program between 1946 and 1949, compared with £11.6 million spent between 1956 and 1959 by its Conservative successor.[14]

The Labour government also made extensive use of its power to control industrial location in the immediate postwar years through a building license system. The government kept a strict control on permits granted for new buildings in undesignated areas, and this attempt to redirect investment did meet with some success. The development areas, representing only 20% of the population, obtained over 50% of all new industrial buildings between 1945 and 1947 (see Fig. 3).[15]

A committee of public servants from various departments was established to decide on the merits of allowing firms to develop or expand new facilities in nondesignated areas, thus depoliticizing the process. But the procedure to obtain a licence was lengthy. Industrialists complained, time and again, not only about the policy but also about the process. The government, however, stood firm against this criticism. It even pressed ahead with still stronger control measures. The Town and Country Act of 1947 introduced a requirement to obtain industrial development certificates from the Board of Trade for all firms wishing to launch new industrial development of more than 5,000 square feet be-

FIGURE 3. The development areas: 1945–1960.

fore planning permission was granted.[16] This provision raised criticism in the private sector, but this time mostly about the delay in obtaining a certificate. However, in some ways, "delay was the policy" in that investors would decide to locate in designated regions simply to avoid the slow process.[17] As well, it was also clear that the committee was quite prepared to take "tough" positions on applications to locate in the more prosperous regions.

The government provided loans and grants to build new factories in the designated areas and redirected some of its own purchases to firms in these regions. It made new provisions for public services and for industrial and local infrastructure, as well as putting in place a policy of urban development. New towns were built, albeit designed to deal more with urban congestion than with regional development. Still, the government did turn to the Town and Country Act to create new towns in designated development areas, the earliest being Aycliffe and Peterlee in the northeast, Chombran in Wales, and Clenrothes in central Scotland.

All in all, the postwar Labour government had set itself ambitious regional development goals and demonstrated a political will to put in place measures to work towards these goals. The chancellor of the exchequer made this clear in his 1946 budget speech when he declared that "the battle for the Development Areas is not yet won, but we mean to win it." He added, "I have told my colleagues that I will find, and find with a song in my heart, whatever money is necessary."[18]

BRITISH REGIONAL POLICY IN ABEYANCE: 1951–1960

The Conservative party, elected to power in 1951, was anxious to limit government intervention in the economy. Consequently, measures to promote regional development now became subject to close review and scrutiny. There was, of course, an ideological basis for this review.

But there was also an economic reason. Levels of employment were now high throughout Great Britain, even in the traditionally less developed areas. The coal and steel industries, as well as the shipyards, were operating at full capacity and the economies of Scotland, Wales, and the northern regions were experiencing solid growth. The regional problem, in the view of many in the Conservative government, was being resolved without government intervention. Thus it pursued regional development with considerably less vigor than had the previous Labour government.

Building licences were abolished in 1954. Although the requirement for industrial development certificates continued, the process was considerably relaxed—so much so that it became fairly easy to obtain a certificate for new development even in the southeast. Consequently, very little in the way of new economic activity was "diverted" to designated areas and, although the "carrot-and-stick" policy instruments of the first postwar Labour government remained on the statute books, they were rarely employed. The government had made it clear that it sought to promote general industrial development and would intervene only to "attract a few industries to those areas hardest hit."[19] Direct government spending for regional development also dropped significantly during the early 1950s. This was true for all government programs for regional development, including grants to firms locating in the designated development areas.

It was not long, however, before the government was jolted out of its complacency. By 1958, areas dependent on traditional industries were experiencing economic decline. The 1958–1959 recession was felt particularly hard in the slow-growth areas and to stem the worsening economic conditions (and with an eye on the electorate), the Conservative government began to reconsider its position on regional development. For one thing, it started to exercise greater control over industrial development certificates. The government also passed the Distribution of Industry Act (Industrial Finance) in 1958. The act added some areas of high unemployment previously not designated under the Development Areas Act. New funds were earmarked for regional development in designated areas, and new areas were designated on the basis of unemployment levels. This approach prompted many observers to argue that British regional policy was now viewed in the context of social, rather than economic, policy, in that the focus was on the problem of unemployment rather than on the strengths and development opportunities of slow-growth regions.

But clearly more action was required. The opposition Labour party called for a return to the approach it had introduced in the immediate postwar years. In an argument replayed several times since, Labour spokesmen insisted that the government had turned Britain into two nations—the haves and the have-nots. The Conservatives countered that the unemployment problem was only local in nature and concentrated in certain pockets. They insisted that the problem could be resolved with appropriate government measures and, once returned to power for a second term in 1959, they quickly identified regional development to be of top priority. It is important to note, however, that, in the election, the economically depressed and heartland industrial areas voted Labour. The Conservatives failed to break through in these areas, although they won handsomely in the Midlands and the South.

MOVING TARGETS AND CHANGING WEAPONS: 1960–1970

Up until the 1960s, the elements, if not their application, of British regional policy had been relatively stable. It is true that some adjustments were made to the policy from time to time and, in the immediate postwar years, some ambitious initiatives had been launched. But changes were not frequent and with the exception of the negative location powers that had been forcefully exercised by the postwar Labour government, they were also not far reaching.

All that changed in the early 1960s. From then until the present, important changes to regional policy would occur every 3 to 4 years, reflecting changing economic or political circumstances, a change in government or simply because things were not working as well as expected.

Certainly in 1960, regional policy took a dramatic turn. The Distribution of Industry Act, which had underpinned British regional development efforts since the war was repealed and replaced by the Local Employment Act (1960). Like its predecessor, the employment act provided for grants and loans to be made for new economic activity in designated regions. But it went further in other ways. The business community could now obtain financial assistance for building factories. In addition, the development areas were abolished and replaced by smaller *development districts*. The term is somewhat of a misnomer in that the areas designated did not so much show prospects for development as an existing or potential high rate of unemployment.

The new area designation process served to deschedule many areas, at least, initially. Under the new scheme, some 14% of the total population was initially covered, as compared to 19% under the development areas.

The new legislation, however, provided for considerable flexibility in designating development districts. Areas could be designated or dedesignated by the Board of Trade without having to obtain parliamentary approval. The board established a benchmark of 4 to 5% unemployment as the trigger that would designate new areas. Still, the areas designated included many of the old problem areas, including part of central Scotland, South Wales, West Cumberland, Merseyside, and the northeast. But changes to area designations were frequent, given the fairly automatic criteria employed, ranging from a coverage of 7.2% of the total population in late 1962 to 16.8% in 1966.

The 1960 Local Employment Act made assistance much easier to obtain and as a result expenditure levels under regional development increased substantially in that decade. Firms were no longer required to show their inability to raise funding from other sources. And, as noted earlier, grants were now offered for the construction of new buildings. Initially, firms were allowed to claim 85% of the difference between the cost of a new building and its actual market value once finished. Thus, slow-growth regions were favored under the scheme because new buildings in economically depressed regions would have a substantially lower market value than those in the more prosperous areas. Later, the program was revised, and a standard grant of 25% of construction costs was made available.

Other important changes were introduced in 1963. It was now possible to obtain grants for new machinery at up to 10% of the cost. Provision was also made for accelerated depreciation to allow firms to amortize investments in plant and machinery against profits. A firm could reduce its profits to zero in the first year by amortizing at an accelerated rate. This initiative, Gavin McCrone wrote, "proved particularly popular with industry."[20]

Still, there were some problems in implementing the regional development programs. In large part, these were due to the continuing designation and dedesignation of areas under the Local Employment Act. In some ways, there was too much flexibility given to the Board of Trade. For instance, areas such as Plymouth and Merseyside were all included initially as development districts. Then, in 1962, they were either dedesignated or stop-listed, which meant that further development could not be encouraged to go there. Shortly afterward, Merseyside, but not Plymouth, was redesignated. This process of designation, dedesignation, and redesignation naturally caused problems for the private sector. A firm might become interested in a particular area, start working on plans to build a factory there, only to find at a crucial stage that the area had become dedesignated. The assistance the firm had counted on was no longer available, and even the industrial development certificate system might be employed to prevent planned expansion. Moreover, a firm deciding to set up in a designated area and hoping to expand in a few years, might well discover that by the time it was ready to expand the area was no longer designated.

In 1963, assuming that new industries locating in development areas would require labor with new or updated skills, the government began to make available funds for a new retraining program. That same year, still other new measures were introduced or existing ones made more generous. Grants, for example, were made available to local authorities to assist with the reclamation of derelict areas. In some instances, the government assumed up to 90% of the cost. Added to this was a series of specific initiatives, such as new public works projects in designated areas and special government procurement from firms or shipyards located in the areas.

But the more important commitments to regional development were not in the form of ongoing regional programs of grants and loans to local authorities or private firms. The most far-reaching intervention was the government's renewed determination to influence and even direct the location of new industry. The control over industrial development certificates was considerably tightened to something like was seen during the immediate postwar years.

In selected sectors, the government went further and initiated discussions with industry to encourage firms to locate in designated regions. An excellent case in point was the automotive industry. The then-president of the Board of Trade served notice in 1960 that he would seek to direct new investment to areas of high unemployment.[21] The government entered into negotiations with individual firms; its position was to oppose all expansion in the south or allow it only if the firm agreed to further expansion in areas of unemployment. The government was successful in this regard and set the stage for the investment pattern of the automotive industry for the next several years. The government later explained that its objective was not simply to encourage growth in slow-growth areas but also to limit inflationary pressure in the Midlands and the South. Once again, this coincided with the emergence of town-planning concerns and several commissions examining the problems of growth and congestion.

The government instituted still other important measures. The prime minister appointed a minister, Lord Hailsham, to be responsible for the northeast. It is hardly possible to overemphasize the importance of this development. It signaled that regional development was now a top political priority and that regional concerns would be brought directly to the Cabinet table. Giving a minister responsibility for a specific region also signified that future regional development efforts for the area would be a highly political and open process. No special ministers were appointed for Scotland or Wales because the secretary of state for Scotland and the Minister for Local Government for Wales would play a similar role. However, a new Scottish Development Department was set up in June 1962.

But it was Lord Hailsham who took the lead both inside government and in public to develop the government's regional policy. Geography and spatial considerations now became far more central to economic policy planning, and a process was put in place that provided an opportunity to question orthodox thinking on economic policy.

Lord Hailsham came to espouse the "growth center" approach to regional planning, as did so many other politicians at that time throughout the Western world and in the less developed countries. As elsewhere, the approach was heralded as a panacea for slow-growth or stagnant regions. Hailsham issued a report in November 1963 that identified various growth centers as the way ahead for regional development policy in Britain.[22] His report called for massive investment in "growth points" in road-building, housing, and other public service infrastructure. At about the same time, a similar study was also released for Scotland.

The growth center approach had obvious political appeal. On the one hand, it sent a signal to economically depressed areas that the government was truly concerned about regional unemployment. On the other hand, it sent out a positive economic message that the approach would serve to build up the regions by focusing on the economic strengths of the designated areas.

But as happened in virtually all countries where the approach was adopted, the growth center concept in Britain was pushed and pulled to cover an extremely wide area. It would apply to most of the northeast and to areas of Scotland. This is, of course, far removed from what François Perroux had in mind when he first propounded the growth pole theory. He had envisaged concentrating on highly selected urban centers that already had strong potential for growth. No matter, the growth center approach constituted a major plank in the government's unsuccessful 1964 election campaign.

The growth center approach was not given much time to prove itself. One of the first things the new Labour government did on assuming power was to do away with the approach, stating instead that it would rely on comprehensive economic planning both at the national and regional levels to a far greater extent than the previous government had done. No more, the new government boasted, would there be a piecemeal approach to regional development.[23]

Shortly after coming to office, the government launched an ambitious series of planning exercises. In addition to Scotland and Wales, which were treated as separate regions for planning purposes, England was divided into eight planning regions. Surveys and development strategies were prepared. Regional development was seen in a highly positive light in that it was considered as supportive to national growth. J. Jones suggests that the decade from the early 1960s to the early 1970s represented "a unique period in which there were thought to be no real conflicts between the regional equity and national efficiency objectives of regional policy. During this period the argument was formulated in such a way that the two objectives were thought to be mutually compatible."[24]

Early in its mandate, the government also introduced new organizations for regional development that were to be, as it turned out, only the beginning of ongoing attempts to find a solution to the problem. The search is still continuing. This, as is apparent elsewhere, is not an experience by any means limited to Great Britain.

Underpinning the government's planning efforts was a new government structure. The Department of Economic Affairs would provide the necessary support and infrastructure for planning the national economy. Regional planning councils were established to assist the exercise at the regional level. These councils were representative institutions, bringing together individuals from local government, trade unions, the universities, and business. Although the councils were advisory bodies only and had no executive power, they were nevertheless assisted by a planning board of permanent government officials. The intention was that the regional councils and their plans would shape the national economic plan.[25]

Few, however, would argue that the experiment proved successful. The councils, it has been explained, "had no powers, were composed of part-timers, were politically unbalanced and badly staffed."[26] They were certainly not able to compete with the entrenched bureaucracy at the center nor, for that matter, were they able to capture the attention and interest of ministers. The failure lay not so much in the concept of integrating regional and national economic planning nor in the lack of political will to make it work. The fault lay, it appears, in the failure of the machinery of government to respond to political direction. The prime minister had made his position clear. He insisted that

> regional development is not a question of industrial location only. The real development we want to see is social development, or urban renewal and urban regeneration, of giving a facelift to some of our old industrial areas . . . . In some parts of the country, we shall have to have planned development machinery on a scale not far short of the Tennessee Valley Authority.[27]

He added that "this job cannot be done from Whitehall. Regional regeneration . . . will require a courageous degree of administrative decentralization." Unfortunately, the required degree of effective decentralization was not forthcoming, and the planning process was unable to deliver what had been promised.

The failure to integrate the nation's regional and national economic planning, however, did not prevent the government from introducing a host of new measures to cope with the issue. In 1966, Labour overhauled its regional development programming. It introduced the Industrial Development Act and extended the assisted areas to cover most of the traditional areas of high unemployment, in particular, large parts of Scotland and Wales. These were the largest areas ever designated and included over 40% of the land area and 20% of the population. The act provided for further revisions to the areas designated on an "as-needed" basis.

The act provided cash grants to firms willing to locate in designated areas. Investment grants of 40% for development areas and 20% elsewhere were made available. For new buildings in designated areas, firms were eligible for a cash grant of 25%. Other measures introduced under the Employment Act were retained, most notably, loans, reduced rents, and assistance for worker training. Moreover, local authorities in designated areas could obtain grants to cover up to 85% of the cost of improving the environment. The government also renewed its commitment to tighten the industrial development certificate process.

Still new measures were introduced later on. In 1967 a new program was designed to subsidize employment in designated areas.[28] Under the regional employment premium program, a direct subsidy was made available to employers for each new employee hired in the manufacturing sector. The premium represented a subsidy of about 7% of the average earnings of employees. Employers were also granted a tax rebate for providing employment in the designated areas. The program was highly controversial and was abolished in 1974 by the Conservative government—only to be reintroduced shortly after by the next Labour government.

D. W. Parsons maintains that regional employment premiums "proved to be the straw that broke the camel's back—the cat amongst the regional pigeons."[29] The nondesignated areas or the "gray areas," which were also experiencing economic decline, began to direct strong criticism at the government's regional policy. Assistance to designated areas was much too generous, they insisted, and it invariably drew development away from their communities. The same year that the program came into force, the government responded to this criticism by appointing Sir Joseph Hunt to lead an inquiry.

This is not to suggest that the government's regional development efforts were considered to be successful even in the designated areas. The movement of people from the north to the south continued. From 1961 to 1966, over 2 million people changed residence, and the south registered important net gains in the population flow. A. J. Brown has observed that during the 1960s, "Scotland showed net emigration to every other British region, the North to every one except Scotland. There is a general tendency for each region to receive from those to the North."[30] Other indicators also favored southern regions. Employment levels, for example, were much higher in the south, as Table 5 shows.

Thus, the promise of integrated regional and national economic planning and the ambitious measures announced by the Labour government since coming to power in 1964 began to turn sour. The government's regional policy was being assailed from all sides—the designated, intermediate, and the prosperous areas were all critical, though for various and

Table 5. *Unemployment Rates in the Regions: 1960–1972*
(Percentage Average of Monthly Figures)

	1960	1962	1964	1966	1968	1970	1972
South East				1.0	1.6	1.7	2.2
East Anglia	1.0	1.3	1.0	1.4	2.0	2.2	2.9
South West	1.7	1.7	1.5	1.8	2.5	2.9	3.4
East Midlands				1.1	1.9	2.3	3.1
West Midlands	1.0	1.6	1.0	1.3	2.2	2.3	3.6
Yorkshire and Humberside				1.2	2.6	2.9	4.2
North West	1.9	2.5	2.1	1.5	2.5	2.8	4.9
North	2.9	3.7	3.3	2.6	4.7	4.8	6.4
Wales	2.7	3.1	2.6	2.9	4.0	4.0	4.9
Scotland	3.6	3.8	3.6	2.9	3.8	4.3	6.5

Source. Department of Employment, May 1973.

often conflicting reasons. The designated areas were largely of the view that the policy was not working well; the intermediate areas felt strongly that their potential for growth was being systematically sapped by overly generous assistance to the designated areas; and the most prosperous areas contended that regional development efforts were playing havoc with national growth and national economic efficiency. Added to this was a strong resurgence in regionalism in Britain. The Scottish Nationalist party, for example, made impressive gains in local elections during this period. The government responded by appointing royal commissions on local government and on the Constitution.

Meanwhile, representations before the Hunt inquiry were largely critical of the government's regional policy. Few voices in support of the current approach were heard. When Hunt did report, he called for a new commitment to regional planning, including an extension of assistance to the intermediate areas. He also recommended the dedesignation of Merseyside. Such recommendations were obviously politically explosive, and coming as they did shortly before a general election was to be called, the government rejected the recommendation on Merseyside but agreed to that which would assist the intermediate areas. Seven new areas were designated, and new funding was made available for the construction of new buildings, for advance factories and for worker training. In addition, new funds were made available to local governments.[31]

Changes were also made in the machinery of government. The prime minister appointed a minister responsible for the northeast, and ministerial responsibility for industry was altered. The Ministry of Technology was enlarged and responsibilities for transport, housing, and local government were reorganized. The Board of Trade was also reorganized and became less powerful. The prime minister himself assumed responsibility for economic affairs and also took on new responsibilities in regional policy and for regional councils. Underpinning these reorganizations and reshuffling was the desire, once again, to strike the right organizational chord to integrate regional and national economic interests and development.

THE ROLLER COASTER ERA CONTINUES: 1970–1979

While in opposition, during most of the 1960s, the Conservatives were highly critical of Labour's approach to regional development, claiming that the government should not have abandoned the growth center concept, and maintaining that it had adopted an uncoordinated, helter-skelter policy that amounted to little more than an increase of spending on a host of initiatives. They argued, time and again, for greater selection and more focus in terms of policy instruments and areas. The Conservatives insisted that the emphasis should be on areas with strong potential for growth rather than on unemployment.

When returned to power, under Edward Heath, the Conservatives quickly announced their intentions to phase out the regional employment program, cut back on the industrial development certificate controls, move away from investment grants, and introduce investment tax allowances.[32] Moreover, the government reported its intention to return to the growth center concept and declared that its regional development policy would not be employed to prop up "losers." Rather, regional policy would now focus on the strengths of the regions instead of on their weaknesses.

But this policy was short lived. D. W. Parsons explains the reversal in policy in this fashion:

> Overnight lame ducks became sacred cows . . . Regional policy under the Conservatives was looking more and more like Labour's approach. Confronted with rising unemployment levels, particularly in traditionally depressed regions, the Heath government responded with all the political sensitivity of a Macmillan or Wilson government.[33]

As early as January and February 1971, the government designated Glasgow, Tyneside, and Wearside as special development areas. Shortly after, £100 million was allocated to new public works projects for designated areas. And that was only the beginning.

In 1972 the government passed a new Industry Act. This act, which introduced an elaborate structure of regional industrial incentives, demonstrates more than any other initiative, the virtual complete reversal of the government's position on regional policy.

An automatic regional development grant (RDG) was established.[34] The grant was adjusted to correspond to the different area designations. For special development areas, assistance of 22% of the building cost and machinery was made available. In the case of development areas, 20% was made available, also for both building and machinery. For the intermediate areas, assistance was only available for building cost, and the level was set at 20% (see Fig. 4). It was also decided that grants were not to be subject to taxation, nor could they be deducted from the cost of assets for depreciation purposes. Responsibility for delivering the program was delegated to regional offices.

The act also introduced a discretionary, project-related assistance in the form of soft loans, equity finance, loan guarantees, or capital grants. The latter was by far the most popular. Assistance was calculated on a cost per job basis, and the amount provided was considered the maximum required for the project to go ahead.

A scheme to encourage office and service industries to locate in disadvantaged areas was also introduced. The assistance was discretionary and project related. Grants were made available to all such firms willing to move to or establish offices in the three kinds of designated areas. Assistance varied, with the offer being more generous for special development areas and least generous for the intermediate ones.

The Heath government also pressed ahead with new spending for the clearance of derelict land. The government paid up to 75% of the cost under this scheme to recreate an attractive environment so as to entice new sources of employment.

The government also used its own expenditure budget to assist designated areas and continued with programs that funded the construction of roads, industrial estates, ports, and so on. It also sought to tilt its own purchasing policy to favor the designated areas. It continued a policy, first introduced in the immediate postwar years, to decentralize government offices—in particular, out of central London to the designated areas. This was in addition to a deliberate policy to locate new government positions outside of London.

1973 saw an important event that would have a strong and lasting impact on British regional policy. In that year, Great Britain became a ful. member of the European Economic Community (EEC). New com-

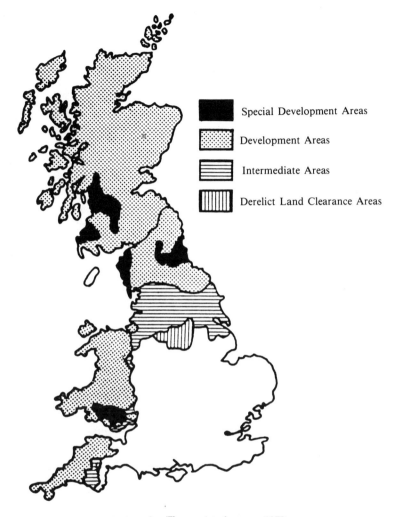

Special Development Areas

Development Areas

Intermediate Areas

Derelict Land Clearance Areas

FIGURE 4. The assisted areas: 1973.

parisons of regional economic well-being were now being made both between nations and regions.

It is well known in its early years that the EEC had a rather uncoordinated approach to regional development. Several agencies had their own instruments—the European Investment Bank and the European Social Fund, to name just two. Some attempts had been made to bring coherence to the various regional programs but they had met with limited success. However, in 1972, the community confirmed that regional policy would in future enjoy priority status.

Britain attached considerable importance to the community's regional policy and held discussions with it before becoming a full member. The Thomson report, released in 1973, argued that a major funding instrument was necessary to reduce regional disparities within the community. In early 1975, after lengthy negotiations, a new European Regional Development Fund was set up, and Great Britain was allocated a major share of the resources. The fund was given £540 million for 1975–1977 with 28% earmarked for Great Britain. Only Italy received more. The fund has been subsequently renewed and granted additional resources.[35]

The fund operates essentially as a grant-allocating agency. The grants are designed to supplement regional development assistance already given by member countries. National governments only can make application to the fund; promoters of specific projects are not eligible. About 20% of the fund allocated to Britain goes to the private sector, with a good part of the remainder allocated to local authorities in designated areas for infrastructure projects.[36]

Britain saw yet another change of government in 1973. While in opposition, the Labour party had reassessed its regional development policy, concluding that a fundamental revamp of the government's role in the economy, particularly at the regional level, was required. A much tighter control of the firms, especially the large multinationals, was thought to be essential. Once back in power, the party, however, began to backtrack and to look once again to the traditional approaches.

The new Labour government did, as it had promised, establish new planning agencies at both the national and regional levels. A National Enterprise Board was set up. At the regional level, development agencies were put in place for Scotland and Wales. The government tightened once again the industrial development certificates and sought to disperse offices away from London. It reintroduced regional employment premiums which the previous Conservative government had phased out. But by 1977 Labour, too, abolished the scheme.[37]

It was soon obvious that the government would be making other cuts in regional programming. It declared that payments under the regional development scheme would be delayed and that mining projects were no longer eligible under the program. Area designation was also cut back with North Yorkshire and Aberdeen being downgraded to intermediate area status.

The government also began to shift resources away from regional programs toward the National Enterprise Board. It was clear that priorities were shifting and regional policy, which had enjoyed prime status in the past under successive Labour governments, was now to be downgraded. The new emphasis was on aid to industry but on a sectoral basis rather than on a regional one.

Hand in hand with its emphasis on sectoral planning, the government turned its attention more and more to urban problems, particularly urban decay. 1977, it has been observed, "was the year when the inner city finally arrived as a political problem."[38] They were now the new economically depressed areas, and the press gave the issue a high profile. The *Sunday Times,* for example, initiated a campaign to save the cities and attempted to do for the inner cities "what its sister paper had done for the depressed areas in 1934."[39] Shortly after the campaign, the government passed the Inner Urban Areas Act and established the Inner Area Program. By the late 1970s, whatever new resources were available were destined for sectoral planning and the inner cities. Regional development policies and programs of the kind Britain had known in the 1960s and 1970s were less and less in vogue.

The stage was set for the coming of a Conservative government under Margaret Thatcher. J. D. McCallum summed up the situation by arguing that the future of British regional policy was at best uncertain: "A consensus nearly fifty years in the making," he wrote, "is probably collapsing: it is unclear what will take its place."[40]

THE THATCHER RETREAT: THE LADY IS NOT FOR TURNING?

On coming to power, the volte-face made on regional policy in the early 1970s by Conservative Prime Minister Edward Heath was not forgotten by Margaret Thatcher. She made it clear that her government would be different and that she "was not for turning."[41] The new conservatism was to be more rigid in its views. Early in her mandate, Mrs. Thatcher and her senior ministers explained that they intended to disentangle the government from the web of industrial incentives and planning. They also rejected out of hand the notion that jobs should go to the regions. People, they insisted, must be encouraged and willing to move to find work.

To be sure, the Thatcher government made important cuts in regional programming. But on regional policy, the lady did turn at least somewhat from her position while in opposition. Contact with political reality saw to this.

The Thatcher government did move quickly after coming to office to end office development permits and industrial development certificates.

The government also abolished regional economic planning councils. Regional development grants were continued, but cuts were made both in eligibility and spatial coverage. Access to the grants was withdrawn for research and development training activities and for maintenance expenditures. The grant-approval process was also tightened up, with grants given only to those projects that could demonstrate need and only when the jobs created were considered new. With respect to geography, the coverage of special development, development, and intermediate areas was reduced from over 43% to about 25% of the British working population. The areas dropped then and subsequently were the predominantly rural, agricultural districts, rather than the declining urban areas (see Fig. 5). Regarding size coverage, minimum value requirements for assets were raised from £100 to £500 for plant and machinery and from £1,000 to £5,000 for building and works. On 1 August 1980, a decision was also taken to eliminate assistance for intermediate areas.

Later, in 1983, the government tabled in the Commons a paper on regional industrial development. The paper argued that "although an economic case for regional industrial policy may still be made, it is not self-evident."[42] But the paper went on to point out that "the government believes that the case for continuing the policy is now principally a social one with the aim of reducing, on a stable long term basis, regional imbalances in employment opportunities."[43]

Later, in 1984, the government announced that it would abolish regional assistance for replacement equipment. Thus, only new equipment would now qualify. In addition, the government placed a ceiling on its regional programming so that grants could not be provided if they represented more than £10,000 per job created. The government declared that it intended to save some £200 million per year by 1987–1988 in regional programming and it did this by abolishing special development areas and downgrading the development areas to intermediate status. Accordingly, the regions would not be eligible for automatic regional development grants but only for selective assistance.

The minister of State for Industry, Norman Lamont, explained in a major policy statement that in future, British regional policy would place greater emphasis on job creation, while at the same time, attempt to improve its cost-effectiveness. He expressed the hope that, after a transitional period, regional policy would cost £300 million less per annum.[44]

To achieve greater cost-effectiveness, the minister announced that the map for designated areas would have two tiers instead of three and that the "inner tier, which will qualify for automatic grants as well as regional selective assistance, will be restricted to 15 percent of the working population."[45]

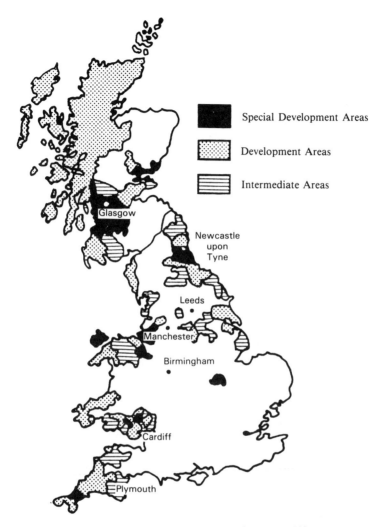

FIGURE 5. The assisted areas as of August 1982.

The basis for designating areas was employment patterns. The minister went on to explain that "it is only right that any policy as expensive as regional policy should be tied more closely to jobs." He concluded by arguing that

the most important feature of our policy is that money will now be spent in the areas with the worst problems and that, in terms of new jobs per pound of expenditure, the new policy will be far more effective than the old.[46]

   The government, thus, essentially retained the position that regional industrial incentives should continue to play an important role in
attempts to influence the location of economic activity. In addition, it
sought to establish a closer link between regional policy and urban development, by attracting private investment into the inner cities. In the
end, the government was to continue with its regional industrial incentives scheme. D. W. Parsons put it in this fashion: "By and large, it
chose to reduce financial resources rather than rid itself of the institutional morass of regional subsidies."[47]
   The government also sought to redraw the designated areas map by
moving away from growth centers and concentrating more on "black
spots." But, as was the case with previous governments, political pressure played havoc with this attempt to redraw the map. Norman Lamont explained that the government "tiptoed through a minefield."[48]
Tiptoe it did, for designated areas went from 27% of the working population in 1983 to 35% in 1985. The West Midlands towns of Birmingham,
Walsall, Coventry, Telford, and Wolverhampton became designated for
the first time. When Britain first introduced regional development programs in the 1930s, these towns had been among the most prosperous in
the country. But by the early 1980s, virtually all areas of Britain could
make a case for special development assistance, and a good number of
them did.
   The Thatcher government also sought to introduce new measures
for regional development. In 1980 it unveiled its intention to legislate a
new program to establish "enterprise zones." In the budget speech, the
chancellor of the Exchequer explained that enterprise zones constituted
an experiment in reducing government intervention in the economy and
allowing private sector firms greater freedom to develop. The central
purpose of the legislation, he explained, was to tackle problems associated with regional, inner city, and derelict land policy. The zones were
to be designated for a period of 10 years, subject to renewal.
   Both new and existing private sector firms were eligible to take
advantage of the program. Measures within the designated zones included exemption from development land tax, 100% capital allowance
on industrial and commercial property for income tax and corporation
tax purposes, abolition of general rates on industrial and commercial
property, exemption from industrial training levy, a minimum of government requests for statistical information, and priority status in dealing with customs.[49] Several areas were immediately designated as enterprise zones, including one on Tyneside, Merseyside, Greater Manches-
ter, London's Docklands, Clydeside in Scotland, and in the lower
Swansea Valley in Wales. The government has continued with the en-

terprise zone approach and has since designated some 20 other zones, widely spread out throughout the country.

All in all, however, regional policy under the Thatcher government did not undergo a complete overhaul. The *Times* argues that regional policy under Thatcher underwent some changes, some updating, but not a "fundamental rethink."[50] One can also speculate whether at least some of the Thatcher changes to regional policy would not have also occurred under another government. It will be recalled, for example, that even the previous Labour government had initiated cuts in regional programming toward the end of its mandate.

Britain in the early 1980s, like other Western industrialized nations, faced the twin problem of high unemployment and inflation. Regional development had few friends in Britain, as elsewhere. In Britain, the problem of the 1980s was not one of regional disparities but of generalized industrial decline. The search for solutions would take place at both the national and international levels. Unemployment was now a problem in the traditionally prosperous areas. If there were still a spatial economic problem in Britain, it was not so much regional, as urban. There was, it will be recalled, widespread rioting in British cities in 1985, principally in protest at the lack of employment prospects for the young. This led to further reviews of what should be done to improve conditions in the inner cities.

Regionalism, as we knew it, was in a headlong retreat politically. Devolution for Scotland and Wales no longer dominated either the media or the political agenda as it once had. D. W. Parsons explains: "One paradigm—the region—has been lost; another paradigm—the inner city—has been found."[51] In addition, new urgent questions were now being asked about Britain's ability to compete internationally, about "national" unemployment, about national recovery, about youth unemployment, and about urban decay.

Given this shift, one may well ask why did British policy and programs also not go in a complete headlong retreat? Why, in other words, did the lady decide to turn on regional policy? The fundamental rethink of British regional policy, as promised, has yet to take place. Why?

There is, of course, the politics of regional policy that invariably influences policy. In the case of Britain, it has dogged both Labour and Conservative governments since the war. They all revised their regional policies or at least those they had adopted while in opposition or on first coming to power. The Thatcher government is no different. It has simply "tiptoed through the minefield" like all governments before it. In Britain, as elsewhere, regional policy has been employed to check regional discontent. And, as elsewhere, regional policy has been successful at the political level but less so at the economic level. Murray Edelman put it succinctly when he wrote that "regional policy is a word that has succeeded but a policy that has failed."[52]

The Thatcher government has admitted as much, arguing that Britain, after many years of effort, has "nothing" to show for regional policy and that regional policy will not solve the problem of regional unemployment.[53] In its white paper on regional industrial development, the government argued that "imbalances between areas in employment opportunities should in principle be corrected by the natural adjustment of labour markets." Yet the report's main conclusion is that "the government is committed to an effective regional industrial policy designed to reduce, on a stable long term basis, regional imbalances in employment opportunities."[54] Clearly, political ideology is one thing, and politics is another, even for the Thatcher government.

There are, of course, other forces at play in British regional policy. Britain must often compete with other countries in attracting new investment. Britain could well decide to do away with its regional programs, but there is no assurance that other countries would follow. Thus eliminating its regional programs could well mean that Britain could no longer compete with other countries for footloose investments.

The EEC Regional Development Fund also constitutes an important constraint on British regional policy. The fund makes available significant resources for regional programming. Britain receives annually an important share of the fund. The Thatcher government admits that it takes the

> contributions [of the fund] fully into account in determining expenditure on [its] regional policy." It adds that it "strongly supports the development of community regional policy."[55]

BRITISH REGIONAL POLICY REVISITED

A review of British regional policy reveals that Cameron's observations, made some 15 years ago, still apply. Regional policy in Britain still resembles "a man with a grumbling appendix." Successive British governments continue from time to time to "change the dosage and hastily add a few new medicines to his treatment."

Among the countries surveyed in this book, Britain has been at the forefront of regional programming. It introduced new and, for the time, imaginative, measures as far back as the 1930s. It came forward with a wide variety of instruments to promote regional development, including control of investment, automatic regional development grants, discretionary top-up grants, regional employment subsidies, tax incentives, infrastructure projects, and so on. It also came forward with a host of government organizations and reorganizations to find the right structure to promote regional development, both in economic planning and in the delivery of programs. And yet Great Britain still faces problems of the same magnitude and in essentially the same areas as when regional policies were first introduced. The policies have not offset the pull of development to the southeast, nor have they been able to arrest the economic decline of designated areas.

This is not to suggest that British regional policies have been without effect. The least that can be said is that regional disparities in Britain would be worse today in the absence of past and present policies. Some comprehensive evaluations of British regional policies have been undertaken and, by and large, they conclude that the various policies and programs have been successful. For example, it is suggested between 1960 and 1981 British regional policy "created a total of 604,000 manufacturing jobs in the development areas . . . [and of these some] 450,000 jobs survived intact by 1981."[56] It is also suggested that the industrial development certificates proved to be particularly effective in that they redirected new jobs without involving significant government expenditures. It is also suggested, however, that for regional policy to resolve British regional problems, it would need to be "two to three" times more effective than it was in the 1960s and 1970s.[57]

But, as this study makes clear, there is not always a direct link between the effectiveness of policy and future policy directions. There are other forces at work. Internal politics and the policies of the EEC, for instance, will continue to have a strong influence on Britain's future regional development efforts.

Now in opposition, the Labour party is again calling for a complete rethink of regional policy. It is making the case for a greater say for local and regional levels in economic planning. As before, the party is insisting that regional policy should not be peripheral to social and economic planning. It must occupy a central position in economic thinking in government. In making the call for a genuine regional policy, the Labour party has considered various options for organizing government to ensure that regional and national economic planning are truly integrated. The Labour party spokesperson on regional development explained that "regional policy is too important to be left to the Department of Trade and Industry in Whitehall."[58]

The Thatcher government is likely to continue to "tiptoe" through the minefield, never convinced that regional policy can be effective but unwilling to abandon the policies and programs. Regional discontent must be accommodated, and a regional policy remains a useful instrument to contain this discontent. If for no other reason, regional policy has to be tolerated for political and social reasons.

The minefield, however, could well become more dangerous. Regional discontent could be on the rise, compelling the introduction of yet new measures. A sudden surge in unemployment in the traditionally depressed areas—which is already high—would certainly place strong pressure on the government to do just that. The Thatcher government would not wish to be seen to be completely neglecting the economic interests of regions from which it draws little support. As it is, the Conservative party is increasingly being viewed as the party of the south and the prosperous regions.

In winning its historic third-term majority government, for example, the Conservatives won only 10 of Scotland's 72 seats in Parliament. Regional discontent is on the rise not only in Scotland but in Wales and in the north. There are, of course, strong historical reasons for Scottish discontent. Still, some observers insist that regional discontent in Britain could be "erased with industrial success." Shortly after being returned to power, Mrs. Thatcher made clear her "concern" over regional problems and stated that her cabinet would carefully look into the situation.[59] This is a sure sign that once again a new batch of medicines may be concocted to appease the grumbling appendix.

Certainly the pull to the southeast is likely to continue, as Britain becomes more integrated in the trading patterns of the European Economic Community. It is true that the costs of locating in that area, in terms of both land and labor, are considerably higher than in other parts of the country. However, the proximity to major markets—that is, to London and Europe—in contrast to the increasing transportation costs and shipping difficulties encountered by firms in the north make it considerably more attractive to set up new centers of production in the southeast. However, a reliance on "free market" economic adjustments may well be misplaced. If production costs become too prohibitive in the southeast, firms may well look to lower input costs just across the channel rather than automatically opting to locate in the north of England. All of this suggests that a reliance on market forces will not be sufficient to ensure balanced growth. It is thus likely that future British governments, if not the current one, will be unwilling to sit by and let market forces call "the adjustment tune."

NOTES

[1]G. C. Cameron, "Regional Policy in the United Kingdom," in Niles M. Hansen, ed., *Public Policy and Regional Economic Development: The Experience of Nine Western Countries* (Cambridge, Mass.: Ballinger Publishing Company, 1974), p. 65. It should be noted that this chapter deals with regional policy in Great Britain. It does not deal with regional development efforts in Northern Ireland.

[2]Gavin McCrone, *Regional Policy in Britain* (London: George Allen & Unwin, 1969), p. 14.

[3]Ibid., pp. 91–94.

[4]Ibid., p. 97. See also B. W. E. Alford, *Depression and Recovery? British Economic Growth 1918–1939* (London: Macmillan, 1975).

[5]See D. E. Pitfield, "The Quest for an Effective Regional Policy 1931–1937, *Regional Studies*, Vol. 12 (1978), No. 2, pp. 429–433.

[6]Ibid.

[7]D. W. Parsons, *The Political Economy of British Regional Policy* (London: Croom Helm, 1986), p. 19.

[8]Ibid., p. 31.

[9]Quoted in McCrone, *Regional Policy in Britain*, p. 102.

[10]Parsons, *Political Economy of British Regional Policy*, p. 51.

[11]McCrone, *Regional Policy in Britain*, p. 107.

[12]Ibid., p. 112.

[13]Ibid.

[14]Quoted in ibid., p. 114.

[15]Ibid., p. 113.

[16]The Committee of Enquiry Under the Chairmanship of Sir J. Hunt, "The Intermediate Areas," Cmmd. 3995, HMSO, 1969.

[17]Parsons, *Political Economy of British Regional Policy*, p. 101.

[18]Quoted in ibid., p. 99.

[19]See House of Commons Debates, *Hansard*, 30 October 1952, col. 1090.

[20]McCrone, *Regional Policy in Britain*, p. 135.

[21]See, among others, Parsons, *Political Economy of British Regional Policy*, p. 146.

[22]*The North-East: A Programme for Regional Development and Growth*, CMBD 2206, HMSO, 1963.

[23]See H. Wilson, *The New Britain: Labour's Plan Outlined by Harold Wilson* (Penguin: Harmondsworth, 1964).

[24]J. Jones, "An Examination of the Thinking behind Government Regional Policy in the UK Since 1945," *Regional Studies*, Vol. 20, no. 3, p. 263.

[25]See, among others, J. Levrez, *Economic Planning and Politics in Britain* (London: Martin Robertson, 1975).

[26]Parsons, *Political Economy of British Regional Policy*, p. 217. He adds that "the planning councils were not to have an economic role, so they were left, like water, to find their own level."

[27]See Wilson, *The New Britain*, p. 40.

[28]See *The Development Areas: A Proposal for a Regional Premium* (London: D.E.A., April, 1967).

[29]Parsons, *Political Economy of British Regional Policy*, p. 217.

[30]A. J. Brown, "Regional Problems and Regional Policy" *Economic Review*, November 1968, p. 80.

[31]See House of Commons Debates, *Hansard* (14 April 1969, cols. 548–553).

[32]See, for example, *Investment Incentives* CMBD 4516, HMSO, 1970.

[33]Parsons, *Political Economy of British Regional Policy*, p. 241.

[34]For a detailed review of regional incentives in Britain, see Douglas Yuill and Kevin Allen, eds., *European Regional Incentives: 1980* (Glasgow: Centre for the Study of Public Policy, University of Strathclyde, 1980), pp. 329–367.

[35]See, among others, W. Green and D. Clough, *Regional Problems and Policies* (London: Holt, Rinehart & Winston, 1982), pp. 56–66. Commission of the European Communities, *European Regional Development Fund—Annual Reports*, Brussels, various dates. Michael Keating and Barry Jones, *Regions in the European Community* (Oxford: Clarendon Press, 1985), in particular Chapter 2. It should be noted that an important part of the fund earmarked for the United Kingdom is allocated to initiatives in northern Ireland.

[36]Ibid.

[37]See Stuart Holland, *Capital versus the Regions* (London: Macmillan, 1976), pp. 249–254. See also Parsons, *Political Economy of British Regional Policy*, p. 244.

[38]Parsons, *Political Economy of British Regional Policy*, p. 250.

[39]Ibid., p. 246.

[40]J. D. McCallum, "The Development of British Regional Policy," in D. M. MacLennon and J. B. Parr (eds.), *Regional Policy Past Experience and New Directions* (Oxford: Martin Robertson, 1979), p. 38.

[41]See, among others, L. Pliatzky, *Getting and Spending* (Oxford: Basil Blackwell, 1982).

[42]*Regional Industrial Development*, Cmmd 9111, HMSO, 1983, p. 4.

[43]Ibid., p. 3.

[44]Regional Industrial Policy, *Press Notice*, Department of Trade and Industry, reference 681, 28 November 1984, p. 2.

[45]Ibid.

[46]Ibid., p. 3.

[47]Parsons, *Political Economy of British Regional Policy*, p. 254. It should be noted, however, that the government did announce a 300 m. cut in regional programming.

[48]House of Commons Debates, *Hansard* (28 November 1984, col. 947).

[49]See *Invest in Britain Bureau* (Kingsgate House, London, Investment Brief No. 21/80, August 1980).

[50]*The Times* (London), 28 November 1984, p. 13.

[51]Parsons, *Political Economy of British Regional Policy*, p. 261.

[52]M. Edelman, *Political Language: Words That Succeed and Policies That Fail* (New York: Institute for Research on Poverty, 1977).

[53]House of Commons Debates, *Hansard* (28 November 1984, col. 945).

[54]*Regional Industrial Development*, Cmmd 9111, HMSO, 1983, p. 11.

[55]*Ibid.*, p. 6.

[56]Barry Moore, John Rhodes, and Peter Tyler, *The Effects of Government Regional Policy* (London: HMSO, 1986, p. 9). See also B. Ashcroft and J. Taylor, *The Movement of Manufacturing Industry and the Effect of Regional Policy* (Oxford Economic Papers, Vol. 29).

[57]Moore, Rhodes, Tyler, *Government Regional Economic Policy*, p. 12.

[58]See G. Robinson, *The Financial Times* (London), 25 January 1985, p. 11.

[59]Quoted in Paul Koring, "Nasty Scottish Snub Jars Thatcher Tories," A Special from London to *The Globe and Mail* (Toronto), 1 July 1987, p. D3.

CHAPTER FIVE

Regional Economic Development Policies and Programs in the United States

A Critical Overview and Implications for the Future

INTRODUCTION

This chapter presents a critical review of the evolution of federal regional development policies in the United States. Virtually all government policies and programs have differential geographic outcomes, but, typically, the spatial impacts are either not the main concern, or they are distributed according to pork barrel political criteria. The focus here is on the more salient activities of agencies specifically created to promote regional development in economically lagging regions. The year 1965 represents a watershed in this regard. At that time Congress established the Economic Development Administration, the Appalachian Regional Commission, and a number of other multistate regional development commissions as part of President Johnson's Great Society program. In so doing, the federal government assumed an unprecedented degree of responsibility for ameliorating spatial structural problems on a national scale. For various reasons that will be considered, this commitment has waned over the years. Nevertheless, there are grounds for believing that regional policy may once again enjoy a revival at the federal level. Be that as it may, there is still a great deal that state and local governments and other countries can learn from the failures and successes of U.S. experience over the past two decades.

HISTORICAL BACKGROUND

If the term *regional policy* is understood to mean a consistent and integrated set of programs designed to influence the distribution of population and economic activity, then the United States has never in fact had such a policy at the national level. However, in a looser sense, federal regional development policies have been present since the early years of the nation. Inspired by such concepts as "manifest destiny," vast territories were opened during the nineteenth century and developed with major federal subsidies and guidance. These areas included the Louisiana, Florida, and Alaska purchases, the Texas annexation, Southwest accessions from Mexico, and Pacific Northwest lands obtained by treaty from Great Britain. As these territories were acquired, surveys established property lines, land record systems were established, and vast land disposal schemes were carried out. Development grants were made in the form of free land, protection for railroads and settlers, and the construction of transportation and communications networks that linked far-flung territories to the national market. In addition, the good husbandry of agricultural resources was encouraged through the establishment of a system of land grant colleges.

During the nineteenth century, federal government policy in effect promoted the realization of the growth potential of rich but undeveloped lands through internal improvements and the encouragement of agricultural settlement by smallholders in new territories. By the turn of the century, however, new issues came to the fore. The federal government began to take responsibility for the protection of human and natural resources against industrial exploitation; the means included the regulation of monopolies, legislation concerning working conditions, the management of resource development, and the regulation of interstate commerce. Yet by the 1920s, the federal government had still not acknowledged any responsibility for maintaining full employment nationally. Nor did it recognize the existence of chronically depressed areas; thus, no efforts were made to identify the causes of such conditions or to develop policy tools for ameliorating chronic regional depression.

New Deal programs in response to the Great Depression of the 1930s were largely intended to stimulate aggregate demand, but a number of significant contributions were made concerning regional economic development. The Public Works Administration attempted to rationalize federal programs in this regard but, like later regional development efforts, it had difficulties in setting and implementing nationally applicable criteria for project selection. Because of the political need to achieve an "equitable" balance in the location of projects among the states, it was not possible to carry out a national schedule of priorities based primarily on economic considerations. The National Resources Board, which was charged with preparing public policies for the development of land, water, and other natural resources, dealt primarily with physical aspects of regional development, but its recommendations contained elements that could readily be applied to area-specific programs. Its lineal descendant, the National Resources Planning Board (NRPB), which was dissolved by Congress in 1943, clearly recognized the actual and potential role of the federal government in influencing the location of private industry. Edgar Hoover, the leading regional economist of the time, was particularly influential in the wartime research of the NRPB. He and others made the federal government aware of economic factors responsible for the existence of depressed areas and in many ways prepared the way for the regional development legislation of the 1960s. Of the various New Deal programs with a pronounced regional dimension, clearly the best known is the Tennessee Valley Authority (TVA). Its regional approach to planning and development served as a prototype for later river basin development programs and, to some extent, for the still later regional commissions established in the 1960s. It should be recognized, however, that although TVA has taken an active approach to regional physical development, it has been very passive in its approach to human resource development, and little is known about the distribution of its benefits among various social and economic groups.[1]

In the postwar years, various legislative and executive efforts to address problems of chronically depressed areas failed for a number of reasons. These included fears of impinging on the private sector and of beggar-thy-neighbor schemes that would redistribute existing production and thereby foster sectional strife. A key controversy, which in one form or another has persisted over succeeding years, arose from the question of how to allocate scarce resources efficiently while at the same time satisfying political demands for geographic equity. Meanwhile, however, regional statistical studies undertaken pursuant to the directives of the Full Employment Act of 1946 were providing an unprecedented data base for regional analyses and for government attempts to deal with the problem of formulating regional policies.[2]

During and after the recession of 1953–1954 representatives from depressed textile, coal, and railroad communities introduced bills for federal assistance to areas with high unemployment rates. Senator Paul Douglas, who emerged as the leader of this effort, offered a bill in 1955 that was conceived as a measure to aid old industrial areas. This proposition did not become politically viable until, in 1956, Douglas joined with Senator John Sparkman, Representative Brooks Hays, and others to form a crucial urban–rural, north–south coalition. It was at last recognized that no depressed area legislation could be exclusively farm–rural oriented on the one hand or urban–industrial oriented on the other. Although the Democratic Congress and the Eisenhower administration agreed in principle on the need for federal assistance to depressed areas, they quarreled over the specific provisions for 5 years without achieving concrete results. After President Kennedy took office in 1961, an accord was finally reached, creating the Area Redevelopment Administration (ARA).

Except for the expansion of targeted areas and the deletion of rapid tax amortization provisions, the new legislation varied little from the original Douglas proposal. Funds were authorized for business loans, public facilities grants and loans, training of unemployed workers, technical assistance grants for planning and feasibility studies, and research. In view of the fundamental assumption that lack of venture capital was the main drawback to business expansion in depressed areas, the Area Redevelopment Act designated approximately one-third of total authorized appropriations for business loans. To assure local commitment and good faith, relevant communities were required to provide 10% in matching loan funds, but in practice many depressed communities had difficulty meeting this requirement. Also, there was a prohibition against loans that would assist businesses in moving from one area to another. The public works provision, though somewhat different in purpose, was well within the nineteenth-century tradition of internal improvements, as well as New Deal resource development programs.

During most of the period covered by ARA operations, over 1,000 counties were eligible for assistance. By 1965, only $323 million had been obligated by ARA; their distribution by project is shown in Table 6. These allocations, which averaged approximately $300,000 per eligible

Table 6. Expenditures by Type under the Area Redevelopment Act: 1961–1965

Type of project	Number	Amount (millions)	Percentage of total
Industrial and commercial loans	405	$176.1	54
Public facilities grants and loans	157	104.1	32
Technical assistance	486	16.1	5
Training courses for workers	1,416	25.6	8
Research projects	44	1.4	1

Source. Sar A. Levitan and Joyce K. Zickler, *Too Little but Not Too Late* (Lexington, Mass.: D.C. Heath Lexington Books, 1976), p. 9.

county, were clearly inadequate to meet the program's ambitious development objectives. In addition, the ARA was given responsibility for administering the Accelerated Public Works Act, which was passed in 1962. Approximately $850 million was spent for about 10,000 projects, but the program, which had only minimal relevance to the depressed area concept, was not extended by Congress beyond its first year.

The ARA experience resulted in numerous criticisms from both opponents in principle and improvement-minded supporters. Effective planning was hindered by ARA's county-by-county approach, which failed to take account of broader geographic economic interdependencies; poor local development plans upon which ARA depended in assessing the feasibility of specific projects; and congressional pressures to designate and assist a large number of eligible areas. The ARA itself was publicly accused by the General Accounting Office of inflating results with respect to job creation and unemployment reduction. To make matters even worse, the program was further hampered by the performance of the national economy, which, by operating well below capacity, produced an inauspicious environment for the development of depressed areas. In the end, debates concerning ARA's effectiveness revealed a number of fundamental tensions that were already present in earlier debates over regional development issues. These involved conflicts between the respective authorities and jurisdictions of federal and state governments, equity and efficiency, planning and the free market, and "place prosperity" and "people prosperity." Nonetheless, the long legislative debates prior to 1965 had promoted an awareness of the problems of economically depressed areas, and the ARA experience established the principle of federal responsibility for promoting the economic development of depressed areas.[3]

THE NATIONAL CONTEXT OF THE REGIONAL POLICY HEYDAY: 1965–1971

Despite the ARA's difficulties, the appeal of a comprehensive program of federal assistance to create jobs and higher incomes for persons living in areas with relatively high unemployment or low per capita income increased during the 1960s. This unprecedented U.S. concern for regional development issues resulted from a conjuncture of social, economic, political, and demographic phenomena. Although fundamental political institutions have remained relatively stable over time, there have been pronounced cyclical changes in the degree to which the federal government has assumed leadership in addressing social and economic problems. For example, the 1920s, the 1950s, and the 1980s represent periods during which the virtues of the free market and private initiatives were emphasized by national administrations. This contrasts with the New Deal programs of the 1930s and the Great Society programs of the 1960s. If President Kennedy did not have much success in terms of persuading Congress to pass liberal social legislation, he did nonetheless popularize the notion that federal regional development efforts were needed for depressed areas. At a time when many political experts still believed that a Catholic could not be elected to the presidency, overwhelmingly Protestant West Virginia gave Kennedy a highly significant victory over Hubert Humphrey in that state's presidential primary election of 1960. Kennedy, like Humphrey, had campaigned on a platform that emphasized the importance of federal developmental aid to west Virginia as well as to other depressed areas in Appalachia and elsewhere. As president, Kennedy's efforts in this regard were consistent with his earlier pledges, but the realization of his legislative objectives came later, when they were subsumed under President Johnson's Great Society initiatives.

Meanwhile, the apparently successful application of essentially Keynesian macroeconomic policy measures during the 1960s was allaying fears of recurrent and lengthy periods of high unemployment and generally depressed economic conditions. As problems of full employment and price stability seemed to be solved, there was a shift of policy interest toward the regional distribution of national wealth and income. It has frequently been observed that regional policies favoring depressed areas have been easier to implement in times of relative aggregate prosperity than during periods of general stagnation. Structural economic problems not only become more evident when there is relatively rapid aggregate growth, but growth itself makes spatial redistribution politically more feasible because the relative losers can still gain in absolute terms. Also, during the 1960s the political case for aid to lagging regions was reinforced by a striking demographic phenomenon: The postwar baby-boom generation was coming of age, and it had a decidedly activist orientation. U.S. society experienced an upsurge of idealism and social concern that was translated into a high degree of support for President Johnson's domestic programs—as well as growing opposition to his Vietnam policies. For a time, however, it appeared that the United States could have both more guns and more butter.

By the late 1960s, the objectives of regional policies were being broadened. The previous emphasis on alleviating problems of depressed areas was expanded to include a more general concern for a more geographically "balanced growth" of the national population. Between 1945 and 1960 all of the net gain in U.S. employment took place in large urban centers. New jobs in smaller towns and cities were offset by rural job losses in agriculture, extraction, and other resource-based industries. Although 400,000 jobs a year were created from 1962 to 1964 in counties with no city as large as 50,000 population, this rate was still only about two-thirds of that necessary to halt net migration from nonmetropolitan areas to large cities.[4] While leaders in rural areas—many of which had been experiencing population decline for decades—had long been seeking federal subsidies for jobs that would stem the loss of young people to the cities, a new element was injected into the migration issue by the urban riots of 1965–1968. Now influential spokespersons in the receiving areas were questioning the absorptive capacity of large cities and at least implicitly were endorsing the balanced growth doctrine. To make matters still worse, considerable publicity was given to Bureau of the Census projections indicating that the national population would grow by 100 million persons by the year 2000 and that most of the net increase would be accounted for by large metropolitan areas. Public residential location preferences also were consistent with the views of the balanced growth advocates. In May 1971, a major national survey concerning people's residential preferences was carried out for the Commission on Population Growth and the American Future.[5] The results indicated that whereas only 32% of the respondents actually lived in a rural area or small town, 53% would prefer such a location. Only 13% of the respondents preferred to live in a large urban area, although 28% lived in such places. When asked whether the federal government should discourage the growth of large metropolitan areas, 52% replied affirmatively and only 33% said it should not. The proportion favoring restrictive policies in this regard was the same in rural areas or small towns, small urbans areas, and large urban areas.

By 1970, a national consensus had formed in response to the seemingly related problems of rural decline and the "urban crisis." The U.S. Department of Agriculture urged the expansion of rural employment opportunities at a rate rapid enough "to absorb the countryside's natural population growth and to provide jobs for those who would prefer to move from impacted city centers to less densely populated areas."[6] The President's National Advisory Committee on Rural Poverty stated that one of the "specific beliefs to which all members of the Commission subscribe" is that "every citizen of the United States must have equal access to opportunities for economic and social advancement without discrimination because of race, religion, national origin, or place of residence."[7] The Democratic party platform of 1968 called for geographically balanced growth and the Republican platform of the same year proposed "to stem the flow of people from the countryside to the city."[8] In the same year, the National Governors' Conference adopted a resolution in favor of "a more even distribution of population." In 1969, the National League of Cities called for a balanced national settlement policy. Similarly, the National Association of Counties, the U.S. Conference of Mayors, the Advisory Commission on Intergovernmental Relations, and the Commission on Population Growth and the American Future all advocated the establishment of a national population distribution policy. President Nixon, in his 1970 State of the Union Message, emphasized the need for a national growth policy in order to "create a new rural environment which will not only stem the migration to urban centers, but reverse it."[9] The Congress responded by passing the Agriculture Act of 1970 and the Urban Growth and New Community Development Act of 1970, both of which endorsed the objective of balanced growth. As Sundquist and Mields have pointed out, by 1970 "at the very least, the concept of national growth policy had been reviewed in every significant political forum the country offered, had drawn considerable support and little opposition, and had been approved by all of them."[10] Yet despite the flurry of activity surrounding the balanced growth issue, the basic regional development programs of the United States remained those established in 1965. These were the Economic Development Administration (EDA), the Appalachian Regional Commission, and the Title V Regional Commissions, which will now be considered in turn.

THE ECONOMIC DEVELOPMENT ADMINISTRATION

The Economic Development Administration was created by the Public Works and Economic Development of 1965. The new agency was provided with the same basic tools as its predecessor—the Area Redevelopment Administration. Public works grants and loans were continued as means for improving local and regional infrastructure. Business loans were again authorized on favorable terms for businesses that experienced difficulty in obtaining private financing. Technical assistance grants were retained to promote efficient development project selection in target areas, and funds were made available for research. These research funds were largely responsible for the considerable growth that regional planning and, in particular, regional economics experienced within major U.S. universities during the late 1960s and early 1970s.

EDA's legislation stated that the agency's mission was to provide the financial assistance, planning, and coordination needed to alleviate conditions of substantial and persistent unemployment and under-employment in economically distressed areas and regions. However, Congress structured the legislation to allow agency administrators to determine priorities and program directions and to give agency policymakers the flexibility to respond to local development problems on an individual basis. In keeping with its mandate, EDA developed five target goals for evaluating the success of its programs. These goals were (1) to reduce the incidence of substantial and persistent unemployment and underemployment characteristics of certain designated and qualified regions, counties, and communities to a level commensurate with the levels prevailing in the national economy; (2) to improve economic development planning, coordinating, and implementing capabilities at the federal, state, regional, and local levels; (3) to provide a basis for improved coordination and continuity for federal, state, and local activities relating to regional economic development and for more efficient utilization of all resources available for regional and local development; (4) to provide a basis for rapid, effective, and efficient expansion of government investment at all levels to promote economic development if and when such expansion is determined to be desirable and necessary; and (5) to develop alternatives to actual patterns of migration of the unemployed and underemployed by expanding economic opportunities in more suitable locations.[11]

The principal innovation in the EDA legislation was the provision for more comprehensive geographic planning areas and greater local participation in the planning process. Under the ARA program, no particular importance had been given to stimulating long-range economic planning by residents of distressed areas. Moreover, ARA's county-by-county approach resulted in excessive fragmentation, and insufficient attention was given to the concentrated development of centers with significant growth potential. In contrast to the ARA approach, EDA created multicounty Economic Development Districts (EDDs). It was recognized that individual distressed counties—termed Redevelopment Areas (RAs)—often lacked sufficient resources to provide a solid basis for development. However, because of economic interdependencies among adjacent areas, it was believed that economic development on a larger scale could be promoted by grouping together within EDDs both RAs and counties that were more healthy economically. EDA thus encouraged groups of counties—usually from 5 to 15 in number—to pool their resources for effective economic planning. In addition, each EDD was required to have a growth center, which was termed a *redevelopment center* if located in an RA or a *development center* if located in another district county, which was usually the case. With the exception of the growth center, counties in the EDD initially were not eligible for project funding from EDA unless they were RAs; nevertheless, all participating counties were expected to benefit from coordinated, districtwide development planning. In 1974, amendments to EDA's legislation expanded funding eligibility to cover all areas within the boundaries of EDDs. Finally, areas requesting EDA assistance were required to submit a long-range Overall Economic Development Plan (OEDP) for local development, based on an assessment of needs and resources. Planning was viewed as important for both economic and political reasons, to assure that development funds would be used efficiently, to provide a mechanism for local inputs into the decision-making process, and to create an EDA constituency.

The efforts of EDA policymakers to set specific goals and define specific priorities were complicated by the fact that the nature and causes of chronic depression and unemployment in various areas of the nation had not been satisfactorily identified when EDA began operations. Data describing economic conditions on a regional or area basis were far from adequate, and in any case there was no consensus concerning solutions to economic problems. One school of thought, for example, argued that external assistance of the type available from EDA was crucial to the building of viable economies in depressed areas, whereas another emphasized the need to build local development capabilities through the involvement of local residents in identifying needs, establishing priorities, and formulating strategies directly relevant to local circumstances. The task of defining goals and priorities within EDA was further complicated by the diversity of economic problems confronting the nation's distressed areas. For example, some areas with high unemployment (often of a temporary nature) had relatively high per capita incomes, whereas some with chronically low per capita incomes had relatively low unemployment rates. Benjamin Chinitz identified seven different types of distressed areas: (1) "rich" and rapidly growing, as exemplified by some high unemployment areas in California, (2) well-to-do mature, such as Pittsburgh, (3) not-so-poor rural, as found in the Upper Great Lakes region, (4) poor depressed rural, which comprised much of the South, (5) Appalachia, (6) large-city ghettos, and (7) Indian reservations. Chinitz argued that EDA should determine an appropriate policy response to each of the types of distressed area problems, pointing out that this task would "demand not only considerable technical sophistication in delineating the correct policy weapons but also a political strategy that is strong enough to prevent federal funds from being allocated to areas that have no potential for economic development."[12]

It is not clear from the record that EDA ever pursued separate yet internally consistent development strategies for various types of distressed areas. Lack of agreement concerning the complex nature of development problems, much less appropriate policy responses, meant that in practice the director and staff members of each program office within EDA set their own priorities and used their own judgment in determining the nature of EDA's mission.[13]

To illustrate the difficulties that EDA encountered in attempting to formulate an overall funding strategy, it is instructive to consider a dilemma that occurred early in the agency's existence. EDA found that areas just meeting the qualifying level for assistance also were the most likely to benefit from national economic growth. The economies of many of these areas improved to a point where they no longer qualified for EDA assistance, and they improved without the benefit of any operating EDA projects. The first evidence of this pattern appeared in the agency's initial annual review of area eligibility in the spring of 1966. In its first 10 months of operations, EDA had approved 650 separate projects, and 324 eligible areas received one or more projects. However, nearly a third of these areas were terminated at the end of the review because their unemployment rates had fallen below the 6% level required for participation. This meant that they were terminated before any EDA projects had advanced sufficiently to be the cause of the economic improvement. Their economies had benefited from vigorous and sustained national economic growth. It was also found that areas in the unemployment range from 6 to 8% had a much higher probability of being terminated than did those with higher rates. The second annual review brought out a similar pattern. Of the 176 areas terminated, 165 were in the 6 to 8% group. In light of these findings, EDA decided that it could put its resources to their best use by assisting places that had failed to benefit substantially from growing national prosperity. These were areas with the highest unemployment rates or the greatest proportion of low-income families.[14]

It was in this context that EDA introduced, as at least an interim measure, its "worst first" policy, which gave priority to projects that promised to have a clear and direct impact on unemployed and underemployed residents of distressed areas. The agency's 1967 annual report stated that

> the 'worst first' policy is the guiding principle for EDA in the use of its resources. It has moved the agency away from the selection of projects simply on the basis of their individual quality and general contribution to economic growth. Instead, EDA is now oriented toward meeting particular geographic objectives.[15]

A system was created for establishing funding priorities, based on the "worst first" criterion, in each of the seven categories of qualified areas. These categories included areas with substantial unemployment, persistent unemployment, substantial population decline, low median family income, and sudden increases in unemployment. The remaining categories were Indian reservations and areas that qualified on the basis of the legislative stipulation that there should be at least one redevelopment area per state. To determine the order of priority within each category, agency officials were to compute the "job gap" in each eligible area. The job gap was the number of jobs needed to lower the unemployment rate or raise the median family income to the level necessary to remove an area from qualification for EDA assistance. The job gaps were then to be used to set target budgets to indicate how much funding EDA would consider in relevant areas during a specific time period.

The "worst first" strategy satisfied Congress and provided a hitherto lacking approach for allocating funds. However, it was frequently ignored in practice by EDA officials, many of whom felt that it was inefficient and retrogressive because a substantial number of the "worst first" areas lacked the initiative and resources to take advantage of EDA projects.[16] In so far as it was implemented, the "worst first" approach was clearly inconsistent with the legislative admonition to invest in areas with significant growth potential, that is, with the notion of clustering investments in the growth centers of EDA multicounty districts.

In view of the lack of success of EDA's "worst first" flirtation, the agency began giving more attention to growth centers in the later 1960s, yet, here too, positive results were elusive. In the early 1970s, EDA carried out an extensive in-house evaluation of its growth center strategy and concluded that its

> experience in funding projects in economic development centers has not yet proven that the growth center strategy . . . is workable. The Agency's approach to assisting distressed areas through projects in growth centers has resulted in minimal employment and service benefits to residents of depressed counties.[17]

A 1974 federal report nevertheless agreed that EDA had not really concentrated its development efforts in appropriate places. It maintained that "the policy of dispersing assistance rather than focusing on those areas with the greatest potential for self-sustaining growth has resulted in much of EDA's funds going to very small communities. Over a third of its public works funds have gone to towns with less than 2,500 people, and over half to towns with less than 5,000 population. There are relatively few kinds of economic activities that can operate efficiently in such small communities, so the potential for economic development in the communities is relatively small."[18] The same report affirmed the notion that future economic development efforts should give priority to areas with the greatest potential for providing higher productivity jobs for the unemployed rather than attempting to create jobs in all areas of high unemployment. Yet there is no compelling evidence that EDA ever heeded this admonition.

EDA efforts to promote local planning initiatives provided valuable staff expertise that, for the most part, had been previously nonexistent. These grants also acted as catalysts to increase communication among competing local town and county jurisdictions. However, the most significant activity of the planning grants program was to increase the participation and cooperation of local political and economic leaders in area economic development activities. Indeed, the degree of involvement of the local power structure was typically indicative of the degree of success of the program. The weakest element in the local planning process was the Overall Economic Development Plan, which rarely set meaningful priorities.[19] Levitan and Zickler found that the results of the OEDP

> normally are long on socioeconomic data, frequently of doubtful relevance, and short on the development of a strategy to implement the goals. In many cases, the goals are 'wish-lists' or backlogs of projects that community leaders have kicked around for years. These documents are not applications for funding and do not commit resources; they only establish eligibility for Economic Development Administration funds. Therefore, they are often prepared by the staff, consultants or local college professors without significant contributions by the community board membership.[20]

When the Nixon administration came into office in 1969, EDA officials ordered the acceleration and expansion of evaluation efforts that had been initiated under the Johnson administration. By the end of 1971, existing programs were strengthened, new legislative proposals were developed, and increased emphasis was placed on interagency coordination. Originally EDA was at least implicitly a rural development agency, but by 1971 it was becoming increasingly involved in demonstration programs intended to create jobs, increase incomes, and stimulate minority entrepreneurship in large urban areas. But for the most part, the agency's activities did not involve major policy changes. In the following years, EDA's mandate would be considerably expanded, though typically without an increase in resources to meet its responsibilities.

THE APPALACHIAN REGIONAL COMMISSION

For 150 years, the Appalachian Mountains were the frontier between European and Indian America in what is today the eastern United States. Under colonial development policy, settlers were discouraged from moving westward because of British concern for monopolizing the fur trade and avoiding conflicts with the Indians. The early settlers who defied this policy sought out remote creeks and mountain hollows to elude both the Indians and the militia, but in so doing, they effectively removed themselves from the mainstream of American life. Nevertheless, for nearly a century the Appalachian settlers maintained a self-sufficient culture that "was in approximate equilibrium, though at a low level of economic activity, with their environment."[21]

Economic and social disaster began for the people of Appalachia when, under the pressures of the Industrial Revolution, the region's rich natural resources began to be discovered and exploited by "outsiders." Instead of purchasing land, paying taxes, and reforesting, timber companies, pursuing short-run profit objectives, bought timber rights at very low prices, cut down the virgin forests, and left the soil on mountain slopes to erode and wash down into the streams. Similar depredations were next undertaken by coal companies, whose absentee owners acquired unrestricted mineral rights at low costs. Mountainsides were stripped to get at the coal, and virtually nothing was done to restore the land. Contaminated water runoff from mined areas severely polluted the streams, and spoil banks that slid down the mountainsides cut off road access and isolated large areas from use by people and wildlife. For years the coal companies dominated local politics, avoided taxation, and escaped from restrictive legislation. The neglect of investment in human resources further deprived local residents of opportunities to improve their circumstances. Central Appalachia, which was particularly dependent on the coal industry, was subject to numerous boom-and-bust cycles over the years. However, the bust became chronic in the 1950s, when oil and gas became the nation's primary energy sources. Coal companies increasingly abandoned their company towns, leaving no viable communities. At the same time, the heavy industry that formed the economic base of northern Appalachia was declining in response to competition from elsewhere. These developments in central and northern Appalachia also had adverse consequences for the closely tied railroad industry. Although some industry was moving to southern Appalachia, this region too was experiencing severe problems by the 1950s. The agricultural sector upon which much of the area depended was rapidly becoming marginal, and the textile sector, southern Appalachia's most important industry, was in decline because of decreased demand and foreign competition.

By 1960 it appeared to many observers that prolonged simultaneous downturn in the economies of Appalachia's subregions had doomed the entire region to chronic depression. In 1960 over 30% of the families living in Appalachia had an annual income of less than $3,000, which was the frequently used benchmark between poverty and a minimally comfortable standard of living. The male unemployment rate was 7.1%, compared with a national rate of 5%. The unemployment situation would have been still worse were it not for substantial outmigration during the 1950s, when net outmigration amounted to 2.2 million persons. There was an absolute decline of 5.1% in the 18 to 64 age group.[22] Even though much of Appalachia had a population density greater than that of the nation, there were relatively few urban centers to provide badly needed schools, health facilities, commercial activities, and jobs. In central Appalachia, only one person in six lived in a town with more than 2,500 population. And the grimy towns and cities that grew up as steel and coal centers in northern Appalachia often lacked the environment and facilities needed to attract and support new development. Thus Appalachia represented an unusual case among depressed regions of industrialized countries. In general, these regions are peripheral to their countries' economic heartlands. Appalachia, on the other hand, is located between two of the most highly industrialized and urbanized regions of the world—the Atlantic megalopolis and the industrial Midwest. With the rapid growth of Atlanta to the south, Appalachia in the early 1960s increasingly appeared to be an island of distress in a sea of affluence.

In 1960 the governor of Maryland convened a group of Appalachian governors in order to initiate a program of development for the Appalachian region. The following year the governors presented a preliminary program to President Kennedy, who directed the Area Redevelopment Administration to give special attention to the region and to assist the governors. However, it was not until 1963 that Kennedy formally endorsed the notion of a comprehensive program for the economic development of the Appalachian region. He simultaneously created a joint federal–state committee, which came to be known as the President's Appalachian Regional Commission (PARC), to prepare legislative recommendations. Early legislation drafts proposed the establishment of a public corporation with powers of eminent domain and the power to raise its own revenues. Arguments for this public authority approach to planning and administration, similar to that of the Tennessee Valley Authority, assumed that Appalachian state and local governments were too weak and the federal government too disorganized to carry out a sustained and coherent development program. However, in 1964, Congress rejected this public corporation approach. An alternative model that in fact greatly influenced the eventual administrative structure of the Appalachian program was the Delaware River Basin Compact of 1961, in which a federal–state commission was created consisting of the four governors of the Delaware Basin states and a federal representative, the secretary of the interior.[23]

The Appalachian program was finally launched with the passage of the Appalachian Regional Development Act of 1965 (ARDA). The ARDA established a regional commission composed of the Appalachian governors (who could be represented by their appointed alternates) and a federal co-chairman at the assistant secretary level who was directly answerable to the president. Action by the commission required the vote of a majority of the state representatives and the federal co-chairman. To carry out its overall planning responsibilities, the commission was authorized to establish a technical staff to be jointly employed and financed by the federal government and the relevant state governments. On their own initiative, the states created a commission position for a states' regional representative, who was employed and paid by the states themselves. Eventually the federal co-chairman, the states' regional representative, and the executive director were designated an executive committee to act in the commission's stead on matters for which they had been delegated authority.

The ARDA stated that it is

> the purpose of this ACT to assist the region in meeting its special problems, to promote its economic development, and to establish a framework for joint Federal and State efforts toward providing the basic facilities essential to its growth and attacking its common problems and meeting its common needs on a coordinated and concerted regional basis.[24]

It was further stipulated that the "public investments made in the region under this Act shall be concentrated in areas where there is a significant potential for future growth, and where the expected return on public dollars invested will be the greatest."[25] Thus, the Appalachian program was to emphasize "economic development," with a strong assumption that this could best be achieved through the provision of "basic facilities," that is, public works in the form of economic infrastructure.

In the debates prior to the enactment of the ARDA it was evident that the states gave top priority to highways in order to overcome the region's isolation. They also gave high priority to dams, reservoirs, and other resource development projects, although they were quite willing to receive "preferential treatment in any other program area where the federal government might be willing to extend it."[26] The similar judgment of the PARC that Appalachia's "penetration by an adequate transportation network is the first requisite of its full participation in industrial America"[27] is reflected in the actual ARDA program funding authorizations shown in Table 7. Of the initial $1.1 billion authorized by Congress, $840 million was allocated to the construction of economic development highways—it was held that they were not a response to effective demand but were rather a means to induce development once in place—as well as local access roads. This heavy emphasis on highway construction was sharply criticized in many quarters, especially in view of Appalachia's pressing human resource needs.[28] However, once in place, the Appalachian Regional Commission (ARC) clearly recognized the necessity for actively addressing these needs.

From the outset the ARC took a comprehensive view of the eco-

Table 7. Funds Authorized under the Appalachian Regional Development Act of 1965 and Appalachian Regional Commission Appropriations through Fiscal Year 1974, by Program

Program	Authorization 1965 (thousands)		Cumulative appropriations 1974 (thousands)	
	Amount	Percentage of total	Amount	Percentage of total
Highways	$ 840,000	76.9	$1,355,000	59.7
Health demonstration	69,000	6.3	257,900	11.4
Vocational	16,000	1.5	169,500	7.5
Supplemental grants	90,000	8.2	333,450	14.7
Mine restoration	36,500	3.3	52,941	2.3
Housing	—	—	9,500	0.4
Land stabilization	17,000	1.6	19,115	0.8
Timber development	5,000	0.5	558	0.1
Sewage treatment	6,000	0.5	6,844	0.3
Administration and other[a]	12,900	1.2	63,058	2.8
Total	$1,092,400	100.0	$2,267,866	100.0

[a]Includes administration, water resource survey, research, and local development district support

Sources. United States Public Law 89-4, Appalachian Regional Development Act of 1965, 89th Congress, 9 March 1965; Appalachian Regional Commission, "Appalachia: Twenty Years of Progress," special number of *Appalachia*, Vol. 18, No. 3 (March 1985), p. 107.

nomic development process, especially in relation to earlier efforts that
tended to equate economic development planning with "smokestack
chasing." In addition to its regional economic development goal, the
ARC adopted a social goal to provide the people of Appalachia with the
health and skills required to compete for opportunity wherever they
might choose to live. It also urged upon Congress the need to broaden
the scope of the ARC's activities in this regard. In 1967 amendments to
the ARDA, Congress established a housing fund to stimulate construction of low and moderate income housing, and in the health program it
placed more emphasis on services, operations, and personnel training,
and allowed the acquisition and operation of existing health facilities.
Further amendments in 1969, 1971, and 1975 authorized the ARC to
expand demonstration programs in the areas of health, nutrition, and
education; to expand its program dealing with occupational diseases
endemic to coal-mining regions; to use its own funds to operate vocational education facilities; and to expand housing assistance.[29] The ARC
also treated the highway program in terms broader than a narrowly
economic development perspective, maintaining that the transportation
system was the matrix within which human resource investments
would prove their effectiveness. Reflecting on his experience as the
ARC's executive director during its first 6 years, Ralph Widner expressed agreement with the critics who had argued that it makes better
sense to invest in people than to invest in the concrete of highways.
Nevertheless, he pointed out, if lack of decent transportation keeps a
child from getting to school, a pregnant mother from getting to a hospital, or a breadwinner from getting a job thirty miles away, "then is such
an investment an investment in people or an investment in concrete?"[30]

One of the more innovative aspects of the ARDA was the provision
in Section 214 for a program of supplemental funds for local financing of
federal grant-in-aid projects, so that local contributions could be reduced
to as low as 20% of a project's cost. The justification for this program was
that many impoverished communities in Appalachia were unable to
participate fully in existing grant-in-aid programs because they could
not afford to contribute the standard matching share; therefore special
funds were needed to supplement local funds and make communities
competitive for grant programs for construction and original equipment.
Over time the range of programs that could be supplemented with Section 214 funds was broadened, though the basic justification remained
the same. The preamble to the ARDA stipulated that the relevant states
were to be responsible for recommending local and state projects within
their borders. As the basic units for planning and fund allocations, the
states were given decision-making authority with respect to the use of

Section 214 resources, subject to the ARC constraints that projects would be justified in annual state development plans and should be related to the social and economic development of Appalachia. By the end of 1972 the states had invested $185 million of Section 214 funds, which also served to leverage even greater federal spending for the programs selected by the states. The percentage distribution of Section 214 allocations by category of project was as follows: vocational education, 23.3%; nonvocational education, 28.2%; health, 30.4%; water and sewer, 14.7%; and airports, 3.4%. In other words, 82% of the total outlays were devoted to human resources (education and health), indicating a pronounced emphasis on this aspect of the development process. Moreover, Kentucky and West Virginia, where human resource problems were relatively great, devoted 100% and 90% respectively, of their Section 214 expenditures to education and health projects.[31]

The data presented in Table 7 permit a comparison of the relative program emphases of the original authorizations of the ARDA of 1965 and the actual cumulative appropriations made for these programs through fiscal year 1974. Although highways accounted for most of the total ARC appropriations (59.7%), the ARC has nevertheless succeeded in bringing about a relative shift of priorities in favor of human resource development. The health and education programs together comprised 7.8% of total 1965 authorizations, whereas they represented 18.9% of actual appropriations through 1974. In addition, the Section 214 supplemental grant programs increased from 16.0% of total 1965 authorizations to 33.6% in terms of actual total ARC appropriations. Thus, for the first time in the history of U.S. regional planning for the development of lagging regions, human resources were in fact treated as a vital aspect of the overall development process.

It will be recalled that the ARDA stipulated that, for efficiency reasons, the investments made under the Appalachian program should be concentrated in areas with "the greatest potential for future growth." A directive from the Congress stated that the ARC should be guided by the assumption that the states were best qualified to determine, in their respective Appalachian areas, the location of places with significant growth potential. In practice, the selection of growth centers was constrained by the nature of the ARC's local development (LDD) program. The LDDs are multicountry areas that serve as the local level planning units within the overall ARC planning system. Within each of the 60 LDDs (their number later grew to 69) into which the region was divided, the states attempted to identify areas where future economic growth would probably occur. The ARC's working definition of a growth center was that it meant a complex consisting of one or more communities or places, which, taken together, provide or are likely to provide, a range of cultural, social, employment, trade and service functions for itself and its associated rural hinterland.[32]

In effect, the ARC's growth center approach was a version of central place theory, that is, it was based on the performance of certain functions, typically of a service nature, without reference to growth or to how the performance of the various functions would give a center growth potential. Nevertheless, this approach could be supported on at least two grounds. First, services in the broadest sense represent the most rapidly growing sector nationally in terms of employment, so that a growth center is increasingly a service center. Also, a central place approach can be pertinent to the efficient delivery of the health, education, and other services provided under the Appalachian program. In practice, the states used widely varying methods for defining "growth areas," which included growth centers as well as adjacent territory with supposed growth potential. The ARC developed a four-level categorization of the growth areas, defined in state plans. Level 1 was defined as the highest level of growth potential in each state; level 4 areas were not deemed to be growth areas, whereas the other levels represented different degrees of intermediate situations. An ARC evaluation indicated that during the first 5 years of its operations, 62% of nonhighway investment funds were located in Level 1 growth areas. Similarly, 32% of the ARC's nonhighway investments went into only 5% of the 397 Appalachian counties, and 55% went into only 15% of the counties. On the other hand, 30% of the counties accounted for just 1% of nonhighway investments. Thus, the ARC "did succeed during its first five years of operation in placing projects in general conformity with its intentions."[33]

By the early 1970s, the major creative decisions involved in the Appalachian program had been made. To be sure, numerous relatively small-scale innovations would be made subsequently, but they did not represent significant changes in the nature of U.S. regional development policy.

THE TITLE V REGIONAL DEVELOPMENT COMMISSIONS

Title V of the 1965 act that created the Economic Development Administration authorized the secretary of commerce to designate, with the cooperation of the states concerned, multistate regions containing similar problems of economic distress or lag. Once a region was designated, the relevant states were invited to participate in a regional commission patterned, at least superficially, on that provided for Appalachia under the ARDA. Eventually eight Title V regional commissions were designated. They included most of the territory of the United States—west of the Mississipi River the only states not participating were Iowa, Nevada, and California—though less than half of the population.

The Title V program was a result of logrolling in the Senate at the time the ARDA was passed. Senators from outside of Appalachia sought comparable benefits for their states. So as to protect the Appalachian program, the Johnson administration agreed in principle to provide comparable institutions for other parts of the country. However, none of the Title V commissions in fact duplicated the ARC. In the Appalachian case, the regional organization resulted from a major spending program; in the Title V program the regional organizations came first, but then the funding failed to follow because of lack of presidential support under succeeding administrations.[34] During their first 6 years, federal spending for all of the five Title V commissions then existing amounted to a little over $100 million, whereas the Appalachian program received $1.3 billion. With so little money, the Title V commissions were unable to elicit much support from the relevant governors, which in turn made it even more difficult to obtain greater presidential backing.

An evaluation of the Title V commissions prepared by the General Accounting office concluded that they had failed to establish priorities for programs and projects, that few of their activities had any multistate impact, and that they had not evaluated the effectiveness of their programs and projects in relation to overall goals. Moreover, the office of federal co-chairman did not have sufficient status to influence the magnitude or direction of other federal development programs.[35] Even though the Title V commissions and the Economic Development Administration were all lodged within the Department of Commerce, there was little or no coordination among their various operations.[36] Given the low level of activity of the Title V commissions, it was already apparent in the early 1970s that their research and planning efforts would in fact have only a negligible impact on regional economic development.

THE DECLINE OF REGIONAL DEVELOPMENT POLICY: 1972 TO THE PRESENT

The unprecedented U.S. regional economic development policy experiments that were initiated in 1965 were gradually eroded during the

1970s. There were a number of social, political, demographic, and economic reasons underlying this evolution. For one thing, the social concern and activism that were manifest in the civil rights and antiwar movements and that also carried over into the antipoverty and regional development programs of the 1960s were abating in favor of more conservative attitudes. The reelection of President Nixon in 1972 was widely perceived as the confirmation of a mandate that discouraged new federal domestic initiatives of any sort. The Nixon administration did in fact oppose renewal of the Appalachian program, which originally had a 6-year authorization, on the ground that it represented an unnecessary additional administrative layer within the federal system. Nevertheless, Congress overwhelmingly voted to renew the ARC and its program. Indeed, at this time there was considerable sentiment, especially in the Senate, for reinforcing the regional commission approach to conducting intergovernmental relations, by establishing and adequately funding a system of such commissions that would cover the national territory.

Meanwhile, the urgency for more geographically "balanced" growth was being called into question by a changing demographic outlook. The rate of national population growth, which had been 18.5% in the 1950s and 13.4% in the 1960s, declined to 11.4% in the 1970s. The Bureau of the Census projected further declines to 9.7% in the 1980s and 7.3% in the 1990s. The bureau revised its total population estimate for the year 2000 from 300 million to 267 million.[37] In addition, there was an unanticipated change in population distribution trends. During the 1970s the historic net migration flow from nonmetropolitan to metropolitan areas was reversed, and, as shown in Table 8, the nonmetropolitan average annual growth rate of 1.3% was greater than the corresponding metropolitan rate of 1%. As a group, northern metropolitan areas with over 2.5 million population experienced absolute population decline during the 1970s.[38] The orientation of the regional development programs created in the 1960s was biased toward shoring up the erosion of nonmetropolitan areas, but now political attention was being drawn more toward the plight of the "mature metropolis." Academic opinion, which had tended to attribute the observed positive association between per capita income and city size to the productivity advantages of large cities, now attributed this relationship to a need to bribe workers with "disamenity premiums" in order to get them to remain among proliferating external diseconomies of urban agglomeration.[39]

In more broadly regional terms, the 1970s were characterized by an outporing of literature contrasting an inevitably rising sunbelt and declining frostbelt. Between 1970 and 1980, there was net outmigration of 2.9 million persons from the Northwest and 2.7 million from the Mid-

Table 8. Metropolitan and Nonmetropolitan Area Population Change, by Region: 1970–1980 and 1980–1984

	Metropolitan area population					Nonmetropolitan area population				
	Total (thousands)			Average annual percentage change		Total (thousands)			Average annual percentage change	
Region	1970	1980	1984	1970–1980	1980–1984	1970	1980	1984	1970–1980	1980–1984
Northeast	43,742	43,291	43,773	-.1	.3	5,318	5,844	5,954	.9	.4
Midwest	40,460	41,550	41,718	.3	.1	16,130	17,317	17,398	.7	.1
South	42,282	51,489	55,663	2.0	1.8	20,531	23,884	24,913	1.5	1.0
West	29,216	35,842	38,792	2.0	1.9	5,622	7,332	7,946	2.7	1.9
United States	155,701	172,173	179,946	1.0	1.0	47,602	54,377	56,212	1.3	.8

Source. U.S. Bureau of the Census, Statistical Abstract of the United States: 1986 (Washington, DC: U.S. Government Printing Office, 1985), p. 20.

west. In contrast, during this period, the South experienced net immigration of 6 million persons and the West 4.1 million.[40] The data in Table 8 indicate that metropolitan areas in the South and West had growth rates twice the national metropolitan growth rate. Metropolitan areas in the Northeast actually declined in population. Nonmetropolitan growth rates were also much higher in the South and West than in the Northeast and Midwest. Various explanations were proposed for these phenomena, including climate, air conditioning, improved transportation and communications accessibility, changing life-styles, the growing number of footloose retirees, differing "business climates," and regional differences in federal spending. Major shifts in economic activity among regions were also seen to be a consequence of changed energy relationships, with stagnation in the North and great spurts of development in the South and West.

The energy crisis brought on by OPEC pricing policies also contributed to an abrupt change in aggregate growth patterns. Between 1960 and 1970, the U.S. real GNP grew at an annual rate of 3.9%; between 1970 and 1973 the corresponding rate was 4.7%. However, from 1973 to 1976 the real GNP grew by only 1% annually.[41] In the face of widespread national stagnation, it was difficult to maintain broad support for regional economic development programs that essentially addressed the problems of only some distressed areas.

The changing environment of the 1970s particularly affected the mandate of EDA. Originally EDA was primarily a public works agency oriented toward the long-run development of lagging nonmetropolitan areas. During the 1970s it was increasingly assigned tasks—in both metropolitan and nonmetropolitan areas—involving the prevention of economic distress, disaster relief, minority business development, and assistance to areas adversely affected by foreign competition or by the closing of plants and military bases. The countercyclical functions assigned to EDA were especially significant in altering the nature of the agency.

The 1971 legislation that renewed the EDA program included a Public Works Impact Program (PWIP) giving the agency responsibility for pump priming undertakings that would maximize short-term employment gains but not necessarily contribute to long-run development. Concern for countercyclical problems had always been implicit in the EDA legislation, but in the original 1965 act, funds appropriated under the Title I criterion of substantial unemployment had been linked to development objectives. The PWIP blurred the link between Title I and development. Priority was given to projects that could be initiated and completed within 12 months, and the requirement that they be justified in an overall economic development plan was suspended. EDA thus assumed "an indirect, and occasionally somewhat involuntary, role in national economic stabilization."[42] The PWIP became "an important part of the Economic Development Administration program, competing for resources and serving frequently dissimilar objectives."[43] Between 1972 and 1985, EDA invested nearly $500 million in 1,438 PWIP projects.[44]

In 1974, Congress enacted a Jobs Opportunity Program that made EDA areas eligible for aid and established a $500 million fund to be administered by EDA to provide public service jobs in urban and rural areas experiencing unusually high levels of unemployment. This purely antirecessionary measure stressed quick-start, labor-intensive projects that could be rapidly completed. Thus, repair, maintenance, landscaping, and beautification projects were given precedence over infrastructure development. An extension of this program was vetoed by President Ford in 1975, but an impetus for an EDA countercyclical role remained nevertheless.

In 1976, Congress, over President Ford's veto, passed a $2 billion Local Public Works (LPW) program, to be implemented by EDA, for construction projects that could produce rapid results in areas experiencing high unemployment. An additional $4 billion was added to this program in 1977 as a major component of President Carter's economic stimulus package. In only 3 months beginning in December 1976, 2,062 projects were approved. By the end of fiscal year 1979, construction had been completed on 7,883 projects, or 72% of the total approved under the two rounds of LPW. EDA had disbursed $5.3 billion, or 89% of the funds appropriated for LPW. EDA outlays for LPW alone exceeded the cumulative total expenditures ($4.8 billion) made on all other EDA activities from 1965 through 1979.[45]

As originally conceived, EDA's resources represented the most clear-cut example of a federal program focused on economic development and aimed at the demand side of the labor market. In keeping with its mandate, EDA initially attempted to be something more than a mere administrator of a grant and loan program carried out on a project by project basis. EDA officials recognized that a logical strategy was a basic precondition to any successful attack on the problems of lagging regions.[46] Nevertheless, the agency never implemented any consistent strategy or set of strategies. In many respects this was more the fault of Congress than of EDA. Congress increasingly gave EDA too many responsibilities that had little to do with long-term economic development, and the designation criteria for EDA assistance became so broad that by 1985 nearly 80% of the entire U.S. population lived in areas qualifying for such aid. Not counting the $6.24 billion that EDA spent for short-term countercyclical public works programs, the agency's total cumulative outlays through 1987 amounted to $6.81 billion (see Table 9), or $310 million per year, a small sum in view of the magnitude of the development problems that EDA was supposed to address. An evaluation of EDA's impact on local areas concluded that although its assistance did make a significant contribution to county income growth (in comparison with a control group of nonaided counties) while the assistance was being given, it was not a significant factor in the postaid income growth of assisted counties.[47] EDA itself recognized that its funding capacity, in relation to the large number of areas qualifying for assistance, led to a wide scattering of funds in relatively small amounts. It acknowledged that its experience

> has clearly demonstrated that the piecemeal approach to project funding followed in the past will generally not result in a meaningful increase in the level of an area's economic activity[48] [and that] its resources, even at the substantially increased levels sought, are inadequate to realize economic growth and stability in more than a handful of areas unless maximum use is made of other public and, particularly, of private investment.[49]

In 1981, President Reagan proposed that the EDA program be phased out. It was argued that EDA did not create "real" jobs and that the proliferation of eligible areas precluded the targeting of resources where most needed. It was further pointed out that aid to localities from state economic development agencies surpassed $60 billion per year, all funded with state revenues. EDA's 1981 budget was reduced by 30%, to

Table 9. Summary of Economic Development Administration Obligated Funds (Excluding Drought Assistance, Local Public Works, and Emergency Jobs Act), Cumulative to 30 September 1987

	Number of projects	Amount (thousands)
Public works	7,107	$3,767,157
Business Development and Trade Act	1,287	1,662,894
Technical assistance	5,690	313,943
Planning grants	7,189	383,200
Economic adjustment	948	681,851
Total	22,221	$6,809,037

Source. U.S. Department of Commerce, Economic Development Administration, 1987 Annual Report (Washington, DC: EDA, 1988), p. xvii.

$454 million, from what had been requested by the Carter administration.[50] In 1986, the Reagan administration was similarly challenging

> not only the rationale but the effectiveness of the government creating jobs and prosperity through taxing, spending, and other forms of wealth transfer. Philosophical arguments aside, the mission of EDA, as decreed by the Congress, is to create job opportunities for the unemployed in areas of high economic distress. This principle is often contradicted by 'add-on' legislation.[51]

The adds-on—pork barrel projects often benefiting relatively wealthy areas with relatively low unemployment rates—for 1984, 1985 and 1986 "represent projects which would have received very low competitive consideration," yet "they total over $65 million, more than the 1985 appropriation for the Economic Adjustment, Planning, Research and Evaluation programs combined."[52] Although the Reagan administration requested a zero program budget for EDA in fiscal year 1985, Congress appropriated $230.7 million to continue the agency.

Unlike EDA, which has had a relatively narrow program focus, and unlike the Title V regional commissions, which had much smaller budgets in relation to regional population, the Appalachian Regional Commission (ARC) has taken a broad view of the economic development process. In addition to its highway program, the ARC has creatively experimented with a wide range of health and education services, with innovative methods of making services available, and with a unique planning process blending national, state, and local perspectives in policy and program decisions. Moreover, throughout the 1970s, the Appalachian region experienced considerable progress.[53] Between 1970 and 1980, 1.5 million new jobs were created, 90% of which were in nonmanufacturing activities. Manufacturing expanded in southern Appalachia, and services grew throughout the region. More than 400,000 new jobs were located on or near Appalachian highway corridors. Per capita income increased from 78% of the U.S. average in 1960 to 85% in 1980. After experiencing net outmigration of 3.3. million persons between 1950 and 1970, there was net inmigration of 1.1 million persons during the 1970s. Inmigration of trained workers and improvements in Appalachian education levels resulted in an upgrading of the quality of the labor force, and there was an increase in the female labor force participation rate. The energy crisis and the concomitant turnaround in the demand for coal contributed heavily to an expansion of employment opportunities in many hard-core poverty areas of West Virginia, Kentucky and Virginia, which had higher in-migration rates than the rest of Appalachia.

Between 1980 and 1983, worldwide recession, an oil glut, and vigorous foreign competition severely affected Appalachia's coal, steel, textile, apparel, and electricity sectors. During this period the region lost
500,000 jobs, and the unemployment rate soared to 16%, one-third higher than the national average. However, by 1985 the situation was again
improving. The jobs lost during the recession were regained, and another 200,000 had been added.[54] It now appears that the base for economic stability that has been established in Appalachia since 1965 is
relatively solid. Despite the continuing problems of some sectors and
localities, the region is not in danger of retrogressing to the conditions
that prevailed prior to the 1970s.

Through fiscal year 1987 the ARC had received cumulative appropriations of $5.4 billion, of which $3.4 billion was for the highway program and $2 billion for all nonhighway programs.[55] Given the magni-
tude of the regional, national, and international economic forces affect-
ing the region, it could not be claimed that these resources, spread over
two decades, were solely responsible for the Appalachian turnaround in
the 1970s. Nevertheless, the ARC's activities were a positive factor in
promoting and orchestrating a significant part of the region's development. When the ARC was established, the Appalachian program was
viewed as a temporary effort to put the region on a path of self-sustained
development. Already, in 1972 and 1973, the ARC and the Title V regional commissions were impeded by the hostility of the Nixon administration, which regarded them as unnecessary layers of bureaucracy
within the federal system. However, in the late 1970s, President Carter
stated his support for regional commissions and called for greater coordination between the commissions and federal agencies. The commissions' federal co-chairpersons were made members of federal regional
councils that were created to promote greater cohesion among federal
programs on a multistate basis. Carter also held that the investment
programs of the regional commissions should be formulated from the
ground up, to reflect substate and state development plans. (Carter
himself had headed a local development district as well as the Georgia
association of development districts before winning elective office.) In
addition, a resolution adopted by the National Governor's Association
in 1978 reflected the virtual unanimity among the governors that the
regional commission should be the future means for better relations
within the federal system. However, preoccupation with macroeconomic problems meant that in practice the regional commissions received
more good wishes than dollars.

The advent of the Reagan administration, with its philosophical
opposition to regional development programs, soon resulted in the abo-

lition of the Title V regional commissions. Reagan also wanted to terminate the ARC and its programs, but the Appalachian governors countered with a unanimous, bipartisan resolution in support of their continuation. The result was a congressional request to the governors for recommendations concerning how the highway program might be completed and the area development program phased out over 3 to 5 years. The governors responded with a report to Congress that agreed to a "reasonable and responsible" finish-up program, if this could be accomplished "in a way that will provide a basis for continued progress in the Region."[56]

The governors' proposal considerably narrowed the focus of the ARC by terminating expenditures for health, education, and recreation construction, community centers, libraries, social service facilities, and multiyear operating grants. The proposal for the highway program called for the completion of a number of critical segments, or 620 miles of the remaining 1,303 miles of the total planned system. Some additional water and health care programs were proposed for the most distressed areas of the region. Finally, the governor's report pointed out that Appalachia had once been "a beautiful Region rich in coal, timber and other resources and populated by self-reliant pioneers."[57] But then severe problems occurred because, among other things, much of the wealth generated by Appalachian resources flowed to corporations outside the region, with little being reinvested in Appalachian communities. The report took note of the fact that outside corporations had cut down the region's "splendid hardwood forests" without benefit of "the conservation and reforestation practices of recent decades" and the fact that "coal, steel, chemical and other industries, while creating jobs in the Region, caused considerable environmental damage in the years prior to the recent establishment of environmental standards."[58] In keeping with the Reagan administration's emphasis on the importance of the private sector and private philanthropy, the report remarked that some corporations have recently shown an increased commitment to the communities in which they do business.

> We believe many corporations and individuals have an interest in remedying some of the past neglect in Appalachia and . . . to help accomplish this, we propose to establish a development foundation for Appalachia [that] would raise funds and invest them to upgrade the Region, helping to offset the loss of funds from ARC and other sources.[59]

Throughout the 1980s Congress has continued to extend the ARC program on a year by year basis, but with a level of funding about half that needed to realize even the governors' modest finish-up proposals.[60] And the continuing existence of the ARC, however emasculated, has seemingly precluded the creation of a comparable private institution.

WHAT HAS BEEN LEARNED?

As pointed out earlier, throughout this century the United States has experienced a 30-year cycle of government efforts to "correct" the perceived harmful consequences of the free market, followed by a reaction against "wasteful" bureaucratic intervention. If the past is any guide to the future, then the 1990s will be a period of increased government activism in the mixed economy. If this turns out to be the case and if regional economic development issues are a part of the agenda, what has been learned from past experience that could help to avoid mistakes and to promote potentially successful initiatives?

Neoclassical economics tends to regard regional policies as sentimental distortions of the superior functioning of the marketplace. However, this need not be the case, especially when the policies are genuinely developmental in nature. Some regional development programs and projects that do not appear to use scarce resources optimally in terms of short-run comparative-static analysis may, in a long-run dynamic context induce considerable development through a process of cumulative causation. For example, during the westward expansion of the United States in the nineteenth century, regional infrastructure development ("internal improvements") policies were actively used as means to extend the frontier and then to integrate frontier regions with the rest of the nation. In short-run, comparative static terms, analysis of the trade-offs between laying a railroad line across a desert or locating it along areas already characterized by relatively dense concentrations of population and economic activity would no doubt have favored the latter option. Yet, in retrospect, it would be difficult to deny that the dynamic consequences of the western railroads, though difficult to quantify, justified their construction from the perspective of long-run national opportunity costs. More recently, at least one aspect of the Appalachian development program suggests that regional policy does not necessarily entail a conflict between national efficiency and equity objectives. This was the decision of the ARC to devote most of its discretionary (nonhighway) investments to upgrading the region's relatively neglected human resources so that Appalachians could better compete for economic opportunities "wherever they may choose to live."

Despite the foregoing cases, it should be acknowledged that many regional policies and programs are frankly based on equity considerations: Something should be done to address the grievances of people in the regions left behind in the process of national economic development. This issue is typically linked to that of population mobility. Equity-oriented arguments for regional policy often regard outmigration as an undesirable phenomenon that should be alleviated by such policy. Sundquist, for example, maintains that in the United States too much emphasis has been given to unemployment and poverty as criteria for designating regions as qualified for assistance.

> Outmigration may be a better measure of the growth disparity that policy should seek to overcome. It should be considered as an addition to, or perhaps even as a substitute for, the criteria now in use.[61]

In contrast, neoclassical economists argue that persons who are dissatisfied with local economic opportunities should move to places where they would be better off. And persons who remain in places with inferior economic opportunities for noneconomic reasons should appreciate their noneconomic rewards without demanding additional economic rewards (subsidies) from the nation at large. There is much to be said for this argument. Yet if one adopts a broadly historical view, it is apparent that the short-run profit motives of groups with privileged economic power did result in devastating consequences for Indians, blacks, and central Appalachians, to name only the more prominent cases. Does society at large owe disadvantaged people and places something to redress the balance of past inequities? And do declining old industrial regions also qualify in this regard?

These questions raise complex economic issues as well as philosophical problems that will not be resolved here. However, if society at large, through democratic political processes, decides that it is desirable to have regional development policies based on equity grounds, then regional economics has a number of tasks with respect to these policies. One, consistent with neoclassical concerns, would be to clarify the national interregional efficiency costs of regional development programs (which may in fact be expensive as well as largely ineffective) so that these costs can be weighed against the reasonably expected benefits. Another task would be the analysis of the intraregional distribution of benefits within targeted regions. If the equity rationale for regional policies primarily concerns persons experiencing low incomes, unemployment, or underemployment, then it is necessary to know the extent to which such groups actually receive the intended benefits. In sum, given the equity constraint, regional policy should seek to attain a "second best" optimum, where the net gain from equity benefits and efficiency losses is maximized. Although this theoretical approach admittedly is limited by difficulties of quantification, it nonetheless focuses attention on the salient variables and their interrelations, which are often obscured by the rhetoric of partisan debate.

For the most part, regional development policies in the United States have emphasized infrastructure investments, which are in turn supposed to encourage private investment in lagging regions. In terms of local benefits, this is a relatively "safe" approach, even if public works projects have only a remote relationship with the location of new industry in a community. If a regional development agency creates an industrial park or lends money for new plant and equipment and the venture does not generate significant employment and income growth, then the failure is obvious. In contrast, if infrastructure investments do not stimulate local development, local residents still have the benefit of improved amenities, and it is difficult to say that the project is a failure.[62] Newman points out, in the context of the Appalachian program, that while no one could be sure that public works projects would contribute to self-sustained growth in lagging regions, "it was clear that better health and education for the people of those areas was a necessary precondition for such development if it was to occur, and, if it did not, individuals could carry them wherever opportunities were available."[63] However, from a local perspective, investment in mobile human resources may also be regarded as more risky than public works projects, because whatever the national efficiency benefits, the local gains may seem small. It is also risky for the development agency if its performance is evaluated in terms of benefits to targeted areas because the benefits that "left" with outmigrants would not be recorded and the true social value of the program would be understated. Viewed in this light, the human resource programs of the ARC have been not only correct but courageous. If regional development policy must deal with political pressures concerning types of investments, the politics of their spatial distribution has been even more formidable. Both of the major regional economic development acts passed in 1965 called for concentration of investments in areas with significant growth potential, yet congressional pressures were largely responsible for de facto investment patterns that were spread widely and thinly. This was especially the case with respect to the Economic Development Administration.

Areas eligible for EDA assistance eventually included 80% of the national population. Ad hoc, add-on projects, largely of a pork barrel nature, and the emergency short-term public works programs that were added to EDA's responsibilities greatly diluted its long-term regional economic development mission. The ARC achieved somewhat better results with respect to spatial concentration, but even here "political pressures on elected officials at all levels from communities denied funds because they were not growth centers were formidable."[64] As one public official put it: "I don't know exactly what a growth center is, but I know there is at least one in each congressional district."[65]

Because EDA activities have increasingly borne little resemblance to a coordinated regional development program with a clear and consistent development strategy, it cannot serve as a model for future regional development planning. The limited experiences of the now-defunct Title V regional development commissions also provide little positive guidance for the future. Moreover, both EDA and the Title V commissions were located within the U.S. Department of Commerce, which effectively precluded regional program coordination at the federal level. The secretary of commerce, or any other cabinet secretary, simply does not have the authority or ability to coordinate the relevant activities of his or her equals in other departments. If any new regional development agency were to be submerged in a cabinet department, the federal presence would be "so inconsequential that sectionalist rivalries may well become dominant in regional programs."[66]

In contrast to the other regional economic development agencies created in 1965, the ARC was a joint federal–state venture, independent of cabinet departments. And despite the moribund appearance of the present ARC, the innovative experiments of its earlier years are still instructive. However, before becoming more specific in this regard, it is pertinent to recall that in the late 1970s there was considerable support within the Carter administration and among the states' governors for multistate regional economic development commissions that would blanket the entire United States. Any future major regional development policy initiatives would probably return to this general approach. Because all parts of the country have perceived regional problems, it is unlikely that Congress would support the creation of multistate regional economic development agencies (REDAs) for only a few areas. Moreover, past experience suggests that the REDAs should be given a broader scope than the regional commissions created in 1965, in both geographic and programmatic terms.

The role of the states would be a pivotal issue in regional economic development planning. Although the U.S. Department of Commerce, among others, faulted the ARC for not preparing a full-blown master plan for Appalachian development, this approach did not appear to be feasible, nor would it in the future. A multistate region does not really exist in the sense of having a government and a common political community. Thus the most expedient way to formulate and implement regional development programs is through the states. This does not imply that a REDA should have only a passive role in planning. Indeed, the ARC actively promoted regional and even state development objectives from a broader perspective than the state governments might have taken. Derthick points out that the ARC staff prefers human resources investments

> to public works or law enforcement. It prefers the innovative to the routine. It prefers concentration of funds to dispersion of funds, to attain programatic purposes rather than the politician's presumed purpose of rewarding followers on the widest possible scale. While the staff serves the states, it tends also to view them as an object of reform.[67]

Moreover, the ARC's states' regional representative "has been no less inclined than other elements of the headquarters organization to view the states as objects of influence, in need of reform in their own interest."[68] While putting pressure on the relevant states, the ARC still realized that in order to be effective a regional development policy must not depart too much at any given time from the aspirations of the constituency it is designed to serve. What is required is

> an evolutionary process of organizational development which enables a regional development program to lead its constituency over time toward increasingly sophisticated strategies. The key to success is the pacing of program development.[69]

In fact, few Appalachian states took full advantage of the potential of the ARC program.[70] In many instances, changes in state administrations adversely affected program continuity, coordination of relevant state agency programs was not achieved, and with the exception of West Virginia, only parts of states were included in the program, which meant that a governor was often preoccupied with other demands in the state. In any future REDA program, the problems of continuity and coordination could presumably be improved, especially if motivated by a budget level sufficient to command attention. And such a program should include whole states, or in exceptional cases, as in that of California, a single state.[71]

Under the ARC program, states were encouraged to accord to their local governments the same kind of partnership in decision making that the states themselves had with the federal government through the ARC. This three-tier, integrated regional planning hierarchy represents one of the more promising and successful innovations of the Appalachian program. To strengthen planning and coordination at the local level, the Appalachian states created multicounty local development districts to foster interjurisdictional cooperation, to realize economies of scale in the performance of community functions, and to enable local priorities and decisions to influence the local investments of federal and state agencies. In 1984, the 69 Appalachian local development districts employed an average of 128 persons and had an average annual operating budget of $530,000. Direct federal funding provided 41% of the budget; 13% came from state sources, 26% from local governments, and 20% from private sources.[72] Any new REDA should work through both the relevant states and substate multicounty planning districts, whose governing boards should include local public officials as well as private citizens representative of a cross-section of local interest groups. Rural areas in particular need to combine their forces within a multicounty planning district framework so that they can more effectively simulate the services that are better developed in metropolitan areas. Enhanced local development possibilities may also require some form of quasi-public entrepreneurship, such as a nonprofit local development corporation willing to pay the price to hold or attract talented leadership. In the South especially, state and local industrial recruitment strategies have done little to stimulate local leadership and entrepreneurship for economic development. Local development organizations that function as "public entrepreneurs" are not widespread, and those that do exist are typically small and underfinanced. Successful examples of "alternative development" have used varying strategies, but invariably local initiative has been the key to success.

> There is a common thread in each case—a local or regional organization which knows the area and involves a cross-section of its citizens.[73]

This also is in keeping with Jane Jacobs's effectively argued thesis that "development cannot be given. It has to be done. It is a process, not a collection of capital goods."[74]

In conclusion, the United States is a collection of heterogeneous regions with differing problems and opportunities.[75] It has been suggested that this diversity has permitted the U.S. economy to adapt more readily to change than has been the case with many European economies.[76] In Schumpeterian terms, in the process of creative destruction, the sheer overall size of the United States and its regional heterogeneity has produced vitality and renewal in some regions (California, New England) even while others (the industrial Midwest, Texas) may, at least for the time being, be faltering with respect to competitiveness. One of the principal reasons why so many government programs are cumbersome and inefficient is that

> general rules and regulations, designed for "average" situations, are inappropriate for communities and areas that diverge markedly from the average. And in a country as large and diverse as ours, with as many programs as we now have, general rules for average situations will lead to multitudes of examples to fill the scrapbooks of collectors of public administrative horror tales.[77]

From this perspective alone, it would seem logical to have a national system of general purpose REDAs, with a focus on development priorities.[78] Some REDAs might concentrate on problems of low income, high unemployment, or industrial conversion, but even in such instances their scope would be much broader than that of an industrial development agency or a purveyor of public works projects. Other REDAs might wish to give major attention to growth management and quality-of-life issues. Yet whatever their development priorities, the REDAs should help to improve the functioning of the federal system so that, in cooperation with the private sector, the economic and social development of their respective regions would be enhanced.[79] If the REDA option were to be implemented, the enabling legislation should allow for considerable program and project flexibility. Regional policy, as regional development—and indeed as life itself—is a continuously evolving process, requiring adaptability, and, with some luck, creativity and novelty.

NOTES

[1]Ray Marshall, "TVA and Social Development," University of Texas Center for the Study of Human Resources, 1972, unpublished paper.

[2]For detailed reviews of implicit and explicit U.S. regional policies prior to the 1950s, see, for example, John H. Cumberland, *Regional Development: Experiences and Prospects in the United States of America* (Paris: Mouton,1971); and Curtis H. Martin and Robert A. Leone, *Local Economic Development* (Lexington, MA: D. C. Heath, Lexington Books, 1977).

[3]For detailed studies of the Area Redevelopment Administration and the debates that led to its creation, see Sar A. Levitan, *Federal Aid to Depressed Areas* (Baltimore: The Johns Hopkins Press, 1964); Cumberland, *Regional Development*, Chapter 7; and Martin and Leone, *Local Economic Development*, Chapter 2.

[4]U.S. Department of Agriculture, *Communities of Tomorrow: Agriculture 2000* (Washington, DC: U.S. Government Printing Office), p. 17.

[5]Sara Mills Mazie and Steve Rawlings, "Public Attitude toward Population Distribution Issues," U.S. Commission on Population Growth and the American Future, *Population*

Distribution and Policy, Vol. V of commission research reports (Washington, DC: U.S. Government Printing Office, 1972), pp. 599–615.

[6]U.S. Department of Agriculture, *Communities of Tomorrow*, p. 17.

[7]President's National Advisory Committee on Rural Poverty, *The People Left Behind* (Washington, DC: U.S. Government Printing Office, 1967), p. xiii. The emphasis is mine.

[8]James L. Sundquist and Hugh Mields, Jr., *Regional Growth Policy in the United States* (Washington, DC: National Rural Center, 1978), p. 8.

[9]Ibid., p. 9.

[10]Ibid., p. 12.

[11]U.S. Department of Commerce, Economic Development Administration, EDA *Handbook* (Washington, DC: U.S. Government Printing Office, 1968), p. 2.

[12]Benjamin Chinitz, "The Regional Problem in the USA," in E. A. O. Robinson ed., *Backward Areas in Advanced Countries* (New York: St. Martin's Press, 1969), p. 61. See also Gordon C. Cameron, *Regional Economic Development: The Federal Role* (Baltimore: The Johns Hopkins Press, 1970), pp. 77–86.

[13]Raymond H. Milkman, Christopher Bladen, Beverly Lyford, and Howard L. Walton, *Alleviating Economic Distress* (Lexington, MA: D.C. Heath, Lexington Books, 1972), p. 13.

[14]U.S. Department of Commerce, Economic Development Administration, *Economic Development Administration Annual Report* (Washington, DC: EDA, 1967), pp. 22–23.

[15]Ibid., p. 23.

[16]Milkman *et al.*, *Alleviating Economic Distress*, p. 33.

[17]U.S. Department of Commerce, Economic Development Administration, *Program Evaluation: The Economic Development Administrative Growth Center Strategy* (Washington, DC: EDA, 1972), p. 5.

[18]U.S. Department of Commerce and U.S. Office of Management and Budget, *Report to the Congress on the Proposal for an Economic Adjustment Program* (Washington, DC: U.S. Department of Commerce and OMB, 1974), p. 25.

[19]Battelle Memorial Institute, *Evaluation of Economic Development Administration Planning Grants* (Columbus, OH: Battelle Memorial Institute, 1970).

[20]Sar A. Levitan and Joyce K. Zickler, *Too Little but not Too Late* (Lexington, MA: D. C. Heath, Lexington Books, 1976), p. 66.

[21]Cumberland, *Regional Development*, p. 91.

[22]Niles Hansen, *Rural Poverty and the Urban Crisis* (Bloomington: Indiana University Press, 1970), pp. 61–64.

[23]Ralph R. Widner, "Evaluating the Administration of the Appalachian Regional Development Program," *Growth and Change*, Vol. 4, No. 1 (January 1973), p. 26.

[24]United States Public Law 89-4, Appalachian Regional Development Act of 1965, 89th Congress, 9 March 1965, Section 2.

[25]Ibid.

[26]Appalachian Regional Commission, "Appalachia: Twenty Years of Progress," special number of *Appalachia*, Vol. 18, No. 3 (March 1985), p. 22.

[27]President's Appalachian Regional Commission, *Appalachia* (Washington, D.C.: PARC, 1964), p. 32.

[28]See, for example, Niles Hansen, "Some Neglected Factors in American Regional Development Policy: The Case of Appalachia," *Land Economics*, Vol. 42, No. 1 (February 1966), pp. 1–9; and John Munro, "Planning the Appalachian Development Highway System: Some Critical Questions," *Land Economics*, Vol. 45, No. 2 (May 1969), pp. 149–156.

[29]Appalachian Regional Commission, "Appalachia: Twenty Years of Progress," p. 105.

[30]Ralph R. Widner, "Appalachia After Six Years," *Appalachia*, Vol. 5, No. 6 (December 1971), p. 19.

[31]Monroe Newman, *The Political Economy of Appalachia* (Lexington, MA: D. C. Heath, Lexington Books, 1972), pp. 148–49.

[32]Appalachian Regional Commission, *State and Regional Development Plans in Appalachia, 1968* (Washington, DC: ARC, 1968), p. 12.

[33]Newman, *The Political Economy of Appalachia*, p. 157.

[34]Martha Derthick, *Between State and Nation* (Washington, DC: The Brookings Institution, 1974), p. 108.

[35]Comptroller General of the United States, *Review of Selected Activities of Regional Commissions*, Report No. B–177392 (Washington, DC: U.S. General Accounting Office, 26 March 1974), pp. 1–2.

[36]David Walker, "Interstate Regional Instrumentalities: A New Piece of an Old Puzzle," *Journal of the American Institute of Planners*, Vol. 38, No. 6 (November 1972), pp. 359–368.

[37]U.S. Bureau of the Census, *Statistical Abstract of the United States: 1986* (Washington, DC: U.S. Government Printing Office, 1985), pp. 11, 14.

[38]U.S. Department of Commerce, *United States Department of Commerce News*, 22 March 1984.

[39]Niles Hansen, "Regional Science and Regional Restructuring: A Critique," *International Regional Science Review*.

[40]U.S. Bureau of the Census, *Statistical Abstract of the United States: 1986*, p. 13.

[41]U.S. Bureau of the Census, *Statistical Abstract of the United States: 1980* (Washington, DC: U.S. Government Printing Office, 1980), p. 440.

[42]Martin and Leone, *Local Economic Development*, p. 58.

[43]Ibid.

[44]U.S. Department of Commerce, Economic Development Administration, *1985 Annual Report* (Washington, DC: EDA, 1986), p. xi.

[45]U.S. Department of Commerce, Economic Development Administration, *1979 Annual Report* (Washington, DC: EDA, 1980), pp. 29, 54.

[46]U.S. Department of Commerce, Economic Development Administration, *EDA Handbook*, p. 2.

[47]B. F. Kiker and Randolph C. Martin, *The Economic Impact on Local Areas of the Program of the Economic Development Administration* (Washington, DC: National Technical Information Service, PB80–146681, 1979).

[48]U.S. Department of Commerce, Economic Development Administration, "The Development of a Subnational Economic Development Policy," *The White House Conference on Balanced National Growth and Economic Development*, Final Report, Appendix Vol. 6 (Washington, DC: U.S. Government Printing Office, 1978), p. 67.

[49]Ibid., p. 68.

[50]U.S. Department of Commerce, Economic Development Administration, *1981 Annual Report* (Washington, DC: EDA, 1982), p. ii.

[51]U.S. Department of Commerce, Economic Development Administration, *1985 Annual Report*, p. vii.

[52]Ibid.

[53]The data presented here are from Appalachian Regional Commission, "Appalachia: Twenty Years of Progress," pp. 76–82.

[54]Ibid.

[55]Appalachian Regional Commission, *1986 Annual Report* (Washington, D.C.: ARC, 1987), p. 13.

[56]Appalachian Governors, *A Report to Congress from the Appalachian Governors Concerning the*

Appalachian Regional Commission (Washington, DC: Appalachian Regional Commission, 31 December 1981), p. 32.

[57]Ibid., p. 44.

[58]Ibid., p. 45.

[59]Ibid.

[60]Appalachian Regional Commission, "Appalachia: Twenty Years of Progress," p. 30.

[61]Sundquist and Mields, *Regional Growth Policy in the United States*, p. 44.

[62]William H. Miernyk, "The Tools of Regional Development Policy," *Growth and Change*, Vol. 11, No. 2 (April 1980), pp. 2–3.

[63]Newman, *The Political Economy of Appalachia*, p. 150.

[64]Appalachian Regional Commission, "Appalachia: Twenty Years of Progress," p. 28.

[65]Ibid.

[66]Monroe Newman, "The Future of Multistate Regional Commissions," *Growth and Change*, Vol. 11, No. 2 (April 1980), p. 16.

[67]Derthick, *Between State and Nation*, p. 94.

[68]Ibid., p. 96.

[69]Widner, "Evaluating the Administration of the Appalachian Regional Development Program," p. 26.

[70]Ibid., p. 27.

[71]Potential opportunities—in an intrastate context—for relating the problems of lagging areas to opportunities in other areas are discussed in Niles Hansen, "Migration Centers, Growth Centers and the Regional Commissions: An Analysis of Expected Future Lifetime Income Gains to Migrants from Lagging Regions," *Southern Economic Journal*, Vol. 38, No. 4 (April 1972), pp. 508–517.

[72]Appalachian Regional Commission, "Appalachia: Twenty Years of Progress," p. 71.

[73]MCD Panel on Rural Economic Development, *Shadows in the Sunbelt* (Chapel Hill, NC: MDC, Inc., 1986), p. 13.

[74]Jane Jacobs, *Cities and the Wealth of Nations* (New York: Random House Vintage Books, 1985), p. 119.

[75]For detailed discussion in this regard, see Niles Hansen, "Urban and Regional Adaptability to Structural Economic Change," forthcoming.

[76]R. D. Norton, "Industrial Policy and American Renewal," *Journal of Economic Literature*, Vol. 24, No. 1 (March 1986), pp. 1–39.

[77]Newman, "The Future of Multistate Regional Commissions," p. 14.

[78]For further discussion of their possible structure and scope, see Benjamin Chinitz, "Regional Economic Development Commissions: The Title V Program" *Canadian Journal of Regional Science*, Vol. 1, No. 2 (Autumn 1978), pp. 124–126.

[79]A study of U.S. trade and industry by Japan's International Trade Institute contends that future U.S. economic growth will depend to a large degree on a national commitment to establish a comprehensive policy for regional development. See Leonard Silk, "Japanese Stress Regions in U.S.," *New York Times*, 20 February, 1987, p. 30.

CHAPTER SIX

Regional Development Policy
The Australian Case

Among countries with distinctly regionalized economic and political
structures, Australia is virtually unique in its degree of indifference to
regional problems and policies, both within the academic community
and among the general public. To an economist brought up in Canada, it
seems extraordinary that highly respected surveys of the Australian
economy and Australian economic development, published since World
War II, should contain not one word about regional problems, regional
development, or regional policy.[1] Regional policy is almost never a major campaign issue. It is seldom debated in Parliament, or discussed on
television or in the press, although the media allocate more time and
space to economic and social issues in Australia than in most countries.

Before we can move toward conclusions on Australian regional policy, we must examine the basic reasons for the Australian tendency to
overlook spatial structures and the spatial distribution of economic and
social problems and activities. The explanation goes back to the begin-
nings of white settlement in Australia; yet regional policy since World
War II cannot be fully understood without this explanation. It is to be
expected that readers outside of Australia will be unfamiliar with some
of the facts. Even readers in Australia, although acquainted with most of
the individual facts, may not have put them together within an analytical framework that illuminates current economic, social, and political
problems.

THE IMMOVABLE FRONTIER

In the economic histories of other large countries of recent settlement, the moving frontier plays a major role. In the United States, and

to a lesser degree in Canada, the progressive westward movement, over
three centuries, spread population, and eventually large cities and industrialization, throughout the entire country. The process created large
disparities in incomes between rich and poor regions, in the United
States exceeding 400%, reflecting differences in product mix and occupational structure in areas at widely differing stages of development. Then
as industrialization and urbanization spread, the regional disparities
dwindled. In Argentina and Brazil, the movement was for centuries
along a north–south axis near the coast, and the interior remained thinly
settled with no large cities, which helps to explain the relative underdevelopment of these countries. Only in recent years, with the construction of Brasilia and the Brazilia–Belem road, and the new interest in
developing the Amazon valley, has there been a significant westward
movement in Brazil. In Australia, however, there never was a significant
movement of the center of population, until recently with discovery of
mineral resources in the north. Population, large cities, and industrialization have never moved far from the coast. A major reason for that
immobility, of course, is the uninviting nature of the interior.

The famous American historian F. J. Turner created a whole school
of thought with his "frontier theory" of development of American society. The following passage illustrates his theory of the moving frontier:

> Stand at the Cumberland Gap and watch the procession of civiliza-
> tion, marching single file—the buffalo following the trail to the salt
> springs, the Indian, the fur trader and hunter, the cattle raiser, the
> pioneer farmer—and the frontier has passed by. Stand at South Pass
> in the Rockies a century later and see the same procession with
> wider intervals in between. The unequal rate of advance compels us
> to distinguish the frontier,—into the trader's frontier, the rancher's
> frontier, or the miner's frontier, and the farmer's frontier. When the
> mines and cow pens were still near the fall line, the trader's pack
> trains were tinkling across the Alleghanies, and the French on the
> Great Lakes were fortifying their posts, alarmed by the British
> trader's birch canoe. When the trappers scaled the Rockies, the
> farmer was still near the mouth of the Missouri.[2]

In the last two decades, there has been a movement to the south as well
as to the west, as scientifically oriented, hi-tech industry sought the sun.

Now consider a contrasting passage from Australian historian Keith
Hancock, who undoubtedly read Turner:

> There is a famous gap in the range of the Blue Mountains, that wall
> of rock and scrub which for a quarter of a century hemmed in this
> colony of New South Wales within the coastal plain. Stand at this
> gap and watch the frontiers following each other westward—the

squatters' frontier which filled the western plains with sheep and
laid the foundations of Australia's economy, the miners' frontier
which brought Australia population and made her a radical democracy, the farmers' frontier which gradually and painfully tested and
proved the controls of Australian soil and climate. Stand a few hundred miles further west on the Darling river and see what these
controls have done to the frontier. The farmers have dropped out of
the westward movement procession, beaten by aridity. Only the
pastoralists and prospectors pass by. In the west centre of the conti-
nent, aridity has beaten even the pastoralists. On the fringe of a
dynamic society there are left only a few straggling prospectors and
curious anthropologists, infrequent invaders of the aboriginal
reserves.[3]

Turner thought that America owes its "rugged individualism" to
the moving frontier. Columbia University economic historian Garter
Goodrich agreed but thought that the impact of the frontier on American
society was so profound, not just because it moved, but because it was a
small man's frontier. As a student of Australian development, he wrote:

Certainly the United States owes its individualism largely to its small
man's frontier; I think it is not fanciful to suggest that Australia owes
much of its collectivism to the fact that its frontier was hospitable to
the large man instead.[4]

Much of the settlement of Australia took the form of "rich squatters" taking up vast tracts of land, hiring very few workers and running
large numbers of animals. Far from pulling population away from the
cities to the interior, this settlement pattern created jobs in the urban
centers, servicing the pastoral economy. Even the mineral discoveries
did not move the center of population as they did in North America. The
early gold discoveries were only a few miles from Melbourne and Sydney. Professor Fred Alexander puts the matter thus:

Use of the term "frontier" to cover gold rushes to such places as
Ballarat and Bendigo, not far distant from the established centre of
Melbourne and considerably within the outer rim of existing pastoral settlement, is unduly stretching the definition given in the
opening paragraph of this essay.[5]

When the irresistible force of immigration met the stubbornly immova-
ble frontier, the only possible result was growth of the six capital cities.
Moreover, these cities and their hinterlands developed together at
almost the same time, almost at the same rhythm, and almost in the
same pattern. It is worth recalling that when the First Fleet arrived from
the United Kingdom in 1788, Australia was undeveloped even in com-

parison with North America when the first settlers arrived there. The North American Indians did have some urban settlements and some stable agriculture, and many of today's cities grew up on the sites of Indian settlements. When the white man arrived in Australia, there were no urban settlements and no stable agriculture. Moreover, there was very little settlement or development before 1820. In that year, Sydney and Hobart were still essentially small convict settlements. Brisbane was established in 1824, the Swan River settlement (Perth) in 1829, Melbourne in 1835, and Adelaide in 1836. Thus the settlements that were to become the state capitals were essentially established within one generation. Moreover, they were all settled by essentially the same kind of people. In all of the colonies most people lived in the capital city from the beginning, whereas the extensive farming and grazing and the mining drew few people into the interior. The cities did not grow much by rural–urban migration because there were practically no rural people to migrate; the cities grew by migration from the United Kingdom. Another very important feature of all of these societies is that from the beginning, the average incomes in the countryside were much the same as in the urban centers; poverty was not primarily a rural phenomenon.

Another feature of the six primate cities worth noting is that they are all ports, and that there are no major ports apart from the six cities (although Darwin, Geelong, and Broome are increasing in importance). For two centuries virtually all overseas trade and all immigration have gone through them. Consequently, the domestic transport system—rail, road, and air—focuses on them, the more so because transport is essentially a state responsibility. Consequently, industries and services wishing to serve the domestic market, as well as those linked to world markets, have tended to locate in the capital cities. The communications system also centers on them.

In sum, then, each state economy consists of a large capital city with a set of manufacturing activities and a wide range of services, and a prosperous hinterland engaged in extensive agriculture and mining, with much the same product mix and occupational structure in all of them. With so high a degree of similarity in the structure of the state economies and so much homogeneity in the societies that developed in each of the six spaces, when "regions" are defined as states, as they usually are, large regional disparities do not appear. Except for Tasmania, which chronically lags somewhat behind the other states, every state has been the richest in the Commonwealth in at least 1 year since World War II, and the relative ranks in terms of per capita income keep changing. Nor are there sharp differences in race, religion, or language to bring interregional conflict of the sort that has plagued other large, regionalized countries. For all these reasons, regional disparities have not been a major political issue, nor a topic that kindles deep emotions or sharp debate. There have been two short-lived movements for separation, one in Northern Queensland and one in Western Australia; but these were more a matter of people wanting to be free to pursue their own interests and development policies, rather than of resentment of people in some societies toward what they regarded as exploitation or as being disadvantaged by being part of a larger political unit. We shall see that identifying "regions" with "states" has been a mistake from the standpoint of economic and social policy; but that is how things have gone. In a confederation where "regions" are states, and disparities among states are not serious, it is not surprising that relations among states, between the federal government and the states, and "regional policy" have not been primarily concerned with regional gaps and regional development.

FISCAL FEDERALISM

Given this background, it is understandable that since the Confederation of six states and the Northwest Territories into a Commonwealth in 1901, discussion of "regional policy," both among social scientists and by politicians and the general public, should have become virtually synonymous with discussion of "fiscal federalism." In *this* field, Australia has shown considerable ingenuity, and on *this* subject the literature is mountainous. However, much of the literature and discussion regarding federal–state financial relations is not really concerned with regional policy as I would define it: supplementing market forces by specific intervention in defined spaces, in order to accelerate or redirect development of those spaces, with a view to reducing regional disparities, eliminating poverty and unemployment, bringing faster or more efficient development of resource frontiers, and to prevent, offset, or retard congestion, pollution, and environmental degradation. Rather, it has been concerned with integrating monetary and fiscal policy, and with maintaining a certain balance in fiscal *capacity* to provide services among states. I shall not, accordingly, attempt to cover the whole of this vast and complex field but will leave that to the specialists, of which there are many; here, I shall concentrate on aspects that have some bearing on regional policy as defined.

In a paper written for the symposium Australian Regional Development, Professor Russell Mathews, former director of the Centre for Research on Federal Financial Relations at the Australian National University and a member of the Commonwealth Grants Commission, points out that there are three types of regional disparities that might be attacked by regional policy: in household incomes, in economic development, and in fiscal capacity. He goes on to say that in Australia, only the last two have been of any importance. Efforts to reduce gaps in household incomes have not taken a regional form. Even the concern for regional development has been indirect and limited to whatever impact equalization of fiscal *capacity* may have on equalization of development opportunities. It is up to the states to decide how fiscal capacity is to be utilized, whether for development or not, and if so, what kind of development. In fact, Mathews maintains that the federal government's financial aid to the states is not even designed to equalize standards of public service; its aim is only to *facilitate* such equalization, and what standards of service are actually provided is for the states to determine.[6]

The Commonwealth Grants Commission was established in 1933. The commission is appointed by the Commonwealth government and concerns itself with revenue sharing through general grants to claimant states. Its function is to assess the needs of the states for such grants in terms of equalization of fiscal capacity. These grants became more than ever important to the states after their abandonment of the income tax field in 1942, and the later judicial finding that sales taxes are excise duties, and so are not available to the states. There are also Special Purpose Grants. Before the war, these were mainly for roads and railroads; but since the war they have been extended to such purposes as acquisition of land for public housing, sewage systems, urban water supplies, and urban public transport. In general, in the postwar period, the Special Purpose Grants have been directed toward the problems of the burgeoning cities and particularly the large metropolitan centers. They have accordingly gone mainly to the more densely populated and more highly developed states. Since the war, the Commonwealth has also assumed major responsibility for higher education. Again, all this assistance is not thought of as being directed toward reducing regional disparities or promoting regional development. It is aimed merely at avoiding the *necessity* for obvious disparities in standards of public service among states.

REGIONAL POLICY: 1945–1987

Let us turn now to those policies that might be regarded as aiming at the improvement of allocation of population, resources, economic activity, and incomes in space, and thus as qualifying as "regional policies."

By and large, Australia's Labor governments have shown mild to keen interest in regional policies and regional development, and the Liberal–National–Country party conservative coalition, when in power, has displayed anything from disinterest to active opposition to such policies. Since World War II, Labor has been in power from 1945 to 1949, from 1972 to 1975, and since 1983; the coalition has been in power in the intervals. The result has been a seesaw effect on regional policy with no very clear trend.

The Curtin Labor government that was in power during the war set up a Department of Postwar Reconstruction in 1942, to undertake postwar planning for a better and avowedly socialist Australia. The blueprint included a planned economy, a good deal of emphasis on housing and city planning, decentralization, and regional planning. The Chifley Labor government that succeeded Curtin maintained these policies, and once the war was over, adopted a policy of regional development in cooperation with the states. Regions were defined and inventories of resources within them prepared. Regional development committees were established and plans prepared for some of the regions. However, most of the powers and instruments for implementing such plans were in the hands of the state and local governments. The states were more interested in using these powers, such as offering subsidies for transport on state-owned railways, to lure industry from other states. In any case, before any serious or effective regional development program got under way, the Labor government went down to defeat in the election of 1949. Labor was not to capture power again for 23 years.

The coalition government under Robert Menzies quickly set about dismantling what little there was of Labor's regional development program. They made it clear that no Commonwealth funds would be available for regional and local development beyond their commitment for assistance with state housing programs. Succeeding Conservative coalition governments maintained this posture, and regional policy was kept in the wings for more than two decades.

At the same time, there was another factor influencing regional policy. Since Confederation, there has always been sentiment in favor of some sort of decentralization policy, and a feeling that the capital cities, especially Sydney and Melbourne, are "too big." The Liberal–National–Country party governments could not altogether ignore this sentiment. Until the mid-1960s, however, decentralization policies were simply directed at promoting growth of any nonmetropolitan centre anywhere. After 1965, there was growing recognition that a program to divert growth from the metropolitan areas to smaller centers would be more effective if it concentrated on a limited number of growth poles, largely as a result of the publication in that year of Professor G. M. Neutze's book, *Economic Policy and the Size of Cities*.[7] Once again, however, the powers for implementing such a strategy were largely in the hands of the states, and it was politically difficult for state governments to restrict their assistance to a small number of designated growth poles. Two state government committees were organized to study the matter, in 1967 and 1969, and both New South Wales and Victoria did designate some growth centers. Before these programs could make much progress, however, Labor, under the leadership of Gough Whitlam, was swept to power, and this government was to embark upon much more ambitious urban and regional policies.

THE WHITLAM LABOR GOVERNMENT: 1972–1975

The short-lived Whitlam regime had a more systematic and articulate regional policy than any government in Australian history—at least on paper. There are not many informed observers who are prepared to argue that it was a great success in practice.

The urban and regional policy was part of a much broader program of economic, social, and political reform. The logic flows from the general philosophy of the Australian Labor Party (ALP) to a new constitutional platform to a new fiscal policy to a new concept of federal–state financial relations to the new urban and regional policy. The philosophy was outlined by Prime Minister Whitlam in a 1972 policy speech[8] and was based on three major objectives of the ALP: to promote equality; to involve the people of Australia in the decision-making processes of our land; and to liberate the talents and uplift the horizons of the Australian people. This concept of participatory social democracy led to a new approach to the constitution, which reversed earlier trends toward greater centralization of powers, accorded recognition to the states as major partners in the federation, maintained that local and regional governments must be treated as essential parts of the federation as well, and regarded the Commonwealth as the coordinator of an expanding system of public services. These views led in turn to a substantial increase in total public expenditures and to large increases in federal grants to states. Within this framework, there was a program to strengthen local governments, establish regional authorities, and to create growth centers.

For the Whitlam government, increased public spending was not a necessary evil forced upon it by unfortunate circumstances, but part of its basic philosophy. It *wanted* to enlarge the role of government in the economic and social life of the nation, expand social programs, and raise labor's share of national income. It also wanted to create jobs. The rate on unemployment was still low on international standards, but it was higher than it had been, and a Labor government could not simply ignore it. For the most part, they seemed to have pursued a rather simplistic Keynesian approach: They wanted to increase social expenditures anyway, and the increased spending should reduce unemployment. There were, however, splits regarding monetary and fiscal policy within the Cabinet and among its advisors. After some internal debate, the antitreasury view of Dr. James Cairns prevailed in the 1973 budget:

> Crucial as the fight against inflation is, it cannot be made the sole objective of government policy. The government's overriding objective is to get on with our various initiatives in the fields of education, health, social welfare and urban improvements. The relatively subdued conditions in prospect for the private sector provide the first real oportunity we have had to transfer resources to the public sector.[9]

Later, when William Hayden replaced Cairns in the Treasury, at a time when inflation and unemployment were increasing together, Mr. Hayden sounded almost like a Friedman-Monetarist. In his 1975 budget speech, he said: "We are no longer operating in that simple Keynesian world in which some reduction in unemployment could, apparently, always be purchased at the cost of some more inflation. Today, it is inflation itself which is the central policy problem. More inflation simply leads to more unemployment."[10] At any rate, total public expenditures rose from 31.3% of GDP in 1972–1973 to 38.8% in 1975–1976 and social expenditures from 14.3% to 21.2%.

The government's policy regarding federal–state financial relations strengthened the states financially but somewhat reduced their independence. The fields where Commonwealth expenditures grew most rapidly—urban and regional development, health, and education—were those that had been traditionally regarded as state responsibilities. The expansion was financed by specific purpose grants that grew at a rate of 64.6% per annum. Some state governments resented this apparent loss of freedom to determine the shape of their own budgets; but, of course, the increased flow of funds for these purposes released state revenues for other purposes. Moreover, general revenue assistance to the states also grew at 18.0% per year, as compared to 8.5% over the previous decade under the conservative coalition.[11] In absolute amounts, specific purpose payments increased from $906 million to $4,213 million and general revenue grants from $1,923 million to $3,112 million over the same period.

Professor Groenewegen states that "the Whitlam government's attempts to upgrade local and regional government to the status of full partners in the federation are at the same time the most interesting of its innovations and the greatest of its failures."[12] The aim of increasing the participation of the Australian people in decision making, he says, was never realized. The new regional authorities that were created "rarely had such independent status and in many cases were little more than new boundaries drawn on the map."[13] Most analysts of the Whitlam urban and regional policies regard them as failures, at least to a very large extent. Why?

Professor R. K. Wilson of Melbourne University reminds us that the objectives of these policies were nothing so simple and clear cut as reducing "regional disparities" in the usual sense of differences in levels of per capita income, unemployment, or incidence of poverty among states or provinces.[14] They included decentralization, which, with 58% of the country's total population in the five larger state capitals at the time, was not an unreasonable aim. In particular, they were directed toward reducing the pressures on Melbourne and Sydney. But they also included among their objectives something brand new, a different concept of causes and cures of inequalities. In his 1972 policy speech, Mr. Whitlam maintained that "in modern Australia, social inequality is fixed upon families by the place in which they are forced to live even more than by what they are able to earn." In other words, inequalities are not due so much to the concentration of ownership of wealth as to disparities in the nature of the places where people live, access to jobs and amenities, costs of land and housing, and provision of social services, education, health, and other facilities. Inequality is accordingly *essentially spatial in origin*. Moreover, because most Australians live in big cities (and because the countryside is not less prosperous than the cities), these spatial disparities occur, not between regions, but *within cities*. Thus "regional policy" must be directed toward disadvantaged suburbs of large cities and particularly toward the working class western suburbs of Sydney and Melbourne.

The left wing of the ALP was not altogether happy with this new formulation of the problem of inequality. They preferred the good old-fashioned Marxist view that inequality springs from the concentration of ownership of means of production in the hands of the capitalist class. Leoni Sandercock maintains that the major source of Whitlam's new concept was the Australian National University's Urban Research Unit, and particularly its director, Max Neutze, and Patrick Troy, who was seconded to the new government by the unit.[15] Whatever the source, it was Whitlam's new philosophy that prevailed. And beyond all that, of course, the urban and regional policies were seen as vehicles for the introduction of Whitlam's participatory social democracy. It was a tall order for a new government whose party had been out of power for 23 years.

The main instrument for the Labor government's new urban and regional policies was the Department of Urban and Regional Development (DURD), created in December 1972. The list of problems identified for DURD in the policy speech was enough to make the bravest of bureaucrats quail: Prices of land and housing were soaring; urban public transport was falling apart; provision of sewerage systems was running far behind needs; journeys to work were too long; city centers were overcrowded and deteriorating; new towns must be created to divert population from the big cities, especially Sydney and Melbourne.

The sewerage and growth center programs were first off the mark. On the border between New South Wales and Victoria are the twin cities of Albury and Wodonga, on the railway line and highway between Sydney and Melbourne. In 1973 an agreement was reached with the New South Wales and Victoria governments to convert Albury–Wodonga into a growth center, and funds were provided for that purpose. Later Bathurst–Orange in New South Wales and Monarto in South Australia were designated for the same purpose. An Area Improvement Program (AIP) was introduced to organize regional bodies, with local representation, to identify regional problems and work out regional strategies for solving them, especially where urban infrastructure and community service were inadequate. This program began with pilot projects in the western suburbs of Melbourne and Sydney that later were extended to 11 other regions. The program was administered by local governments in each of the regions, and these in turn were assisted under the Grants Commission Act of 1973, which provided funds to the states for redistribution to those local governments that were experiencing difficulties in maintaining the standards set by other communities in the region or in other regions. In 1975 grants were made to 885 local councils under this program.

There was also to have been a Land Commission program, to set up public land development agencies in each state with enough clout to influence prices of land and the distribution of development in different areas. This program ran head on into opposition of state governments, especially those where a Liberal government was in power. Dr. Sandercock points out that although the federal government could create growth centers, purchase inner city land for urban renewal, and relocate government offices in city suburbs, most of the purposes foreseen for the land commissions required the cooperation of the states. She adds,

"Frequently that cooperation was simply not forthcoming. It is as unrealistic to expect a State Liberal government to abolish land speculation as it would be to expect a State Labor government to abolish welfare housing, just because a federal government (of the opposite political complexion) says it must."[16]

Another venture that did not get very far was the Australia Assistance Plan. Under the AAP, the Social Welfare Commission was to establish regional organizations, with representation from the Commonwealth, state and local governments, trade unions, employers' organizations, and nongovernment organizations concerned with social welfare to monitor and plan social services in the region, advise government departments, and carry out modest projects with federal funds. Such organizations were set up in all states but Tasmania and Western Australia, but the program had barely started when the Fraser government abolished it in 1976.

The Whitlam government's brave schemes for upgrading local governments also ran into obstacles. Local governments are creatures of the states, and the state premiers resented the apparent encroaching on their authority implicit in according more responsibility to the local councils. The government's plan to give local governments direct access to the Loan Council was defeated by the states, and when the government went to the people with a referendum to provide for a constitutional amendment that would achieve the Labor government's aims, that was defeated too.

The aims of the Whitlam regime's urban and regional policies were clearly very ambitious, perhaps even romantically so. There have been various attempts to explain the relative failure of the program. Dr. Sandercock makes the point that the essential character of the program was such that it was bound to run into stiff opposition, not only from the state governments but from the established Canberra bureaucracy as well. As a new department, she says, DURD recruited staff from outside the public service, many of whom had been engaged in "grass roots urban action," trying to bring about change through community action or the education system—"Young Turks," in effect. Of them, she says:

> These people did not sit easily in inter-departmental committee meetings with the more conventional career public servants from the established departments. DURD gained the reputation, not only among other federal departments but also with those State departments involved in negotiating programmes with DURD, as the abrasive department. Missionary zeal, moral outrage, and shorts and thongs, were not styles of negotiation that got far in the dour, pseudo-neutral, quiet-suited world of the Canberra bureaucracy.[17]

Apart from its abrasive "house style," DURD's "radical interventionist economists" were bound to clash with the sober neoclassical, monetarist, fearful-of-inflation economists who peopled old-line agencies like the Treasury.

Another problem for DURD was that—like the Department of Regional Economic Expansion (DREE) in Canada 4 years earlier—it never became the superministry that many of its more left-wing supporters hoped it would be. They wanted DURD to have control over the spatial allocation of expenditures on such things as housing, public transport, conservation, and the environment. But the Labor caucus elected 27 persons to the Cabinet, and there had to be ministries for all of them. Finding itself confronted with separate departments of Transport, Housing, Environment, Education, Services and Property, Health, Tourism and Recreation, DURD wanted at least to have a dominating influence on the spatial distribution of their activities and expenditures. Here again, DURD clashed inevitably with the Treasury, which was used to being the only department with power to influence other departments; and in such clashes—again, as with DREE in Canada—the Treasury nearly always won.

Wilson[18] regards this failure to integrate urban and regional planning within one agency as the main reason for DURD's failure. He speaks of "a paralysis of planning," describes the growth center at Monarto as "an expensive disaster," cites Geelong as an example of failure due to disagreement between state and federal governments. He also raises questions about the validity of the whole concept of decentralization, and cites William Alonso, of Harvard, one of the foreign experts called to advise the government on its urban and regional policy, as expressing doubts as to whether any of Australia's metropolitan centers, even Sydney or Melbourne, is really "too big." Wilson also presents figures of expenditures that cast light on the actual nature of the program as carried out (see Table 10). Of the amount spent for growth centers, $24 million was spent in Sydney, the rest in Albury/Wodonga, Bathurst/Orange, and Monarto. Altogether, a good deal more money was spent under the program in the established large metropolitan centres than elsewhere.

P. N. Troy[19] also stressed the lack of coordination and bureaucratic opposition as causes of difficulties with the Labor government's program of urban and regional development. Joan Vipond[20] puts more stress on the changing urban situation in Australia, particularly the decline during the early 1970s in both the fertility rate and the rate of immigration, which together produced a significant reduction in the rate of population growth and forecasts of size of metropolitan centers. In

Table 10. DURD Expenditures by Sector: 1972–1975

Sector	Expenditure
Sewerage backlog	$260 million
Growth centers	140 million
Land commissions	100 million
AIP	36 million
Urban renewal	28 million

Source. Robert Wilson, *Australian Resources and Their Development* (Sydney: University of Sydney, Department of Education),
p. 198.

addition, some "polarization reversal" was taking place; Sydney and
Melbourne were growing at a rate below the national average. The rate
of inflation in land and housing was slowing down. These trends made
the government's urban and regional policies seem less necessary and
less urgent. Also the manufacturing sector was stagnant, so that attracting industry to the growth centers seemed less urgent too. Vipond also
points out that the slowdown in growth of Sydney and Melbourne had
little to do with development of the growth centers. Albany/Wodonga
and Bathurst/Orange had together less than 150,000 people and were
growing less rapidly than the coastal towns of New South Wales and
Queensland.

In retrospect, despite the underlying lofty idealism, breadth of vision, and brilliance of conception, there does seem to have been something inchoate and half baked about the Whitlam program on urban and
regional development. After 23 years in the wilderness, the Labor party
lacked the experience and the skills to implement smoothly and quickly
a program of major reforms. The bureaucracy lacked them too because
no such program had been under way for over two decades, and many
of the top people in the public service were highly suspicious of the
whole venture. For all the reasons set forth, there was little in the way of
scholarly tradition and applied research in Australia on which the government could draw. Indeed, when it comes to that, the body of received doctrine on urban and regional development is none too ample
anywhere. And the Whitlam regime was not given the time to learn by
doing.

THE FRASER REGIME: 1976–1983

In the whole history of parliamentary democracy, there can be few
cases where a change in government was brought about in so abrupt

and traumatic a fashion and where it ushered in so drastic a change in basic ideology and policies of the party in power, as the replacement of the Whitlam Labor government by the Fraser Liberal–National–Country party government. In July 1975, an ALP Senator for Queensland died, and the Queensland Premier, Sir Joh Bjelke-Petersen, flouting tradition, appointed a replacement who was aligned with the Opposition. That action gave the Liberal coalition a majority in the Senate. At that time, the mounting inflation was causing concern throughout the country, and many members of the general public, as well as the official Opposition, were disturbed by the government's unorthodox methods of financing its deficits abroad. Malcolm Fraser, who had assumed leadership of the coalition the previous March, warned that the Senate would not pass the Supply Bills called for in Mr. Hayden's Budget Speech of August 1976 and asked for a general election. The government refused, and the ordinary business of government came to a grinding halt. In November, the Governor General (Sir John Kerr) used his prerogative and dismissed the Labor government, naming Fraser acting prime minister. In December, Fraser won a smashing victory at the polls, with majorities in both houses.

This series of events brought a rapid and complete reversal in all the things that the Labor government stood for: the basic ideology, the attitude toward the constitution, the fiscal policy, the approach to federal–state financial relations, and urban and regional policy.

Fraser is a remarkably thoroughgoing and consistent conservative, even for a leader to the Liberal–National–Country party. He is member of the "squattocracy," Australia's "rich-squatter," country squire, large landowner class. Barry Hughes, at the time economic advisor to the South Australia government, has gone so far as to label him a physiocrat:

> In many respects Fraser is an old-fashioned physiocrat. Physiocracy descends from the eighteenth century French school of economists who believed that economic wealth sprang from the land. Agriculture was what kept the country going, and everything else, particularly government activities, represented an unproductive burden on the economy.[21]

Fraser was unblushing in his demands for a cut in real wages and in the share of wages in national income, to raise profits and provide the stimulus to private investment that could reduce unemployment. He is also a devout Friedman-Monetarist, convinced that unemployment cannot be reduced below its "natural" rate and only by curbing inflation and reversing inflationary expectations can unemployment be reduced at all. This view blended nicely with his overriding conviction that government, and particularly central government, should be kept as small as possible.

Mr. Fraser's basic philosophy was well expressed in his speech opening Parliament in 1976:

> At the root of the economic crisis is a steadily increasing tax burden required to finance, at the expense of the private sector, an ever growing public sector. Measures to deal with this crisis will advance Australia toward the long-term goal of a society based on freedom.
>
> The government's strategy to achieve its objectives can be summarized as follows: (i) there will be a major redirection of resources away from government towards individuals and private enterprise; (ii) the internal structure of the government is being made more economical and effective; a responsible Cabinet system has been instituted which will permit effective and coordinated decisions to be taken and implemented; (iii) historic reforms will be made to reverse the concentration of power in the federal government.[22]

Given this general economic and social philosophy, it is not surprising that the Fraser government's approach to federal–state financial relations included returning to the states as much as possible of the responsibility for social programs. The policy announced on coming to power involved an income tax revenue-sharing arrangement with the states, enabling legislation to allow the states to place a percentage surcharge or rebate on personal income tax for residents of the state (to be administered by the Commonwealth) and reduction of specific purposes payments (on which the Whitlam government had so much relied for financing social programs) and their replacement by general revenue grants. It also established State Grants Commissions to distribute grants to local governments and reduced the equalization component of these grants, thus renouncing the principle of basing grants to local governments on relative needs, embraced by the Whitlam regime. Groenewegen summarizes these changes as follows:

> To put it briefly, the Fraser government's new federalism can be seen as part of its attempt to reduce the size of the public sector. . . . The federalism also acts as a brake on State expansion by making expenditure increases more dependent on state-induced rises in tax rates, which increases the political cost of such government expansion. A smaller public sector obviously allows greater opportunities for the expansion of private interests. Moreover, such expenditure reduction allows the reduction of taxation, particularly that levied on the higher income groups who tend to support the conservative parties.[23]

Within this general policy framework, it would have been totally inconsistent for the Fraser government to continue the Labor government's ventures in urban and regional development, and it did not. Budget allocations for the Urban and Regional Development and Environment were immediately cut from $408 million to $251 million, and further cuts followed in later budgets. DURD was replaced by a new Department of Environment, Housing, and Community Development, broader in the scope of its functions than DURD but with less money; Sandercock says it was set up "solely for the purpose of simplifying and reducing expenditure on urban programs."[24] The lands commission budget was immediately cut by almost two-thirds, and further cuts followed. Outlays on the growth centers were immediately cut from $64 to $19 million. In the last fiscal year of the Fraser administration, 1982–1983, all that remained of the growth centers program was $1.3 million for Albury/Wodonga. Funding for Monarto virtually disappeared as early as 1975–1976 and disappeared altogether in 1980–1981. In 1980, the Bathurst/Orange Development Corporation was selling off its land because population growth in that "growth center" was so slow.

With urban and regional development turned over to private enterprise and the states, what happened? An overriding element was the restrictive influence on any kind of development of the continuing battle against inflation and balance of payments deficits. The Fraser government found that it is not all that easy to reduce inflation and unemployment simultaneously. Indeed, there were years when they increased together, and interest rates remained high. For the most part, the states reverted to the use of incentives to lure industry away from other states, no matter where they might settle within each state. Several states enjoyed mineral discoveries, and all were eager to attract private enterprise to exploit and process their resources. None of the states developed a really coherent urban and regional policy. In New South Wales, a major effort was made to stem the tide of migration from the inner city of Sydney to the outer suburbs, so as to make sure that the existing infrastructure was fully utilized and avoid the need for a new infrastructure on the fringes of the metropolitan area. A Committee of Review of the Bathurst/Orange growth center pointed to the needs for resources of urban centers that were growing naturally, especially those on the North Coast. Melbourne was worried about the threatened traditional industries in its center (textiles, clothing, footwear) and related congestion and pollution. Adelaide was worried because its manufacturing base, motor vehicles and white goods, was narrow and threatened by foreign competition. Throughout Australia there was concern about the need for structural adjustment called for by Australia's commitments under GATT and UNCTAD agreements, with their threat of growing competition from imports from developing countries. It cannot be said, however, that these worries crystallized into an integrated policy to deal with them, at either the federal or the state level.

One result of turning over "regional policy" and regional development to the state governments is to further reduce competition and competitiveness in the national economy as a whole. Since World War II, Australia, together with New Zealand, has been one of the most highly protected economies in the world, both by tariffs and by quantitative controls of imports. Professor Fred Gruen of the Australian National University points out that this protection does more damage to efficiency in Australia than it does in her OECD partners, which also have high levels of protection because of the small size of the Australian economy:

> As shown earlier, these [other OECD countries] have grown much more vigorously than Australia in the last quarter of a century. One reason we suffer more from protection is that protection is much more damaging in a relatively small economy like Australia and that the biggest economies like the Common Market, the United States and Japan are not affected nearly as adversely by tariffs and other forms of protection. . . . This was probably a major factor in enabling many of the original member countries to "pass" Australia's per capita output level. Another reason our protection may be more harmful is that it is in industries where substantial economies of scale are possible.[25]

When "regional development" is limited to the efforts of state governments to bid enterprises away from other states by artificial (nonmarket) means, the effective size of the market, in which open competition takes place, is still further restricted. Protectionism through state governments takes various forms:

1. Offering subsidized state transport to enterprises agreeing to settle and operate within the state.
2. Offering preference to enterprises within the state for government purchasing, thus virtually guaranteeing a market to enterprises that settle and operate within the state.
3. Regulations, standards, provisions for the health of humans, animals, and fruits and vegetables that virtually eliminate interstate trade in eggs, milk, fruit, vegetables, and live animals.
4. State arbitration commissions that set "margins for skill" for various trades and occupations (to be added to the basic wage determined by the Commonwealth Arbitration Commission)

that may bear no relationship to real differences in value of marginal product.
5. Building codes that inhibit interstate trade in prefabricated housing and building materials.

How serious the aggregate impact on the national economy is of such misguided interference by state governments in the operation of the market, all in the name of "regional development," would be difficult to measure. The point is, however, that Australia's state governments have shown themselves as having little interest in either the efficiency of the *national* economy or the welfare of particularly disadvantaged *communities* within each state. Perhaps from the standpoint of the political survival of individual state governments, this stress on employment creation and income generation *within the state,* no matter where, reflects sound political judgment. But it also provides a justification for the Whitlam government's attempt to provide the Australian people with a balancing act that did not quite come off: to exercise firm control and direction of regional and national development at the federal level, while at the same time making the states more equal partners in the federation and bringing local governments, communities, nongovernmental organizations, and various interested individuals and groups into the decision-making process with regard to the spatial distribution, the pace, and the pattern of development.

THE EXCAVATION OF REGIONAL DISPARITIES

Despite the Fraser government's apparent disinterest in regional policy and regional development, it was during its administration that an event occurred that was to transform the Australian picture where regional disparities are concerned. For the purpose of the 1981 census, the Bureau of Statistics set up 60 statistical divisions, which were, in effect, true regions. Some of the major results are presented in Figures 6, 7, and 8. They demonstrate that despite the similarities in economic and social structures among the states, there are indeed substantial gaps among smaller defined spaces, which come closer to the economic or analytical concept of "regions." For example, income per capita ranged from $7,600 in the Pilbara (a mineral boom region in the northwest of the country) to $4,500 in Southern Tasmania. The differences in rates of unemployment are much greater, ranging from 2.7% in Upper Great Southern Western Australia to 10.6% for Richmond Tweed.

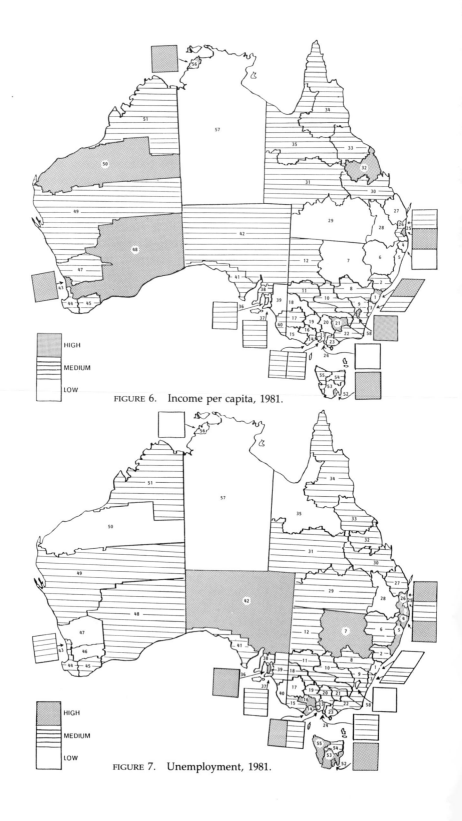

FIGURE 6.   Income per capita, 1981.

HIGH
MEDIUM
LOW

FIGURE 7.   Unemployment, 1981.

HIGH
MEDIUM
LOW

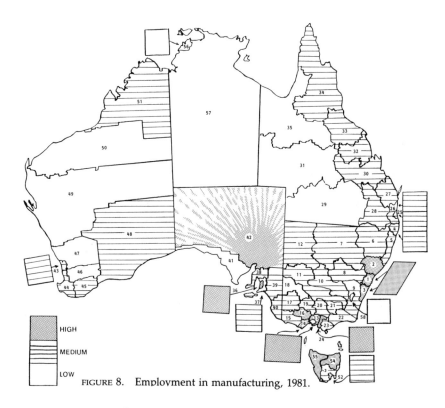

HIGH

MEDIUM

LOW

FIGURE 8. Employment in manufacturing, 1981.

1981 CENSUS OF POPULATION AND HOUSING LIST OF STATISTICAL DIVISIONS

NEW SOUTH WALES

1 SYDNEY
2 HUNTER
3 ILLAWARA
4 RICHMOND–TWEED
5 MID-NORTH COAST
6 NORTHERN
7 NORTH WESTERN
8 CENTRAL WEST
9 SOUTH EASTERN
10 MURRIMIDGEE
11 MURRAY
12 FAR WESTERN

VICTORIA

13 MELBOURNE
14 BARWON
15 SOUTH EASTERN
16 CENTRAL HIGHLANDS
17 WIMMERA
18 NORTHERN MALLEE
19 LONDON-CAMPASPE
20 GOLBURN
21 NORTH EASTERN

22 EAST GIPPSLAND
23 CENTRAL GIPPSLAND
24 EAST CENTRAL

QUEENSLAND

25 BRISBANE
26 MORETON
27 WIDE BAY–BURNETT
28 DARLING DOWNS
29 SOUTH-WEST
30 FITZROY
31 CENTRAL WEST
32 MACKAY
33 NORTHERN
34 FAR NORTH
35 NORTH-WESTERN

SOUTH AUSTRALIA

36 ADELAIDE
37 OUTER ADELAIDE
38 YORKE AND LOWER NORTH
39 MURRAY LANDS
40 SOUTH EAST
41 EYRE
42 NORTHERN

WESTERN AUSTRALIA

43 PERTH
44 SOUTH WEST
45 LOWER GREAT SOUTHERN
46 UPPER GREAT SOUTHERN
47 MIDLANDS
48 SOUTH EASTERN
49 CENTRAL
50 PILBARA
51 KIMBERLEY

TASMANIA

52 HOBART
53 SOUTHERN
54 NORTHERN
55 MERSEY–LYELL

NORTHERN TERRITORY

56 DARWIN
57 BALANCE

AUSTRALIAN CAPITAL TERRITORY

58 CANBERRA

The breakdown into statistical divisions also reveals differences in economic structure among states. Western Australia has neither a low-income region nor a high-unemployment region. Neighboring South Australia has no high-income region and one low-income region. Most of its regions suffer from high unemployment. Victoria shows no very clear pattern. It has regions with high, medium and low incomes, and with high, medium, and low unemployment. Tasmania has no high income region except the capital city, Hobart; the rest have medium or low incomes. Still more significant, Tasmania has no region with low unemployment, and most of its regions have high unemployment. In Queensland, all regions have low or medium incomes except for the capital city, Brisbane, and the urban center Mackay. Queensland also has no region with low unemployment, although some have medium unemployment; the rest suffer from high unemployment. The Northern Territory has a "dualistic economy." Its capital city, Darwin, has high incomes; all the other regions have low incomes. On the other hand, unemployment is low throughout.

When cast in terms of regions, moreover, the differences in occupational structure are far more substantial than they are for states. For example, only South Australia, Victoria, and New South Wales have any regions with high employment in manufacturing. Disparities among individual regions in this respect are enormous. Illiwara, New South Wales, has 29.8% of its employment in manufacturing, Central West Queensland 1.3%. Upper Great Southern Western Australia has nearly half of its labor force in agriculture, (48.6%), Canberra half of 1% of its labor force. South Australia, Victoria, and Queensland have regions with high employment in agriculture; Tasmania, New South Wales, and the Northern Territory do not.

Clearly, no central government policy applied uniformly throughout the land can hope either to solve the problems or realize the potential of regions so diverse as these. The Australian economy is in fact a loosely integrated collection of some five dozen or more variegated regional economies, and the behavior of the national economy is a complex set of interactions among these regional economies and of the interaction of each with the outside world. There is no reason to expect that all of these economies will react in the same way to a particular central government monetary, fiscal, or trade policy, or even to particular state policy. Solving the problems and realizing the potential will require a set of policies that are to some degree tailormade for each region. Even policies defined in terms of sectors will not do the whole job; societies are not located in sectors but in spaces, and individuals, households, and groups live in spaces, not sectors.

THE HAWKE LABOR GOVERNMENT

The replacement of the Fraser Conservative government by the Hawke Labor party government brought no such abrupt changes in direction of government policy as did the replacement of Whitlam by Fraser. Instead, the first major action of Hawke as prime minister was to assemble representatives of employers, labor, agriculture, and other social groups to work out an accord on wages, prices, and other important aspects of economic policy. In some respects Hawke has been more successful in pursuing conservative policies than his predecessors: wage restraint, deregulation, privatization, limitation of price increases, a cautious antiinflationary monetary and fiscal policy. The reaction of the Australian public to these policies is reflected in Hawke's reelection in 1986. As Gruen puts it:

> Since [1983] the Accord has worked well to restore a more favorable economic climate and to give us very high growth rates by current OECD standards—although these very high growth rates have created their own problems. We are now confronted with a current account deficit that is not sustainable for long.[26]

Nor did the return of the Labor party to power bring a rapid reintroduction of the various facets of regional policy associated with the Whitlam regime. Politicians have long memories, and the contribution of Whitlam's ambitious regional policies to his premature downfall have not been forgotten by politicians on either side of the House. The new figures on regional disparities have not been given much publicity, they have not been widely discussed, and the Hawke government has not tried very hard to make political capital out of them. Instead, work on regional government proceeded quietly in the Department of Local Government and Administrative Services (DOLGAS). It should also be said, however, that the implications of these figures are not fully appreciated, either within or outside of the government. It is too little appreciated that the recently revealed regional disparities present the Australian government and the Australian people with an opportunity as well as a problem.

At time of this writing, the major effort of the Hawke government regarding regional policy was the "Country Centers Project," undertaken by DOLGAS. According to an official DOLGAS pamphlet,[27] "the Country Centers Project arose from the federal government's concern to address realistically the problems faced in Australia's country towns." Krystov Zagorsky comments that in this context, "realistically" means "on a very modest scale."[28] The modesty is no doubt partly the result of still-fresh memories of the difficulties encountered by Gough Whitlam's more ambitious programs along similar lines; so long as the "Country Centers" program is small enough in scale, friction with the state governments can be avoided. The same principle applies to the Treasury and other old-line agencies of the central government. DOLGAS has identified 75 regions, as opposed to the Bureau of Statistics' 60. The regions are essentially the zones of influence of urban centers of 10,000 or more population, and some of them cross state boundaries. On the whole, they are defined in more clearly operational terms, as "planning regions," than the statistical divisions. Yet so far, there are only 11 centers where local liaison committees have been established and where federal funds are provided for running expenses and for professional research assistance to identify development problems and potential.

The main objective of the centers is to produce local action development plans, to design strategies for self-help, and to generate development schemes that can be implemented either by government or by private enterprise. Such schemes are envisaged as mainly the product of local knowledge and local ideas but as consonant with the objectives of state and federal governments. Thus far, the program is low-key. However, DOLGAS had a competent and ambitious staff, whose goals were perhaps closer to those of the Whitlam regime than to those thus far announced by the Hawke administration.

Since its return to office for a third term (the first Labor government in Australian history to do so), the Hawke administration has been restructured, and the number of cabinet portfolios reduced. DOLGAS has been disbanded, and its local government and regional development division moved to the new Department of Immigration, Local Government and Ethnic Affairs (DILGEA). The department has built up what may well be an unrivalled data bank, covering more than 500 socioeconomic variables for each of their 75 regions. The country centers project is continuing, still directed primarily toward rural problems and still limited to 11 centers, 1 in Tasmania and 2 each in the other states. In 6 months of operation, the 11 centers identified 58 business opportunities, of which 19 were considered worth pursuing, and for which business plans have been prepared for 7. These are not exactly calculated to bring dramatic changes in the structure of the regional economies involved: export of hay; aquaculture; table grapes; fruit and vegetables marketing; honey, bee, and pollen production; and cattle hide tanning.[29]

The country centers project is part of the economic and rural policy statement of April 1986, which provided a modest $210 million package for "improving macro-economic and sectoral performance."[30] The new department, in discussing the program, is careful to distance itself from the Whitlam regime:

> In recent years, the economic policy framework of the government has focussed on stimulating aggregate income growth at the same time as reducing the country's reliance on borrowed funds. . . . In this new economic climate, past regional and decentralization policies have been inappropriate and too expensive. No longer can government undertake spending to compensate for short-run income loss, or to encourage economic and employment growth through expensive job creation, infrastructure and growth centre strategies. Many of the earlier regional programs, as a result, have been abandoned.
>
> Under these circumstances, regional policy had been seen as a minor adjunct to industry policy—a matter primarily of state responsibility. . . . However, broad-based macro-economic and sectoral policy measures have not fully met government growth targets or the expectations of local communities.[31]

At the level of the 11 centers, the department apparently did not find all that much local initiative or regenerative capacity. The liaison committees organized to identify development opportunities, they say, took two quite distinct forms: a guided community consultation structure in which hired consultants played a subordinate role and a consultant-centered structure in which hired consultants shouldered the bulk of the burden. The department clearly favors the former; for one thing, they say, all too frequently, "This consultant-centred structure favoured particular interest groups in the centres studied."[32] But whichever the structure, "it became apparent through the CCP that there was virtually no spontaneity demonstrated by local communities to progress their identified opportunities to commercialisation."[33] They noted a general lack of business skills, business information, and advice networks at the local level. Risk finance is available, but access is inhibited by poorly packaged proposals. Better results are attained when regional *networks* of entrepreneurs can be created.

At the very least, however, the work of the regional development branch has added greatly to the store of knowledge about the Australian economy. They are publishing a series of studies of Australian regional development, which "detail the great diversity of Australia's regional economies, their very different structures of production and ownership, and their highly variable levels of economic performance.[34] . . . The country centres project has shown that the adjustment prescriptions in many communities is different. It has demonstrated that there exists considerable variation in social and economic structure, performance, potential and needs of regions across Australia."[35]

The general conclusion seems to be that the centers are too small in scale and too narrow in scope for effective operation of a regional policy. More effective seems to be Australia's experiments with planning and development in larger regions. A good example is the Geelong Regional Commission. Its authority covers the city of Geelong and eight other municipalities, with an aggregate population of 183,000 people. The region is on the south coast, just 72 kilometers southwest of Melbourne. Geelong grew up in the mid-nineteenth century as a wool center, and later profited from the gold discoveries near Ballarat. Its port is the sixth largest in Australia and is second in terms of grain handling. Today, Geelong is primarily a manufacturing town. Manufactures account for one-quarter of its employment but half of its value added. Retailing and other services account for the rest of Geelong's economic activity. It benefits from the presence of Deakin University (established in 1977), the Marine Science laboratory, and the Australian Animal Health laboratories.

The commission is composed of five members appointed by the Victoria governor-in-council, and one councelor for each of the nine municipalities. It has a full-time chairman for a period not exceeding 5 years. For a community of less than 200,000 people, it has a considerable staff. It has four divisions, each with several full-time professional staff members: economic development, planning and design, development and construction, administration and finance. Biggest of these is the economic development division, with a director, a regional economist, and 11 other professional officers.

In 1985–1986, the commission received grants of $1.8 million from the State of Victoria and $260,000 from the nine municipalities. It also obtains funding for particular projects from the federal government through such programs as the community employment program. Some financial resources are derived from sale or rental of properties owned by the commission. The scale of the commission's operations is such, however, that it has to rely mainly on borrowing on commercial terms to finance its capital development projects. In Australia, municipal as well as state borrowing is controlled by the Commonwealth Loan Council, and the commission has borrowed the maximum permitted under Loan Council Policy. As of 30 June 1986, its debt was $18.1 million.

A good many of Geelong's manufactures are "traditional" products that have been in difficulties in industrialized countries everywhere: textiles, base metal products, coal products, food and beverages, tobacco products, chemicals and petroleum products, automobiles. Nonetheless, in recent years, the Geelong region has succeeded in expanding its value added in manufactures at the same rate as the Australian average. This success is at least partly due to the work of the commission. One of its most interesting ventures has been the purchase of manufacturing plants from enterprises facing difficulties. One of these was a firm manufacturing transmission components with 170 workers. The commission bought the factory for cash and then sold it back on the basis of a long-term loan, enabling the company to keep going. The biggest such venture, however, was the purchase of the International Harvester works. The company had reduced its number of employees from 2,300 to 600 and was threatening to close down altogether. The commission borrowed from the Victoria Government State Development Fund and bought the plant. It then leased the space to manufacturers of prefabricated housing, footwear, and agricultural machinery. The agricultural machinery company now leases about half the total space and was organized by the commission itself, with funding from the Victoria Economic Development Corporation. In short, the commission has played a genuine, active, and successful entrepreneurial role.

Another of the commission's ventures is the City by the Bay Plan, a $30-million redevelopment scheme designed to restore and revitalize the central core of the city of Geelong. A national wool center, including a wool museum, was opened on 21 December 1988, as part of Australia's Bicentennial Year celebrations.

The commission has also moved to build upon one of the region's major resources: its beaches and coastline. It has encouraged tourism, recreation, sports, and industry related to these. When the Rip Curl Company (manufacturers of surf boards and related products) complained that they could not find space to expand in Torquay (a seaside resort within the region) and threatened to move to Queensland, the commission negotiated the purchase of 5.7 hectares at Torquay. Not only did Rip Curl stay, but other companies moved in, and in 1986 the surfing-equipment industry at Torquay had a turnover of $30 million and employed 300 people. Since then, the commission has embarked on a multi-million-dollar tourism, recreation, and retail center named Surf Coast Plaza, and the Australian Surfriders Association has made the plaza its Australian headquarters.

The sophistication regarding regional development displayed by the commission and its staff also appears in its approach to attraction of new enterprises to the region. Rather than casting bait in all directions and welcoming all newcomers, as Canadian provinces tend to do, the commission has made careful studies of the region's advantages and shortcomings, to determine what industries "belong" in the region. These include, according to the commission, "port related industries, capital-intensive industries, leisure and tourist industries, . . . and downstream industries related to textiles, metal processing, petrochemical machinery manufacture, and indigenous agriculture and mariculture products." The commission sees the region's strengths as follows: the strength, stability, and linkage of the industrial skill base; the presence of leading scientific and postsecondary educational institutions; the availability of a sheltered deep water port; the "near-yet-far" advantage of proximity to Melbourne; the proximity of surf beaches, Corio Bay, and the Otway ranges; and the quality of life of the Geelong region. On the basis of these, the commission analyses its "target" industries further, for compatibility with the regional plan, attractability, promotion, delineation of the target market, competitive opportunity, and environmental change needed. It then opens discussion with the target industries and tries to remove any obstacles to their locating in the Geelong region.[36]

The commission has recognized the special need of small enterprises for high-standard industrial building and has established four industrial estates near the city of Geelong for that purpose with "unit factory" complexes. It convened a group of investors to take advantage of innovative research being done at Deakin University and to commercialize its products and formed Geetech Propriety Ltd. It has worked with the federal government to establish a regional airport.

All in all, the Geelong regional commission has displayed an impressive degree of that very entrepreneurial and managerial talent that the regional development branch found so woefully lacking in the rural centers program. The difference in scale is no doubt part of the explanation, but it is not the whole of it. As G. A. McLean of the commission itself modestly phrases it in his study for DOLGAS,[37] "Whereas the Geelong Regional Commission is not unique in Australia, nevertheless it is one of the few statutory authorities which has successfully combined the functions of land use planning and economic development." Indeed, it provides a model, which not only could be usefully replicated in Australia but effectively emulated in other large regionalized countries such as Canada and the United States.

Among the factors contributing to its success would appear to be these:

1. The commission itself is small, with just 14 members, all knowledgeable regarding the region's needs and potential, represent-

ing diverse interests of the region, and being able to tap the expertise of other members of the community.

2. The commission is backed by a sizable, full-time, permanent and professionally trained staff.
3. It has been able to get support from federal, state, and local government, apparently without engendering conflict among the three levels.
4. Its decisions and activities are based on thorough knowledge of the human and natural resources of the region and appreciation of both the possibilities for and limitations of the region's development.
5. Although taking advantage of the various related programs at the state and federal level, its program has remained an essentially local undertaking.

This list of factors seems rather simple, but it is not easy to find them in operation in other industrialized countries.

THE GEELONG REGION DEVELOPMENT STRATEGY

In June 1988, the Geelong Regional Commission published a 110-page volume entitled *Directions: The Geelong Region Development Strategy.* The document might well be regarded as a model of long-term planning for the development of a small but dynamic regional economy and its community. It is the product of 4 years of hard work, which generated hundreds of pages of individual studies, documents, and reports on particular aspects of the region's development, which were then distilled into the strategy. The project has its genesis in the 1984 *Economic Strategy* of the state government of Victoria, which recognized the importance of the development of the Geelong region as a part of the strategy for development of the state as a whole and provided general guidelines for the design of such regional strategies. The preparation of the strategy involved not only the commission, its staff, and a special study team but also the local governments of the region and the community as a whole. It also had the cooperation of state government departments.

The document presents a 5-year plan and a 10-year "vision," under the following chapter headings: The Context of Change, with projections for the world economy and for the Geelong region; Assumptions, providing the framework within which plans can be made for 5 to 10 years, essentially a forecast of major trends, such as "there will be no loss of a major employer to the region" and "the Port of Geelong will not grow significantly in terms of tonnage throughout or direct employment"; Regional Issues, restating strengths and weaknesses, opportunities, and threats for the region; The Ten Year Vision, setting forth regional goals and subgoals; The Five Year Implementation Plan, with a precise schedule for undertaking specific projects in both the public and the private sectors, and a still more detailed program for the current fiscal year, 1988–1989; and finally, Monitoring and Evaluation. There is also a physical framework plan, showing in map form the evolution of land use during the planning period.

The thoroughness, care, and professional competence with which the background studies were carried out is apparent from the documents themselves. Equally evident is the prudence with which the people ultimately interested in the results of implementing the strategy were brought into the planning process itself. Similar exercises for every major region of Australia would go far toward solving the problems of Australia's "seven deadly economic sins" that cannot be solved by macroeconomic policies at the national level alone.

CONCLUSION

It may seem to some readers that an undue amount of space has been accorded to what is, after all, a very small-scale program for the development of a small and not terribly important region. However, the reason I have covered the Geelong case in such detail is that I am convinced that it is only through programs of this sort that Australia can solve its tightly interwoven economic problems. Elsewhere I have referred to these problems as "Australia's seven deadly economic sins."[38] The seven are:

1. An unsuitable and inefficient industrial structure, produced by a century of industrialization behind very high walls of protection.
2. A wage structure that bears little relationship to relative levels of productivity, as a consequence of a high degree of monopoly, strong trade unions, and compulsory arbitration.
3. An unfavorable balance of payments and mounting foreign debt.
4. An extraordinary degree of concentration of population in the capital cities.

5. Lagging technical and scientific education and a lack of entrepreneurship.
6. An excessively large role of government in the economic life of the nation and correspondingly mastadonion bureaucracies.
7. Simultaneous unemployment and inflation.

Since the brief Whitlam regime, a succession of governments has endeavored to deal with these "sins" by remote control, through a highly aggregative and orthodox monetary policy, plus a rather ineffectual fiscal policy and a modicum of sectoral policy. These have not served to reduce the burden of sin for two reasons: Contrary to the impression one may get by looking only at states, the Australian economy is a highly disintegrated collection of small regional economies; and the seven sins burden these regional economies in very different degrees and are combined in very different proportions. No monetary, fiscal, and sectoral policy applied uniformly throughout the land can possibly deal with these variations in economic and social problems from one *place* to another. The federal and state governments can provide funds and technical assistance, but the planning, policy formulation, and implementation for regional development must be carried out at the level of the region or community, along the general lines illustrated by the Geelong Regional Commission.

Reverting to the general theme of this book, it seems that the world, or at least Australia, will need to change again before such a program could be launched and effectively carried out. From what we have seen in the Australian story, and in the other stories as well, it does not seem likely that such a sweeping change in development strategy will take place without another swing of the pendulum of prevailing economic and social philosophy. Such a swing, in the Australian case, would obviously have to be in the general direction of the Whitlam regime. At time of writing there was no sign of such a swing. On the contrary, the Hawke government had just announced a "minibudget" continuing its march to the right, reiterating its faith in privatization, deregulation, and reduced federal and state government expenditures: reducing corporation income taxes and adding a threat that any increases in wages beyond government guidelines will kill all hopes for personal income tax cuts. The Conservative coalition was still floundering in its effort to remain to the right of labor and still announce policies that are both sensible and attractive. It is too bad that the Liberals do not have the wisdom and courage to become liberals, leapfrog over Labor in the opposite direction, show a concern for people and their problems where they are, and announce policies to solve these problems at the regional and local level.

NOTES

[1] See Heinz Arndt and W. Max Corden, *The Australian Economy* (Melbourne: F. W. Cheshire, 1963); J. Nieuwenhuysen and P. Drake, eds., *Australian Economic Policy* (Melbourne: Melbourne University Press, 1977); and Robert Jackson, "The Australian Economy," *Daedelus, Australia: Terra Incognita*, Winter 1985; Helen Hughes, *Australia in a Developing World* (Boyen Lectures), Sydney, Australian Broadcasting Corporation, 1985; Lawrence Krause, *The Australian Economy: A View from the North*, (Washington DC: Brookings Institution, 1984).

[2] F. J. Turner, *The Frontier in American History.* (New York: Henry Holt, 1920), p. 12.

[3] Sir Keith Hancock, *Australia*, 1940, p. 405.

[4] Carter Goodrich, "The Australian and the American Labour Movement", in *The Economic Record*, November 1928, pp. 206–207.

[5] Fred Alexander, *Moving Frontiers* (Melbourne: Melbourne University Press, 1947), p. 28.

[6] Russell Mathews, "Fiscal Federalism and Regional Development", in B. Higgins and K. Zagorsky, eds., *Australian Regional Development* (Canberra: Government Printing Office, 1987).

[7] Max Neutze, "Economic Policy and the Size of Cities", in J. Nieuwenhuysen and P. Drake, eds., *Australian Economic Policy* (Melbourne: Melbourne University Press, 1977).

[8] E. Gough Whitlam, "1972 Policy Speech," in *On Australia's Constitution* (Melbourne, 1977). See also Peter Groenewegen, "Federalism," in Patience and Head, *From Whitlam to Fraser* (Melbourne and Oxford: Oxford University Press, 1979).

[9] James Cairns, *Budget Speech*, 17 September, 1974.

[10] William Hayden, *Budget Speech*, 1975.

[11] Groenewegen, "Federalism," p. 57.

[12] Ibid.

[13] Ibid., p. 60.

[14] Robert Wilson, *Australian Resources and Their Development* (Sydney: Department of Education, University of Sydney, 1980).

[15] Leonie Sandercock, "Urban Policy," in Patience and Head eds., *From Whitlam to Fraser*, (Melbourne and Oxford: Oxford University Press, 1979), p. 145.

[16] Ibid., p. 152.

[17] Ibid., pp. 150–151.

[18] Robert Wilson, *Australian Resources and Their Development* (Sydney: Department of Education, University of Sydney, 1980), p. 198.

[19] Patrick Troy, "Federalism and Urban Affairs, 1972–75," *Royal Australian Planning Institute Journal*, vol. 14, January 1976, pp. 15–20.

[20] Joan Vipond, in B. Higgins and K. Zagorsky, eds., *Australian Regional Development*, 1987.

[21] Barry Hughes, "The Economy," In Patience and Head, eds., *From Whitlam to Fraser* (Melbourne and Oxford: Oxford University Press, 1979), pp. 38–39.

[22] M. Fraser, "Governor General's Speech Opening Parliament, 1 February 1976, *House of Representatives Debates*, 1976, pp. 12–13.

[23] Groenewegen, p. 68.

[24] Sandercock, "Urban Policy," p. 155.

[25]Fred Gruen, "How Bad Is Australia's Economic Performance and Why?", (Shann Memorial Lecture), *The Economic Record*, June 1986, p. 187.

[26]Ibid., p. 193.

[27]DOLGAS, Canberra, 1986, *The Country Centres Project.*

[28]Krystov Zagorski, "Federal Policy of Regional and Urban Development: The Australian Case." Paper delivered to the XIth World Congress of Sociology, New Delhi, August 1986 (Canberra: Australian National University), 1987.

[29]DILGEA, Canberra, *Australian Regional Development: 8-1 Country Centres Project 1986,* 1987.

[30]Ibid., p. 11.

[31]Ibid., pp. 12–13.

[32]Ibid., p. 16.

[33]Ibid., p. 21.

[34]Ibid., p. 29.

[35]Ibid., p. 30.

[36]DOLGAS, Canberra, *Australian Regional Development: 7. Geelong Experience,* 1987, pp. 34–35.

[37]Ibid., p. iii.

[38]Benjamin Higgins, "Conclusions: Implications for Policy," In B. Higgins and K. Zagorski, eds., *Australian Regional Development* (Canberra, Government Printing Office, 1988), Chapter 12.

CHAPTER SEVEN

Integration of National and Regional Policy

Malaysia

The countries lumped together as "less developed," or "Third World," differ widely in level and pattern of development, structure of their economies, degree of regional and technological dualism, culture, and ideologies. Regional policies differ accordingly. However, there is one feature of economic and social policy in Third World countries that unites them and distinguishes them from the "industrialized market economies," taken as a group: They have official and formal national development plans. Reducing regional disparities is sometimes an objective of regional policy; it is never the be-all and end-all of regional policy. Rather, regional policy and planning are viewed as integral parts of national strategies for enhancing the economic and social welfare of national societies as a whole. Moreover, since the mid-1960s, more and more less developed countries (LDCs) have turned to regional policy and planning as the most effective technique for assembling national policies and plans for development.

In this chapter and the next we consider regional policy of two especially important cases—Malaysia and Brazil. These countries were selected partly because the author of these chapters has been personally engaged in the planning of regional development in both of them but mainly because both represent particularly large-scale efforts at regional development and both have a rich and varied experience with regional policy. Also, they are both near the top of the income scale among developing countries and so are more readily comparable with industrialized countries than most LDCs.

We begin with Malaysia, for two reasons: No other country has

opted more clearly and articulately for the construction of national policies and plans as aggregations of regional policies and plans; and Malaysia is possibly the best illustration in the world of a major theme of
this book, namely that the degree to which national economic and social
policy takes on a regional form depends on the extent of the overlap
among income and welfare differences, differences in occupational
structures and product mix, differences in language, religion, and
culture, and differences among spaces. In Malaysia the overlap has been
virtually total, and this overlap has been the single most important
factor in informing not only regional policy but national economic and
social policy in general.

THE 1969 RIOTS

In May 1969 an event occurred in Malaysia that changed not only
regional policy but the whole approach to national social and economic
policy, from that time to the present day. The event was an outburst of
bloody race riots in the capital city, Kuala Lumpur, with violent clashes
between Malays and Chinese. The riots shook the Malaysian government, and the Malaysian people, to the very core. Until the violence
erupted, it had been possible to maintain the complacent belief that
together, "the bargain"—the agreement that government, both legisla-
ture and bureaucracy, would remain in the hands of the Malay majority,
whereas the Chinese (and Indians) were allowed complete freedom in
commerce, industry, and finance—and the development strategy of accelerated growth and trickle down would maintain equilibrium among
ethnic groups and gradually remove inequities.[1] This pleasant illusion
was shattered by one day of violence on 13 May 1969.

BACKGROUND OF THE RIOTS

Four overlapping polarizations lay behind the riots: rich versus
poor, Malay versus Chinese and Indian (or Muslim versus non-Muslim),
urban–rural occupational structure, and spatial disparities (regional
gaps).
   The rich versus poor polarity was identified by the Malaysian population with Chinese versus Malay. Except for the royal families and a few
merchants, the majority Malay population was poor in comparison with
the Chinese, who constituted about 35% of the population and also in
comparison with the smaller Indian and European populations.

The rich–poor dichotomies overlapped with the urban–rural dichotomy as well. The royal families were rural based, but they maintained urban residences, and in any case there was only a handful of them. The Chinese were in the cities, dominating the commerce and finance, and to some degree industry as well, whereas the Malays were in the *kampungs* (villages) and on the land. Of course there were poor Malays in the cities as well, and about half of the estate workers were Indian. In 1980, 35% of estate workers were classified as poor (see Table 11). Despite this blurring at the edges, however, a clear enough picture emerges of Rich–poor = Chinese-Malay = urban–rural.

As can be seen from Tables 12, 13, and 14, the Muslim–non-Muslim polarity, which obviously coincides with the Malay–non-Malay polarity, also coincides with the rural–urban and poor–rich polarities.

Behind the differences in income and occupation of the various ethnic groups were vast differences in ownership of assets. As may be seen from Table 15, in the corporate sector, the Malay majority owned only 0.3% of the assets in agriculture and 0.9% of the assets in industry. Even in the noncorporate sector, Malays owned only 2.3% of the assets in industry. In noncorporate agriculture, the Malays did own 47.1% of

Table 11. Peninsular Malaysia: Number of Poor Households by Sector: 1980

	Total households ('000)	Total poor households ('000)	Incidence of poverty (%)	Percentage among poor
Agriculture				
Rubber small holders	425.9	175.9	41.3	26.4
Palm oil small holders	24.6	1.9	7.8	0.3
Coconut small holders	34.2	13.3	38.9	2.0
Padi farmers	151.0	83.2	55.1	12.5
Other agriculture	172.2	110.5	64.1	16.6
Fishermen	42.8	19.4	45.3	2.9
Estate workers	112.5	39.5	35.2	5.9
Agricultural total	963.2	443.7	46.1	66.6
Nonagriculture				
Mining	32.6	11.1	34.0	1.7
Manufacturing	301.1	55.4	18.4	8.3
Construction	56.3	12.0	21.3	1.8
Transport and utilities	137.2	31.5	23.0	4.7
Commerce and other services	793.6	112.4	14.2	16.9
Nonagricultural total	1,320.8	222.4	16.8	33.4
Total	2,284.0	666.1	29.2	100.0

Source. Government of Malaysia, *Fourth Malaysia Plan,* Kuala Lumpur, 1981, p. 333.

Table 12. *Peninsular Malaysia: Mean Monthly Household Income of the Lower Four Deciles[a]: 1970, 1976 and 1979 (in M$)*

	Malay	Chinese	Indian	Others	Average for all ethnic groups
1970	56.76	135.93	112.48	44.72	75.90
1976	101.95	247.27	197.21	107.08	142.19
1979	140.35	280.11	263.43	154.37	186.19

[a]This refers to the lowest 40% of households in the size distribution of income.
Source. Government of Malaysia, *Fourth Malaysia Plan*, Kuala Lumpur, 1981.

Table 13. *Peninsular Malaysia: Employment by Race and Sector: 1980*

	Malay (%)	Chinese (%)	Indian (%)	Total employment ('000 in sector)
1. Primary	66.3	19.9	13.0	1,539.1
2. Secondary	39.8	51.1	8.5	1,244.7
3. Tertiary	47.0	41.6	10.5	1,480.6
Total	51.9	36.5	10.8	4,264.4

Source. Government of Malaysia, *Fourth Malaysia Plan*, Kuala Lumpur, 1981, p. 46.

Table 14. *Employment in Agriculture in Peninsular Malaysia: 1975 and 1980*

	1975		1980	
	Agricultural workers		Agricultural workers	
Community groups	('000)	%	('000)	%
Malay	1,029.1	69.6	1,020.2	66.3
Chinese	282.8	19.1	306.1	19.9
Indian	154.4	10.5	199.4	13.0
Others	11.6	0.8	13.4	0.9
Total	1,477.9	100.0	1,539.1	100.0

Source. Government of Malaysia, *Fourth Malaysia Plan*, Kuala Lumpur, 1981.

Table 15. *Ownership of Assets in Modern Agriculture and Industry, Peninsular Malaysia: 1970*

| Ownership | Modern agriculture[a] (planted acreage) | | | | Industry[b] (fixed assets) | | | |
| | Corporate sector | | Noncorporate sector | | Corporate sector | | Noncorporate sector | |
	('000 acres)	%	('000 acres)	%	$	%	$	%
Malaysians	515.0	29.2	697.6	94.1	559.7	42.8	167.2	97.6
Malay	5.0	0.3	349.3	47.1	11.2	0.9	3.9	2.3
Chinese	457.0	25.9	243.3	32.8	342.3	26.2	158.0	92.2
Indian	4.9	0.3	74.8	10.1	1.5	0.1	3.9	2.3
Others	48.1	2.7	13.2	1.8	187.2	14.3	1.4	0.8
Government[c]	—	—	17.0	2.3	17.5	1.3	—	—
Non-Malaysians	1,249.6	70.8	44.0	5.9	747.3	57.2	4.1	2.4
Total	1,764.4	100.0	741.6	100.0	1,307.0	100.0	171.3	100.0
Percentage of total	70.4		29.6		87.4		12.6	

[a]Modern agriculture covers estate acreage under rubber, palm oil, coconut and tea. FELDA is included in this category—under the noncorporate sector. Ownership is in terms of total planted acreage.

[b]The industry sector covers manufacturing, construction, and mining. Ownership is in terms of fixed assets. Total excludes unallocatable assets amounting to $25.2 million.

[c]Government ownership of 17,000 acres in modern agriculture is included in the noncorporate sector, whereas its ownership of $17.5 million of fixed assets in industry is included in the corporate sector.

Source. Fisk and H. Osman-Rani, eds, *The Political Economy of Malaysia* (Kuala Lumpur: Oxford University Press, 1982), p. 154.

the assets, but this figure was less than their share of total population, and it included the large holdings of the royal families and of the Federal Land Development Agency (FELDA) as well as the small holdings of the peasants. The major owners in the plantation sector (corporate agriculture) were foreigners, but Chinese holdings were substantial. A similar situation prevailed in corporate industry, although here foreign domination was somewhat less marked. In noncorporate industry the domination of the Chinese was overwhelming.

But just how unequal was income distribution in Malaysia in the 1970s? Table 16 shows figures for a "peer group" of countries with per capita incomes of $1,700 to $2,230 in 1984, taken from the *World Bank World Development Report 1986*. The countries in this group for which income distribution was most equal are a rather mixed bag: Yugoslavia, South Korea, and Portugal, in that order. The most unequal distributions are found in Brazil, Panama, and Mexico, followed by Malaysia. Thus Malaysia finds itself in the middle of its peer group in this respect. Moreover, Malaysia's per capita income puts her in the upper income group of the developing countries. All in all, the degree of inequality in Malaysia in the late 1960s and early 1970s was scarcely enough to explain the eruption of violence, *had it been evenly spread among spaces and societies.*

Even if we consider the last polarity—disparities in terms of space— it is unlikely that by itself it would have led to serious trouble, in the light of the otherwise favorable pattern of regional development. Let us glance briefly at this development as it took shape after the arrival of the British.

Table 16. Income Distribution: Malaysia and Peer Groups

Year	Lowest 20%	Second 20%	Third 20%	Fourth 20%	Highest 20%	Highest 10%
Brazil (1972)	2.0	5.0	9.4	17.0	66.6	50.6
Portugal (1973–1974)	5.2	10.0	14.4	21.3	49.1	33.4
Malaysia (1973)	3.5	7.7	12.4	20.3	56.1	39.8
Panama (1970)	2.0	5.2	11.0	20.0	61.8	44.2
Mexico (1977)	2.9	7.0	12.0	20.4	57.7	40.6
South Korea (1976)	5.7	11.2	15.4	22.4	45.3	27.5
Yugoslavia (1978)	6.6	12.1	18.7	23.9	38.7	22.9
Argentina (1970)	4.4	9.7	14.1	21.5	50.3	35.2
(Indonesia (1976)	6.6	7.8	12.6	23.6	49.4	34.0)

Source. World Bank, *World Development* (New York: Oxford University Press, 1986), pp. 226–227.

REGIONAL DEVELOPMENT LEADING TO REGIONAL DISPARITIES

The establishment of the rubber industry in Malaya by the British at the end of the nineteenth century introduced a pattern of development led by modern-sector plantations, agriculture and mining, and later forestry. In the 1920s and 1930s, regional planning became a major aspect of colonial development policy. This policy consisted largely in pushing back frontiers, and region after region was intensively studied, in terms of soils, hydrology, slopes, forest inventories, and the like. Regional planning, in other words, was mainly land-use planning. This tradition continued into the postwar period, and even into the postindependence period.

Development was export-oriented from the beginning of British interest and has continued to be so after independence. In fact, import replacement has played a much smaller role in development strategy than in most LDCs. In the interwar period, exports were dominated by rubber and tin. Later other products such as palm oil, iron, hardwoods, and cocoa, and, later still, petroleum and manufactures were added. All of these products except manufactures were tied to particular spaces by their physical characteristics: where the minerals and forests were located and where the soils, slopes, rainfall, and so forth were suitable for rubber, palm oil, pepper, and other plantation products. The favorable locations were different for different products, and the succession of products that became important for export led to a species of moving frontier.

INDEPENDENCE: MALAYA BECOMES MALAYSIA

By the time Malaya gained its independence in 1957, British colonial policy had had both good and bad results. The good results provided a basis for enough stability to deal with the bad results.

Apart from the establishment of a prosperous export sector, one of the most favorable aspects of the colonial period was that it was so short—much shorter than in other countries in Asia. Consequently economic penetration by the British was rather shallow. As a result, indigenous entrepreneurship (particularly among the Chinese and Indian populations) was not destroyed to the degree that it was in other countries. Indigenous entrepreneurs shared in the development of land and mineral resources. At the attainment of independence, half the population had already been drawn into the modern sector (as compared to 7% in Indonesia, for example).

More important, the population explosion that followed European settlement (as a result of improved health and reduced incidence of internal wars among rival rulers) also came late; Malaysia has never suffered from population pressure on the land. As late as 1980 only 30% of the cultivable land was in use.[2]

Moreover, Malaya's experience under colonial role was not only short but relatively amicable; as a consequence, in contrast to her neighbors—Indonesia, Burma, and the countries of Indochina—Malaysia suffered less ideological conflict and confusion; a clear choice was made for ties with the Western world, private enterprise, a generally liberal ideology, British-style legal institutions, and parliamentary democracy. From the moment of independence, the country had an "outward" rather than an "inward"-looking world view; it has been open to both foreign aid and foreign investment and has benefited a good deal from import of technology and scientific, professional, and technical skills as well as import of capital. This set of conditions in turn provided some stability in which to deal with the more unfavorable legacies of the colonial period.

British development policy in Malaya created a major problem in that each new wave of rapid development of the modern sector, coupled with the sparse population, brought a wave of immigration of Chinese and Indians; over time, both these populations became a larger proportion of the Malayan total. The separation of Singapore, with its vast Chinese majority, shortly after independent Malaysia was created, helped to defuse this explosive situation by improving the ratio of Malays to Chinese (the inclusion of Sabah and Sarawalk in the Malaysian Federation also reduced the proportion of Chinese in the total population).

EMERGENCE OF REGIONAL INEQUALITIES

Meanwhile, however, the pattern of regional development initiated during the colonial period was leading to regional inequalities. The moving frontier was resulting in an unfavorable distribution of economic activity and population in space. By the time manufactured exports became important in the 1970s, there was a distinct pattern of spatial development along a north–south axis to the west of the central mountain spine of the country, from Penang through Kuala Lumpur to Johore Bahru (see Figs. 9 and 10). All the major cities were on this axis, the

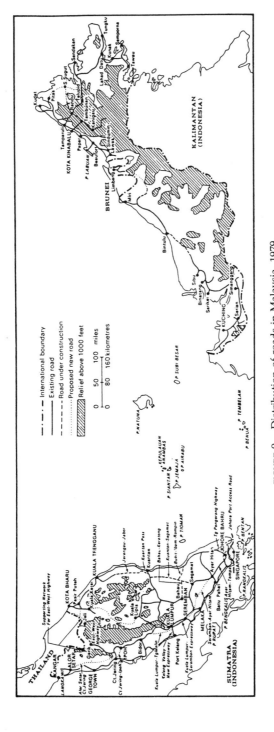

FIGURE 9. Distribution of roads in Malaysia, 1979.

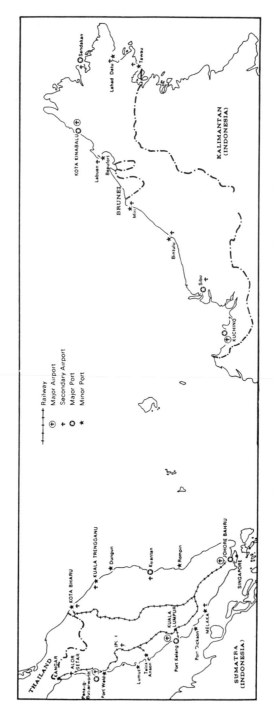

FIGURE 10. Distribution of railways, ports, and airports in Malaysia, 1979.

transport and communications systems followed it, the main plantation sector was just east of it, much of the mining followed the same pattern (see Fig. 11). As manufacturing grew, it was natural that it should locate on the same axis, where the population, the domestic market, the financial and other services, the roads, railroads, and good harbors were— also the good schools. The British left behind relatively good education and health systems, which facilitated the expansion of the modern sector. Although these facilities were spread to some extent throughout the country, they were nonetheless more prevalent and of higher quality along the western axis. This concentration of development between the west coast and the central mountain range was to become a major concern of regional policy, especially because the poorest states with the highest concentration of Malay population were on the east coast.

SPATIAL ASPECTS

Now we can put together the overlap of all the factors discussed with regional imbalance. Because wealth is associated with modern sector industry and services and because these are found in the west coast states, especially in Selangor and Penang, wealth is found in this region and these states. Poverty, on the other hand, is associated with small-scale agriculture and fishing and is found in the east coast states, especially in Trengannu and Kelantan. Wealth is associated with urban occupations; and all the big cities are on the west coast axis, especially Kuala Lumpur and Penang, with Johore Bahru increasing in importance (see Table 17). The Chinese are in the cities, and especially in the larger cities, so they are situated on the west coast axis, too, especially in Kuala Lumpur, Penang, and Johore Bahru, whereas the Malays are in the countryside, with the highest degree of concentration in the east coast states, especially in Trengganu and Kelantan (see Table 18). It follows that the purest concentration of Islamic religion and culture is to be found in the east coast states, especially in Trengganu and Kelantan-purest, that is, in terms of percentage of population, although not necessarily in terms of absolute numbers. Conversely, the percentage of population with other religions and cultures is to be found in the west coast states, especially in the large west coast cities.

The way in which all these polarities aggregate in terms of regional disparities in per capita income, occupational structure, and urbanization is shown in Table 19. The per capita income of the richest state, Selangor, was more than three and a half times as high as that of the poorest, Kelantan. Selangor is also three times as urbanized as Kelantan;

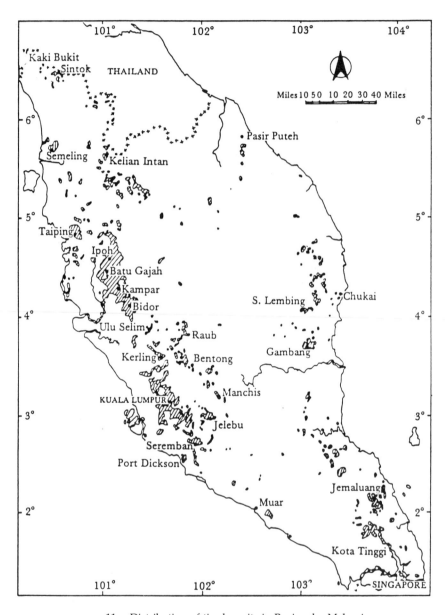

FIGURE 11.   Distribution of tin deposits in Peninsular Malaysia.

Table 17. Urbanization by State and Region: 1970

Geographical area/state	Total population ('000)	Urban population ('000)	Percentage urbanized	Number	Average town size ('000)
1. South-West	2,516.3	938.4	37.3	10	93.8
Malacca	404.1	101.5	25.1	1	101.5[a]
Selangor	1,630.7	733.2	45.0	6	122.2
N. Sembilan	481.5	103.7	21.5	3	34.6
2. Central Perak	1,569.2	431.8	27.5	8	54.0
3. North	1,851.4	515.7	27.9	8	64.5
Penang	775.4	395.0	50.9	5	79.0
Kedah	955.0	120.7	12.6	3	40.2
Perlis	121.0	—	0	0	0
4. East	1,596.7	308.6	19.3	12	25.7
Kelantan	686.3	103.3	15.1	5	20.7
Trengganu	405.5	100.5	27.0	3	36.5
Pehang	504.9	95.8	19.0	4	24.0
5. South Johore	1,277.0	336.0	26.3	7	48.0
Total	8,810.3	2,530.5	28.7	45	56.2

[a]Includes conurbation.

Source. Reproduced with permission from Ove Simonsen, *Regional Framework for Resource Allocation in Public Sector Programs,* Nagoya, United Nations Centre for Regional Development, Working Paper 70–10, November, 1979.

the capital city and Malaysia's largest, Kuala Lumpur, is there. Penang is more urbanized still, but that is because it is a small state, consisting mainly of the two cities of Georgetown and Butterworth. Selangor also had the most advanced production structure, followed by Penang. The three poorest states, Kelantan, Trengganu, and Kedah/Perlis, had the least advanced structures of production. In sum, as a glance at Figure 11

Table 18. GRP per Capita and Percentage Malay Population: 1970

	GRP per capita	Percentage Malay population
Southwest	M$ 1,214	33.8
Central	778	34.3
North	615	54.1
South	660	50.1
East	500	82.3

Source. FENCO and van Grinkel Associates, *Pahang Tenggara. Master Planning Study,* Kuala Lumpur (DARA), 1972.

Table 19. GDP per Capita, Sectoral Shares of GDP and Urbanization by State: 1970

	GDP per capita		Sectoral shares of GDP (%)[a]			Urban share of population (%)[b]
	($)	Index	A	I	S	
Selangor	1,520	167	14	38	48	45
Penang	939	103	18	22	60	51
Perak	911	100	29	35	36	28
Negeri Sembilan	907	99	37	25	38	21
Pahang	855	94	42	23	35	19
Johore	835	92	40	21	39	26
Malacca	761	83	31	10	59	25
Ledah/Perlis	605	66	58	12	30	13
Trengannu	536	59	38	22	40	27
Kelantan	420	46	43	12	45	15
Pen. Malaysia	912	100	29	28	43	29

[a]Sectors: A: agriculture, forestry, fishing; I: mining, manufacturing, construction, utilities; and S: transport, commerce, government, other services.
[b]Minimum urban concentration: 10,000 persons.
Source. Government of Malaysia, *Second Malaysia Plan, 1971–1975*, Kuala Lumpur, 1970.

will show, the more prosperous and more highly developed states are on the west coast, the poorest and least developed on the east coast.

REGIONAL POLICY: 1970–1988

After the race riots of May 1969, the government, with the general support of the people, moved with extraordinary alacrity and perspicacity. They realized that henceforth the problem of regional disparities, with all its related polarities, would have to be tackled directly and head on, rather than counting on mere growth of national income to solve it. By the same token they realized that if the economic disadvantages of the Malay population were to be eliminated, high growth of national income was not enough. Malays would have to be drawn into the high-productivity, high-income activities, which were mainly urban, and they would therefore have to receive education and training that would permit them to make this transition. These joint realizations crystalized in the New Economic Policy (NEP), which was incorporated into The Second Malaysia Plan for 1971–1975 as Chapter 1. There the new strategy was summarized as follows:[3]

> Comprising two prongs, the NEP seeks to eradicate poverty among all Malaysians and to restructure Malaysian society so that the iden-

tification of race with economic function and geographic location is eventually eliminated, both objectives being realized through rapid expansion of the economy over time.

This process involves the modernization of rural lives, a rapid and balanced growth of urban activities and the creation of a Malay commercial and industrial community in all categories and at all levels of operation, so that Malays and other indigenous people will become full partners in all aspects of the economic life of the nation.[4]

This two pronged approach was translated into two sets of policies. One of these was defined in terms of assistance to Malays, wherever they happened to be. The other was defined in spatial terms and expressed in a series of regional development plans. The first set of policies took the form of legislation and institutions designed to help indigenous people ("Bumiputras") to get into urban occupations, especially industry, commerce, and finance, including ownership and management of enterprises in these fields. These ventures were moderately successful, as we shall see. However, they do not really come under the heading of regional policy; they were regional only insofar as the Malay population is more heavily concentrated in some regions than in others. For this reason we shall not go into these policies here but will direct our attention to the specifically regional policies.

With the introduction of the NEP, the concept of regional development changed. It was no longer merely a matter of contributing to growth of national income by opening up and settling resource frontiers, wherever the potential appeared to be good. There were still frontiers to develop, certainly; but henceforth regional development was to be designed to contribute to the objectives of the NEP: to reduce regional disparities and thus reduce disparities among ethnic groups; to raise incomes of Malays, wherever they might be; to draw Malays into urban centers while retarding migration to Kuala Lumpur and other major centers—that is, to create or expand urban centers in retarded regions; to draw Malays into industry, commerce, and finance, not just as employees but as owners and managers as well; and to improve levels of health and education of the Malay population.

As Kamal Salih (then dean of the School of Comparative Social Science at the Science University of Penang) has pointed out, the new strategy initiated with the Second Malaysia Plan was a major step that "can be expected to become a major pillar in the country's development strategy in subsequent plans." He notes also that it

is associated with recent official awareness of the important role of regional development in national planning, and a policy shift from

purely sectoral planning, which has marked much of the country's
programming in the past. It is part, in fact, of what is now becoming
a more definitive national policy for regional development, and even
more of a national industrialization policy for the next twenty years.[5]

It was a tall order. The Economic Planning Unit (EPU) in the Prime
Minister's Office, despite a sizable and very competent staff, aided by a
large and semi-permanent team from the Harvard Development Advisory Service (now Harvard Institute for International Development), including such distinguished development economists as Donald
Snodgrass and Jack Knecht, could not possibly handle it. So the government turned to the international development community for assistance: technical assistance in the preparation of a series of regional
development studies and capital assistance for implementing the development plans that came out of the studies. By and large, a different
donor was chosen for each region, and consequently there was a different team for studies and plans for each region. Continuity and coordination of the complex administrative framework was provided by the staff
at EPU and by overlapping membership on the Steering Committees
that were appointed for each project (see Fig. 12).

THE JENGKA TRIANGLE

The Jengka Triangle scheme was the first of the new-style regional
development projects, which were concentrated in the eastern states
(see Fig. 13). It was launched toward the end of the period covered by
the First Malaysia Plan as a World Bank project.

Jengka started as a typical resettlement scheme of its era. That is, it
consisted essentially in cutting down one kind of trees (tropical hardwoods) and planting another (rubber and palm oil). After 1970, however, the Jengka project quickly adapted to the objectives of the NEP and
the Second Malaysia Plan. Most of the settlers in the scheme were Malays, and accordingly Malays reaped most of the benefits. The pattern of
settlement was more urbanized than had been the case with the earlier
Federal Land Development Agency (FELDA) schemes, and a special
study was undertaken of the urban center of Jengka as the growth pole
of the region. Also, more attention was paid to the planning of health
and education for the region than was typical of the earlier FELDA
projects. The World Health Organization had just completed its systems
analysis approach to public health planning and chose the Jengka project as the vehicle for its first test run application. It was an interesting

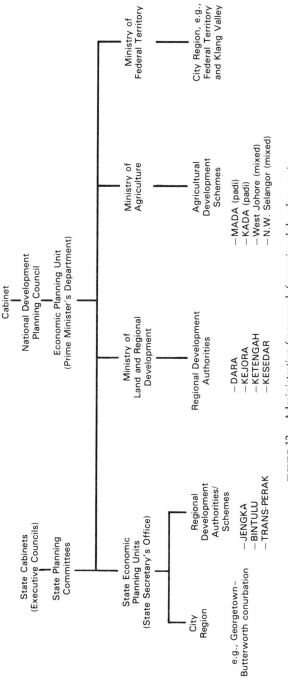

FIGURE 12.   Administrative framework for regional development.

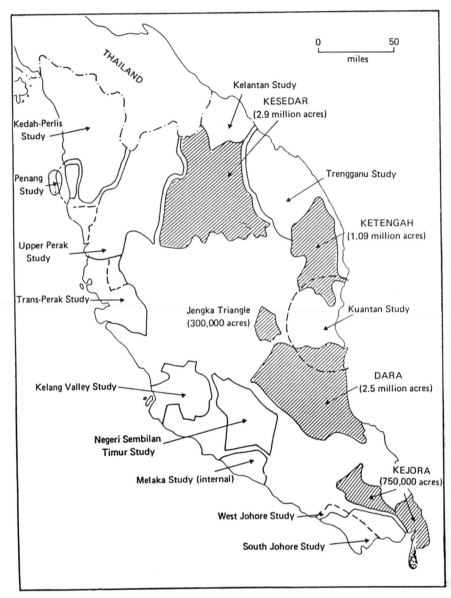

FIGURE 13. Location of regional development authorities in Peninsular Malaysia and areas covered by various master planning studies.

case because the settlers in FELDA projects were not a normal sample of the population. Young childless couples were preferred as settlers by FELDA; the settlers came mainly from the poorer east coast states where special health conditions prevailed; and the range of occupations in such land settlement schemes was narrow. The school system for Jengka also presented special problems for similar reasons.

The project attracted a good deal of attention and as a resettlement scheme is generally considered to be a success. Khalid Husin of Malaysia's Ministry of Land and Regional Development maintains that "in terms of new land development JENGKA is spectacularly successful."[6] The scheme may be regarded as a transitional one between the old era of regional development and the new.

JOHORE TENGGARA

The Johore Tenggara project, with a high-powered planning team from the University of East Anglia and financed by British foreign aid had barely started when the NEP and the Second Malaysia Plan (SMP) were taking shape. Its ideology and methodology were accordingly more closely attuned to the NEP and SMP from the beginning. Planning for the region was integrated with urban planning on the one hand and with national planning on the other. If there were a growth pole for the region, it was obviously Johore Bahru, and a separate urban development study was undertaken for that city. Johore Bahru seemed to live in the shadow of Singapore on the other side of the bridge, rather than being stimulated by that vigorous metropolitan center. An international airport and a deep-water port were planned to help rectify that situation.

PAHANG TENGGARA

The Pahang Tenggara study, for which the present writer served as senior economist, started in 1972. Both the NEP and the SMP were accordingly already launched, and both were constantly in the minds of members of the team. We were also in frequent contact with our neighbors to the south in the Johore Tenggara project, and a good deal of intellectual cross-fertilization took place. The ideology and methodology of the Pehang Tenggara project were also influenced by the fact that I was simultaneously a member of the "Unified Approach" team set up under the auspices of the United Nations Research Institute for Social

Development (UNRISD) in Geneva, and I was anxious to make Pahang Tenggara a case of application of the unified approach.

The "Unified Approach" was the major recommendation of the United Nations Expert Group of Social Policy and Planning in National Development, which met in Stockholm in September 1969 under the co-chairmanship of Gunnar Myrdal and the author. It led promptly to Economic and Social Council Resolution 1494 (XLVIII) of 26 May 1970 and General Assembly Resolution 2681 (XXV) of 11 December 1970, urging member nations to pursue the unified approach in their development planning and policy. Other U.N. resolutions to the same effect followed. A project was set up within the UNRISD to translate the concept into operational terms. The basic ideas were dropping the distinction between economic and social development; the blurring of jealously guarded lines of distinction among U.N. Specialized Agencies; recognition that sectoral programs cannot be effectively planned or implemented in isolation from each other; the need for bridges among sectoral departments of government; need for an interdisciplinary approach to analysis of development problems and processes; planning for all objectives of development directly and simultaneously, with full cognizance of interactions among them; need to reexamine the development problem as a total societal process; and emphasis on the "style" of development most suitable to each society's values, aspirations, and circumstances.

My teammates, the EPU, and our steering committee were all sympathetic to the idea of applying the unified approach; it was in tune with the dominant themes of development planning ideology of the time. Finally, the Pahang Tenggara project incorporated a specific and comprehensive growth pole strategy. Growth poles were in the air at the time also; some of the growth poles incorporated into regional plans were, indeed, far too much in the air, including those of Pahang Tenggara, as we shall see.

The Pahang Tenggara project has attracted a good deal of attention and generated a substantial literature.[7] The salient features of the project which aroused such interest were as follows:

1. Scale. Pahang Tenggara is much the biggest regional development project yet attempted by the Malaysian government and one of the biggest anywhere. The region has over 1 million hectares, half of which were to be cleared and planted, the rest to be used for forestry or left in present uses. Some 550,000 people were to be settled, compared to the 50,000 then living in the region. The plan called for 36 new towns with populations ranging from 5,000 to 150,000 by 1990. The plan alone cost $4,000,000 (U.S.) at 1970–1973 prices and took a team of over 50 profes-

sionals more than 2 years to complete. The planning phase was financed by the Canadian International Development Agency, and the team was Canadian except for some Dutch tropical agriculture experts and a contingent of Malaysians. Implementation of the plan was expected to cost $1 billion, public and private. DARA, the regional development authority for Pahang Tenggara, has received much the biggest budget allocations from the government (see Table 20) and has much the biggest staff (Table 21), of all the regional development authorities.

2. In line with the Unified Approach, sociocultural factors were accorded high priority. Because the future settlers were not in the region, a sociological survey was mounted in the areas from which they were expected to come, to determine their values, attitudes, aspirations, and desires. The survey was organized and conducted by the sociology department of the Science University at Penang, using graduate students from the areas surveyed.

3. As a result of this survey, the physical and sociocultural environments were accorded high weights in the objective function. Within the latter, as well as standard considerations such as education, nutrition, health, and recreation, were a concept of "quality of life," based on the sociological survey and diversity of occupation, to give heed to the NEP goal of widening the occupational structure of Malays. Increasing income and reducing unemployment were also included as objectives.

4. To improve the chances of achieving these sociocultural objectives, a much more urbanized settlement pattern than was normal for FELDA projects was recommended. The settlers, including plantation workers, should live in towns of not less than 5,000 people and preferably in cities of 10,000 to 20,000, with two regional centers of 150,000 and 50,000 respectively. (No one was to spend more time commuting to work than the normal trip of half an hour on foot or by bicycle for workers living on plantations. The savings in provision of education, health, and recreation facilities, and the like would more than offset the cost of motorized transport to and from work) (See Fig. 14.)

5. Given the goals of the NEP, the team argued that it could not justify planning a system that would create poor Malay families. Incomes should approximate the national average to begin with and should rise at the same rate as the national average. On this principle, it persuaded the government that allocations of land per family should be raised from the then-current standard of 3 hectares to 6 hectares. This principle was later extended to other regional development schemes, including Johore Tenggara (KEJORA). Because the economic activities recommended were entirely in the modern sector and mostly in the modern export sector, family holdings of this size could yield incomes

Table 20. Financial Allocation for Resource Frontier Development: 1971–1980 (M$ million)

	Second Malaysia Plan (1971–1975) allocation			Third Malaysia Plan (1976–1980) allocation				Total allocation (1971–1980)			
	Dara	Kejora	Ketengah	Dara	Kejora	Ketengah	Kesedar	Dara	Kejora	Ketengah	Kesedar
Operating expenses[a]	3.75	3.09	1.8	31.0	15.3	17.95	5.15	34.75	18.39	19.75	5.15
Development expenditure	102.0	74.24	5.3	427.78	203.03	133.89	38.99	529.78	277.27	139.19	38.99
Infrastructure	35.0	20.64	1.0	162.62	51.69	68.17	1.45	197.62	72.33	69.17	1.45
Housing[a]	—	—	—	60.0	16.2	11.84	—	60.0	16.2	11.84	—
Roads[a]	29.0	29.0	—	115.09	77.04	—	7.12	144.09	106.04	—	7.12
Water supply[a]	8.0	8.0	—	33.01	28.08	13.11	—	41.01	36.08	13.11	—
Electricity	—	—	—	19.39	4.58	6.08	—	19.39	4.58	6.08	—
Loans	30.0	16.6	4.3	37.67	25.44	34.69	0.3	67.67	32.04	38.99	0.3
Land development schemes[b]	—	—	—	—	—	—	30.12	—	—	—	30.12

[a] = loans; [b] = grants; U.S. $1.00 = M$2.4 approximately.

Source. Federal budget 1980.

Table 21. Manpower Allocation in Regional Development Authorities: 1979

	Dara			Kejora			Ketengah			Kesedar		
	Number of Posts	Filled	Vacant	Number of Posts	Filled	Vacant	Number of Posts	Filled	Vacant	Number of Posts	Filled	Vacant
A. Managerial & professional	85	68	17	33	24	8	29	20	9	20	14	6
Expatriate officers	5	5	—	3	3	—	8	3	5	—	—	—
B. Executive and semiprofessional	56	52	4	26	23	3	16	13	3	13	8	5
C. Clerical & technical	185	151	34	96	88	8	63	60	3	78	42	36
D. Industrial & manual group	299	178	121	173	140	33	66	37	29	55	30	25
Total	635	504	176	331	278	52	182	133	49	166	94	72

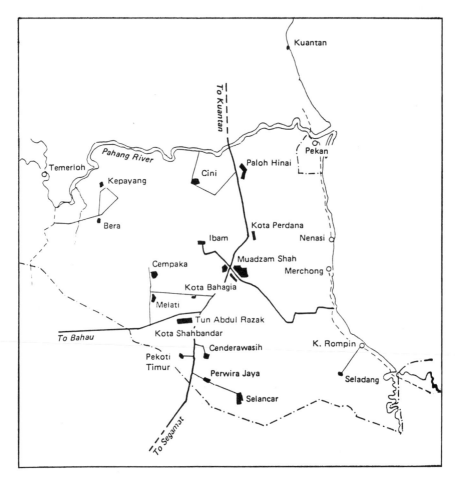

FIGURE 14.   Dara (Pahang Tenggara) settlement pattern and roads.

near the national average. (In the event, with the rise in rubber and palm oil prices after the oil crisis, they yielded incomes for a time well above the national average).

6. As in Jengka, the special characteristics of the settler population required tailor-made plans for education and health. The WHO applied its new systems analysis to the region.

GROWTH POLE STRATEGY

In terms of adaptation of regional policy to a changing world, of special interest is the story of the application of the growth pole concept.

The only city that seemed to hold out some promise of becoming a "growth pole" for the east coast region was Kuantan. It had only 75,000 people but was growing rapidly and industrializing in a dynamic way. It was linked to Kuala Lumpur by road and by air. It also happened that both the prime minister and the director of EPU came from there and had a keen interest in seeing the city grow and modernize.

Kuantan lacked a good harbor. The Pahang River there was shallow and silted up every year. Ships of any size had to moor offshore and unload by lighter. However, as part of their program of foreign aid, the Netherlands was building a deep water port just north of the city, with a special technique for constructing moles right in the sea. Our idea, therefore, was that Pahang Tenggara should be used to strengthen Kuantan as a growth pole. Development would begin in the northern part of the region, along an axis from the proposed new regional capital at Muadzam Shah and Kuantan. Building the new city and the road connecting it to Kuantan would be given top priority, and as production of export products got under way, it would flow along the new road to the new port. As the obverse of this policy, the road from Muadzam Shah to the south and the one to the west toward Bahau would be delayed. We wanted to avoid linking Pahang Tenggara development to the west coast axis and the ports of Kelang and Johore Bahru.

When I visited 6 years after the beginning of implementation of the program, exactly the opposite had taken place. Muadzam Shah, which was supposed to become the major urban center of the region, had only 2,000 people, whereas Tun Adbul Razak, which was supposed to be a secondary centre, already had 10,000. The roads to the south and to the west were further advanced than the one to the north. As the new port was being completed, the mole tilted and cracked, dumping the buildings on top of it into the sea. Such production as there was by that time was flowing out through Port Kelang and Johore Bahru, just what we hoped to avoid.

A number of factors had conspired to bring about this change in strategy. First of all, the markets for rubber and palm oil had changed drastically, and palm oil had become a more attractive investment than rubber. Palm oil had been planned for the south of the region, rubber for the north. Consequently the south was developing more rapidly. The southern forestry complexes were also developing more rapidly than those in the north. The roads were constructed as joint ventures between the Department of Public Works and various private contractors; it so happened that the contractors working in the southern part of the region were more efficient than those working in the north. It also happened that FELDA had already cleared a good deal of land in the south when the project began, especially in the "nucleus estates."

Despite all these imperfectly foreseen or unforeseen events, had the Malaysian government been adamant in the pursuit of our growth pole policy, it could have stuck to the plan. But the economic situation in general had changed in ways that made the growth pole strategy less attractive. When the Master Plan was put together, employment creation was accorded top priority, according to the government's stated policies. But in its early years, the major problem faced by DARA was labor shortage. The outburst of industrialization had accelerated rural–urban migration and made rural–rural migration appear less attractive. Palm oil is less labor intensive in the early years than rubber, making palm oil still more attractive as compared to rubber, thus shifting activity toward the south. Kuantan had become a boom town and had nearly doubled in population, but the boom had little to do with the opening of Pahang Tenggara and was largely *sui generis*. Moreover, whereas the planning team had expected expansion of Kuantan to generate spread effects to the north, to the lagging states of Trengganu and Kelantan, it was becoming clear that such spread effects were not going to appear; except for attracting migrants to take jobs in the city, Kuantan's new prosperity had little impact on the states to the north. Solving their problems would require direct action within those states themselves.

In sum, we had been a bit naive in our application of growth pole strategy. The present writer is perhaps more to blame for that than any other member of the team, but no one made a serious effort to argue me out of the idea. And certainly we were not alone. Similar overconfidence in simplistic growth pole theories was being demonstrated all over the world at that juncture of history.

POSTSCRIPT ON PAHANG TENGGARA

I am indebted to Wong Tai Chee, who is completing a PhD dissertation on Malaysian resettlement schemes for the Department of Human Geography of the Australian National University, for some important recent information, derived mainly from the 1985 and 1986 annual reports of DARA. The most interesting and the most baffling facts about DARA's recent development are these:

1. The total population of the region in 1986 was 103,450 compared to the plan forecast of 332,700. Fulfillment of plan targets was therefore less than one-third.
2. Nonetheless, the development of agricultural land was 47% over target (as of 1984), and over $500 millions had been spent.

3. About three-quarters of the population were engaged in agriculture (80% in 1984, probably a bit less in 1986).
4. The labor shortage was such that some 50,000 Indonesian workers had been employed.
5. With a population of 21,655, Bandar Tun Razak, which, according to the plan, was to have been the region's second city, was much the biggest city in the region. The second was Bera with 12,423. Muadzam Shah, which was to have been the region's major metropolitan center, was fifth with 7,754 (see Table 22).

The differences between the urban structure that is actually emerging and the one foreseen in the Master Plan have already been explained, at least to some degree. The most puzzling question arising from these new figures is, "How could so much overfulfillment in terms of agricultural land development be accompanied by such underfulfillment in terms of total population and urbanization?" Without another revisit to the area, the present writer can only guess. An important factor, obviously, is the unexpectedly rapid industrialization and rise in per capita incomes in the country as a whole and the improvement in transportation both in the country and the region. Together, these forces have meant that less processing of the output of the region has taken place inside its borders, and more outside. Also, it seems, people working in the region have been able to go to nearby and larger towns outside the region for shopping and urban services, instead of being dependent on urban centers within the region as expected. Accordingly, the construction of facilities within Pahang Tenggara's urban centres lags behind targets laid down in the plan. A larger proportion of the population consists of temporary workers, and a smaller proportion of permanent settlers, than was foreseen 17 years ago. The Mahatir government has not been greatly perturbed by these new developments, because the aim of drawing Malays into urban occupations is being met by migration of Malays into cities of more than 75,000 people rather than by urbanization of the countryside (see Table 23). The change in governmental attitudes is reflected by FELDA's decision in 1985 to replace individual ownership of land by settlers with a "share system," which effectively transforms small holders into wage workers. On the surface, this change in policy seems like mystifying retrogression. The old system seemed to work pretty well; in 1985 FELDA accounted for 45% of the land holdings in the region (see Table 24). It could very well be, however, that in a period of rapid industrialization and urbanization in the country as a whole, "land hunger" has become a less important incentive for migra-

Table 22. Occupational Structure of Townships With More than 5,000 Population in Pahang Tenggara

Township	Agricultural jobs	Percentage	Percentage of Master Plan	Nonagricultural jobs	Percentage	Percentage of Master Plan
Bandar Tun Razak	2,563	80.4	30.9	626	19.6	69.1
Bera	2,048	81.4	52.1	467	18.6	47.9
Cini	2,291	78.3	52.1	634	21.7	47.9
Kepayang	1,630	79.3	52.1	426	20.7	47.9
Muadzam Shah	1,250	46.6	52.1	1,435	53.4	47.9
Perantau Damai	1,117	92.9	52.1	85	7.1	47.9
Total	10,899	—	74.8	3,673	—	25.2

Source. (a) DARA, Pahang Tenggara Regional Masterplanning Study, 1972, p. 152, Table 14.1b, for percentage of Master Plan (b) DARA, Annual Report, 1986, p. 36, for all other figures.

Table 23. Settlements with More than 1,000 Population in Pahang Tenggara (1986) and Kesedar (1985)

Pahang Tenggara[a]		Kesedar[b]	
Settlement	Size	Settlement	Size
Bandar Tun Razak	21,655	Kuala Krai	12,757
Bera	12,423	Gua Musang	5,497
Cini	12,372	Jeli	2,553
Kepayang	11,928	Manek Urai	2,422
Muadzam Shah	7,754	Kemubu/Dobong	2,232
Perantau Damai	6,204	Ciku	1,346
Bandar 21	4,306	Bertam	1,329
Mentiga Timor	3,704		
Kota Bahagia	2,803		
Perwira Jaya	2,691		
Tembangau	2,681		
Selancar	2,527		
Bandar 34	2,287		
Ibam	2,075		
Kota Perdana	1,858		
Cendarawasih	1,682		
Melati	1,060		
Paloh Minai	1,024		

[a]Pahang Tenggara, *Annual Report*, 1986, p. 35.
[b]Kesedar, *Annual Report*, 1985, pp. 162–165.

Table 24. Distribution of Land Ownership in Pahang Tenggara and Kesedar

Ownership	Pahang Tenggara (hectares)	Percentage	Kesedar (hectares)	Percentage
Public				
FELDA	138,753	44.8	38,803	27.2
Joint-venture	21,575	7.0	—	—
Public estate	27,741	8.9	15,197	10.6
Kesedar land schemes	—	—	16,078	11.3
Kesedar rehabilitation schemes	—	—	25,277	17.7
Private				
Estate	103,037	33.2	20,350	14.3
Small holdings	18,870	6.1	27,062	18.9
Total	309,976	100.0	142,767	100.0

Source. Adapted from DARA, *Annual Report*, 1985, p. 16; Kesedar, *Annual Report*, 1986, p. 13.

tion; FELDA is competing for migrants against wages in the city, not small-scale farming in the villages.

Time will tell. It seems that the Pahang Tenggara tale is not yet entirely told.

KESEDAR

The Kelantan Regional Development Authority (Kesedar) is worthy of mention if only because it is in such sharp contrast to DARA. (See Tables 25 and 26.) It is small scale and modest in its aims. In a way it is a throwback to earlier resettlement schemes. It provides only 3 hectares of land per family, plus a household lot for diversified subsistence farming and cooperative fish farms. Because of the rough terrain and steep slopes and because of the employment-creation priority of the program, rubber is the cash crop. Nearly half the allotment—1.2 hectares—is to be devoted to upland paddy, to provide subsistence until the rubber trees mature. Settlers undertake a loan as payment for their land. Until this load is paid off, expected net family income will not reach even M\$ 2,500. Expected income will then—after 23 years—rise to M\$ 5,000, but by that time the rubber trees will be getting old and will soon need replacement, so income drops again. It is not really a very glamourous prospect for the settlers, even if the average income of people coming into the scheme is expected to be only M\$ 50 per month before they come. As the author has stated elsewhere,[8]

> In effect, the Pahang Tenggara Project aims at converting desperately poor peasants into "kulaks" or middle income farmers, while KESEDAR aims at converting desperately poor peasants into poor peasants. Even at M\$ 5,000, family income will be far below the national average 25 years hence.

One wonders even if such projects are consistent with the new economic policy.

Of course, the scheme will turn a few poor peasant families—450 families in the first 3 years—into landowners, a matter of great importance to them. And it will make them better off than before. But it will not significantly reduce gaps between Malays and non-Malays, and it does not provide opportunities for settlers to move into urban occupations as DARA does. It settles more people per thousand dollars spent than DARA does, but the estimated internal rate of return is considerably lower. KESEDAR is being financed by the World Bank. It is a little surprising that the bank found the project attractive. As industrialization proceeds, as rural–urban migration replaces rural–rural migration,

Table 25. Distribution of Agricultural Land in Pahang Tenggara and Kesedar

Land Use	Pahang Tenggara		Kesedar	
	Hectares	Percentage	Hectares	Percentage
Palm oil	241,369	17.9	56,910	39.9
Rubber	33,199	10.9	77,173	54.0
Fruits	23,090	7.4	—	—
Cattle ranch	5,939	1.9	—	—
Diversified crops	4,241	1.4	8,684	6.1
Research farm	1,012	0.3	—	—
Tea	526	2.2	—	—
Total	309,976	100.0	142,767	100.0

Source. DARA, *Annual Report*, 1985, p. 15 and Kesedar, *Annual Report*, 1986, p. 13.

and as Malaysian per capita incomes rise, justification of projects like KESEDAR, which despite its labor-intensive character cost M$ 35,000 per family settled, will be increasingly hard to justify.

REGIONAL POLICY AND THE THIRD MALAYSIAN PLAN

The idea of using regional plans as building blocks for the national development plan was already in the air when the Second Malaysia Plan for 1971–1975 was completed, but the idea had not yet taken clear shape

Table 26. Industrial Projects in the Pahang Tenggara and Kesedar Regions

Type of industry	Pahang Tenggara (unit)	Kesedar[a] (unit)
Palm oil (primary processing)	30	2
Rubber processing	—	2
Tea processing	1	—
Food, drink, or tobacco processing	1	4
Sawmill, pulp and paper processing	2	22
Nonmetallic (mineral processing)	1	1
Total	35	31

[a]Based on 1982 data.

Source. (a) DARA, *Annual Report*, 1985, p. 120, Master Plan Review: Status Report II, Lembaga Kemajuan Pahang Tenggara. (b) Kesedar, *Annual Reports*, 1985, p. 87, Table 21.

and did not much affect the form or content of the plan. But by the time of the midterm review in 1973 the EPU had explicitly recognized the relationship between spaces, sectors, structures, and societies, notably the relationship between regional gaps and disparities between ethnic groups. As work on the Third Malaysia Plan got under way, the EPU was ready to experiment with the idea of aggregating the various regional plans into the national plan. By that time both the Johore Tenggara and the Pahang Tenggara schemes had been launched. The writer was brought back to Malaysia to work directly within EPU on regional aspects of the third plan. Ove Simonsen, another member of the Pahang Tenggara team, and a physical planner with a broad and deep knowledge of the social sciences, transferred to EPU as World Bank/UNDP advisor on regional planning. Dan Usher of Queens University, Canada was brought in to work on industrial incentives in regional policy, and other foreign experts were added to the regional planning unit within EPU.

Behind the effort to integrate regional and national planning was certainly a kind of growth pole strategy, but it was less naive than the notions that underlay plans for individual regions, in Malaysia and elsewhere in the world, at that time. It was recognized that in order to achieve a certain, defined pattern of regional development, as distinct from a policy of merely encouraging growth in one individual region after another, it is necessary to plan the growth of the entire urban structure. There was also some recognition that it is not enough to select certain urban centers as growth poles and then build some social infrastructure and try to lure some private enterprises to those centers; it is necessary to plan the transmission lines and the receptors at the other end, as well as the generators. Accordingly, the EPU launched a massive study of Malaysia's urban structure and of all kinds of flows among cities. The analysis of various cities and their impacts on regional and national economies was farmed out to Malaysian universities (see Fig. 15). From these studies emerged a strategy. Policy would be directed toward slowing down the growth in the Kuala Lumpur-Port Kelang area to a pace some 30% lower than that which was expected in the absence of such policies. That would still be a high rate of growth. Penang would be left to its own dynamic devices; its growth would be neither encouraged nor discouraged. An effort would be made to resuscitate the economy of Malacca. Johore Bahru would be stimulated to grow faster through investment in infrastructure and incentives to private enterprise. The Big Push, however, would be in the east coast cities, and especially in Kuantan. In addition, small and medium-sized towns in the poorer regions of the west, north, and south, which were smaller

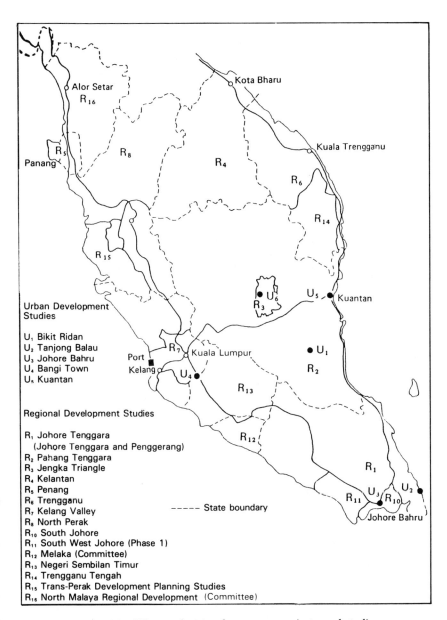

Urban Development
Studies

U₁ Bikit Ridan
U₂ Tanjong Balau
U₃ Johore Bahru
U₄ Bangi Town
U₅ Kuantan

Regional Development Studies

R₁ Johore Tenggara
   (Johore Tenggara and Penggerang)
R₂ Pahang Tenggara
R₃ Jengka Triangle
R₄ Kelantan
R₅ Penang
R₆ Trengganu
R₇ Kelang Valley
R₈ North Perak
R₁₀ South Johore
R₁₁ South West Johore (Phase 1)
R₁₂ Melaka (Committee)
R₁₃ Negeri Sembilan Timur
R₁₄ Trengganu Tengah
R₁₅ Trans-Perak Development Planning Studies
R₁₆ North Malaya Regional Development (Committee)

FIGURE 15.   Urban and regional programs, projects, and studies.

and weaker than they would be in a "normal" (rank-size rule) hierarchy, would be stimulated to more rapid development.[9]

Thus all regions were to be encouraged to grow, but some would receive more encouragement than others. Note too that there was no effort to redistribute economic activity, industry, or income *from* rich regions to poor ones, as there has been in much of Canadian regional policy. Development of each region would take place within the context of a plan, and the plans would result from careful and exhaustive study. No economic activity would be encouraged in any region unless there were a clear long-run comparative advantage for that activity in that region. Government assistance might be available to help new enterprises survive start-up difficulties but that was all. The Canadian concept of offering incentives as a kind of bribe to induce enterprises to locate in a designated region *instead* or where they wanted to go in the first place, with no careful examination of the question as to whether or not they belonged in the disadvantaged region, was quite foreign to the Malaysian strategy of the period.

Even in Malaysia, "the best laid plans of mice and men gang aft aglee," and things did not work out in quite the way that the regional planners would have liked. The experiment was new. There was little in the experience of Malaysia, or indeed of other countries, to guide us. We soon found out that in order to integrate regional plans into a national plan it is better to have that idea before the regional planning itself begins. As it was, the various regional plans were prepared by different consulting firms, from different countries, under different foreign aid programs, at different times, with different scopes and methodologies, even with somewhat different objectives in mind. It was almost impossible to add them up. The regional planning unit in EPU was too small, even with all the foreign assistance, to handle the mass of data coming in from the field and to assure some modicum of uniformity in the regional planning process.

In some ways that were worse, our *theory* was not very rigorous or refined, let alone tested. It was not the rigorous and refined theory of François Perroux that was being applied. That theory runs in terms of the tendency of development through market forces to lead to polarization, concentration of dynamic, innovative enterprises in certain spaces, generating spread effects to a global "economic space," spaces defined as "fields of forces."[10] We were trying to formulate regional policies to alter the spatial distribution of economic activity in accordance with stated goals of national policy. In other words, we were not content to leave the location of spread effects to the market and let them fall where they might, even outside the country. We wanted spread effects to end up in certain spaces, to benefit particular societies. We did not really know how to do that, and there was no very convincing and generally accepted literature, no received doctrine, to guide us. In this situation, the macroeconomic division of EPU, secure in its Keynesian armor, and not too happy with this newfangled idea of using regional plans as building blocks for national plans, was able to go its customary well-trodden way and have more impact on the actual plan document than was intended in the new strategy. Our path was relatively new and untrodden and full of pitfalls. One of these pitfalls was that the urban studies proved to be much more complex than anticipated and took much more time to complete than expected. Some of them reached the EPU too late to be of much use in preparing the third plan.

In reviewing Malaysia's regional policy in a changing world, it might be said that Malaysia reacted to internal events and external ideas. Of course, events in the outside world, such as changes in prices of rubber, tin, palm oil, and petroleum, and revisions of foreign exchange rates, have changed the details of regional policy, too. But major changes in strategy have been adjustments to the changing internal situation. Ideas, however, have come from abroad. Malaysians with university education have been trained abroad or have been trained by people who were trained abroad. As in other developing countries, economic policy, including regional policy, is made much more by "experts," advisors, consultants, and planners, many of whom are foreign, and much less by bureaucrats, than is the case in most industrialized countries. Such people like to think that there are ideas, ideologies, and sound theories behind the advice they give. The "experts," advisors, consultants, and planners who formulated regional policy during the period 1969–1985, both Malaysian and foreign, were in constant touch with the ebb and flow of world thought in the field. Moreover, Malaysians have made major contributions to that thought and to the international literature. Malaysians have played a major role in the conferences, seminars, and workshops of the United Nations Centre for Regional Development in Nagoya and have made substantial contributions to its publications. Thus in saying that Malaysia reacted to ideas from abroad, we are far from saying that Malaysians had no original ideas of their own; we are saying rather that in contributing original ideas they started from the same *international* corpus of literature, theory, doctrine, ideas, and debate as people in other countries who were concerned with regional policy. It was not a matter of foreigners pushing alien ideas down their throats; Malaysians and foreigners were members of the same international community of professionally trained people concerned with regional policy.

Thus Malaysia, like most LDCs, and a good many industrialized countries as well, struggled with application of the growth pole concept during the late 1960s and early 1970s. Malaysia broke away from simplistic concept of implanting one growth pole to develop one region and moved on to a concept of systems of interactions in space sooner than most countries. The experimentation, the adaptation to changing internal situations and changing ideas the world over, continues, and regional policy becomes ever more refined.

The changes in government in Malaysia have brought no fundamental changes in regional development policy. There is a basic continuity between the third plan and the fourth and fifth. The first chapter of the fifth plan reiterates the overriding importance of the NEP in regional and national development policy, stating that the NEP has dominated development policy since 1971. It also documents the considerable progress that has been made in achieving the objectives of the NEP in 15 years. Income disparities have been reduced among ethnic groups, as between urban and rural populations, and among regions. Bumiputra real income per capita has risen from 65% to 78% of the national average. The per capita income of the Indian population is just equal to the national average, the per capita income of the Chinese still somewhat above it. The per capita GDP of the poorest state, Kelantan, has risen from M$ 989 to M$ 1,740. Bumiputra's share in the ownership and control of the corporate sector has risen from 4.3% to 17.8%. National unity is said to be "still the overriding goal," and therefore the major effort to remove glaring imbalances among major ethnic groups must be continued. The whole of Chapter 3 of the plan is called "The NEP: Progress and Prospects."

In his foreword to the plan, Prime Minister Mahatir Bin Mohamad states once more that his government wants development to occur through activities of the private sector, but scolds private enterprise for not being enterprising enough.[11] "The private sector will have to provide the dynamism in the economy," he says. "Government involvement in the economic sector should be minimized. Commerce and industry is best left to the private sector." But he has no profound admiration for the actual performance of private enterprise.

> Hitherto the private sector has been interested only in a very narrow field, namely, finance, property development, and estates. If manufacturing is tried, it is largely in import substitution where protection is demanded. For real growth, the Malaysian private sector must venture into manufacturing for export.[12]

Mahatir is presumably directing his criticism to indigenous Malaysian enterprise; Malaysia has been extremely successful in expanding exports of hi-tech manufactured products, but most of the technology and capital for these has come from abroad. Dr. Mahatir's statement, however, illustrates the pragmatic approach in many LDCs to questions of relationship between government and private enterprise. Ideologically his government prefers private enterprise, but that philosophy does not blind them to the deficiencies of private enterprise when it comes to development, nor prevent them from stepping in to fill the gap with public enterprise when need be. Malaysia is often presented as an example of successful development in a market economy, and in a sense it is; private enterprise is not hampered by excessive or misguided regulation and control. But between 1970 and 1985, when Malaysia's dramatic expansion took place, private investment increased by 10.6% per annum, whereas public investment increased by 14.4%. The share of public investment in the total rose from 30% in 1970 to 50% in 1985.

Malaysia is also a country that has not entirely abandoned Keynesian policies to promote growth and reduce unemployment. During the slump of 1981 and 1982, the plan states,[13] increased government expenditures were deliberately used to counteract it. With the strong growth of the export sector in 1983 and 1984, restraint was exercised to avoid inflation. Unemployment has in fact been held to moderate levels (better than Canada): 5.7% in 1980 and 7.6% in 1985. Yet prices rose on average only 2.8% per annum during the Fourth Plan, and in 1985 fell slightly, a much better record than Canada's. The whole trade-off curve, in other words, was more favorable in Malaysia than in Canada.

From 1981 to 1985, because of the world recession, growth of real GDP fell to 5.8% per annum. The outlook is not favorable for 1986–1990, the plan states, so the strategy for the next 5 years must be to sustain this kind of "moderate growth." The actual growth of GDP was 5.2% in 1987 and 7.4% in 1988.[14] Many industrialized countries, including Canada, would be happy with this kind of "moderate growth."

RESULTS

Whatever has been the role of regional policy in the whole picture, the history of Malaysia's development since 1969 is a spectacular success story. Shifts in economic policy, including regional policy, have been largely a matter of adaptation to ever brighter pictures of Malaysia's potential. For the period 1965–1984 the growth rate of per capita na-

tional income was 4.5%, one of the highest in the world. The growth of
GDP averaged 6.7% per year from 1965 to 1973 and 7.3% from 1973 to
1984. In the latter period, both industry and the manufacturing component grew at 8.7%. Despite rapid industrialization and urbanization,
even agriculture expanded at a rate of 4.2% per year, better than most
LDCs. Structural change was also rapid. The share of agriculture in total
employment fell from 30 to 21% between 1965 and 1984, the share of
industry rose from 24 to 35%, and of manufacturing from 10 to 19%. The
share of services remained essentially unchanged, falling slightly from
45 to 44%. Investment grew at 9.1% per year during the first period and
11.4% during the second. All this was accomplished with a commenda-
bly low inflation rate: 1.2% for 1965–1973 and 6.2% for 1973–1984. The
figures for registered unemployment were also low but may underesti-
mate the actual amount of total unemployment. All in all, it is a praise-
worthy development effort. And as we have seen, income distribution
compares favorably with most other countries in a similar phase of development. Terrence McGee has contended that not only is Malaysia
already an "industrialized country" but that it has already entered the
phase of mass consumption.[15]

It is worthy of note that the expansion of manufacturing has been
accompanied by an upgrading of quality. Malaysian manufacturing is
becoming increasingly hi-tech. Not only is Malaysia one of the 20 leading exporters of manufactures in the world, it has become the world's
largest single exporter of electronic components. Over half the new
manufacturing jobs created during the 1970s were in electronics. Malaysia is the biggest supplier of integrated circuits to the United States,
produces 14% of the world supply of semiconductors, 40 to 70% of the
world's supply of 64K chips. The city of Penang alone is the world's
leading exporter of these chips.[16]

Malaysia has also made progress in the specific goals of the NEC.
The country as a whole has become considerably more urbanized; the
proportion of total population living in urban centers increased from
26.5% in 1957 and 28.8% in 1970 to 37.5% in 1980 (Table 27). The urban
share of the Malay population increased from 27% in 1970 to 37.4% in
1980. The Malay share of the urban population grew from 21 to 38% of
the population, the Chinese share fell from 63 to 50%, and the Indian
share fell slightly from 13 to 11%. In cities with more than 75,000 population, the Malay share rose from 14% in 1957 and 22% in 1970 to 40% in
1980. For the same census years, the Chinese share was 66, 61, and 48%,
the Indian share 15, 15, and 11%.[17] In the five major urban regions—
Kuala Lumpur-Port Kelang, Penang, Johore Bahru, Melaka, and Ipoh-
Taiping—containing 32% of the population of Peninsular Malaysia in

Table 27. Urban Population Change by Ethnic Group in West Malaysia:
1921–1990 (by Percentage)

Group	1921	1931	1947	1957	1970	1980	1990[a]
Malay	18.4	19.2	21.1	21.6	27.1	37.4	45.6
	(54.0)	(49.2)	(49.5)	(49.8)	(52.7)	(55.1)	(58.1)
Chinese	60.2	59.6	62.3	63.9	59.0	50.6	43.7
	(29.4)	(33.9)	(38.4)	(37.2)	(35.8)	(33.9)	(31.4)
Indian	17.8	17.8	13.8	10.7	12.8	11.3	10.1
	(15.1)	(15.1)	(10.8)	(11.2)	(10.7)	(10.3)	(9.9)
Others	3.6	3.4	2.8	3.8	1.1[b]	0.7	0.6
	(1.5)	(1.8)	(1.3)	(1.8)	(0.8)	(0.7)	(0.6)
Total	100.0	100.0	100.0	100.0	100.0	100.0	100.0
Urban percentage to total percentage	14.0	15.1	15.9	26.5	28.8	37.5	41.1
Total population (million)	2.91	3.79	4.91	6.28	9.15	11.47	12.97

[a]Projected figure; [b]the sharp decline was a result of the Malayanization policy in employment following the independence in 1957. Figures within brackets indicate percentage of total population.

Sources. (a) Department of Statistics, Kuala Lumpur for 1921–1970; (b) Fourth Malaysia Plan, 1981–1985, p. 79, for 1980 and Fifth Malaysia Plan, 1986–1990; pp. 134–35, for 1990.

1980, 37% were Malays, 49% Chinese, 13% Indian and 1% others. The former urban–rural–Chinese–Malay polarization has been considerably diluted.

Even more striking is the change in occupational structure among Malays. The proportion of Malays in the manufacturing labor force rose from 19.6% in 1957 to 28.9% in 1970 and 53.5% in 1980. Conversely the share of Chinese in manufacturing employment fell from 72% to 65.2% and then to 45.5% in 1980.[18] The proportion of primary employment accounted for by Malays and Chinese respectively scarcely changed between 1970 and 1980, but in the secondary and tertiary sectors, the proportion of Malays rose, and the proportion of Chinese fell. More important, the role of the primary sector in the employment of Malays declined, and the importance of the secondary and tertiary sectors increased. Thus the polarization of occupational structures of Malays and Chinese has also become less sharp. Meanwhile, substantial structural change has taken place in the economy as a whole (Table 28).

There is also some evidence of regional convergence. In 1985, the gap in per capita GDP between the richest state (Selangor) and the poorest (Perlis) had fallen to about 114%. The incidence of poverty also declined more rapidly in the poorer states than in the richer ones.[19]

Table 28. Change in Employment Structure in Peninsular Malaysia: 1947–1985
(by Percentage)

Year	Primary[a]	Secondary[b]	Tertiary[c]	Annual growth rate[c]	Total[a,b,c]
1947	66.2	13.5	20.0	—	99.7
1957	59.0	16.0	25.0	3.4	100.0
1970	46.8	23.6	29.6	3.7	100.0
1975	41.4	26.1	32.5	6.5	100.0
1980	36.1	29.2	34.7	5.0	100.0
1985	35.7	28.0	36.3	6.0	100.0

[a]Agriculture; [b]mining, manufacturing, construction, and transport; and [c]wholesale and retail trade, banking, public administration, education, health, defense, and utilities. *Sources.* 1947 and 1957 data are calculated from *1957 Population Census*, p. 30; 1970, 1975, and 1980 data from Department of Statistics, Kuala Lumpur, and from Kuala Lumpur, Government of Malaysia, *Fourth Malaysian Plan, 1981–1985*, 1980, Table 3-10; and 1985 data from Kuala Lumpur, Government of Malaysia, *Fifth Malaysia Plan, 1986–1990*, 1980, Table 4-3, for 1985.

Less progress had been made in terms of Malay ownership and management of industrial enterprises, but even there the situation had improved. By the end of 1985, the share of Malay ownership in commercial and industrial corporate enterprises has risen to 17.8%, as compared to 4.3% in 1971.[20] Altogether, the overlapping polarizations that caused so much tension in 1969 have been greatly diluted since. Very important is the fact that the succession of governments since then have been *seen* by all major ethnic and social groups as making a sincere effort to resolve the tensions. There has been no renewed outbreak of racial violence.

At time of writing there is more threat to this new "entente cordiale" from outside than there is from inside the Malaysian economy and society. Export-led development is splendid when world markets are expanding. But since the recession of the 1980s, Malaysia's main customers have been experiencing serious difficulties of their own. In the electronics industry, which has been so important a leader in Malaysia's industrialization, there have been retrenchments and layoffs, due not only to world recession but to an apparent entry of United States firms into a new product cycle, involving more vertical integration and concentration of activities, especially R & D, and less decentralization. Textiles and rubber products too are in a phase of relative stagnation. These trends have inevitably slowed down the rates of expansion and structural change in the Malaysian economy. In this situation, achieving further gains in the objectives of the NEP become more difficult, and maintaining the social stability of the last decade and one-half becomes proportionately more complicated. However, in 1988 unemployment was down slightly from 8.2% in 1987 to 8.1%; and the rise in consumer prices was still only 2.7%.[21]

CONCLUSION

There is of course no way of isolating the contribution of regional policy—positive or negative—to the impressive economic and social performance of the Malaysian society during the last 15 years. Those who oppose any intervention in the market designed to alter the spatial pattern of economic and social development can always argue that the performance would have been better yet without the interference involved in regional policy. No one can prove them wrong beyond a shadow of doubt. Conversely, those who believe that regional policy within the international capitalist system, with private enterprise and especially multinationals playing the major role in decision making, can result in uneven development, "development of underdevelopment," and continued exploitation and poverty could argue that the intervention involved in Malaysian regional policy did not go nearly far enough. It may be a bit easier to cast doubt on these arguments than on the neoclassical ones, but they, too, cannot be proved wrong beyond a shadow of doubt. They obviously include elements of truth, and no one can say precisely what would have been the pattern of Malaysian development if the postwar Communist uprising had been successful.

But although no one can say what would have happened with no regional policy, or with a "socialist" regional policy, the present writer is convinced that the regional policies that were in fact carried out were in large measure responsible for the success of the NEP and of the series of national development plans implemented since 1970. First of all, there are the well-established interactions between the seriousness of regional disparities and performance of the national economy:[22]

1. Countries with large and growing regional gaps tend to have a low level and slow rate of development; those with small and diminishing gaps tend to have a high level and rapid rate of development.
2. Countries with large regional gaps have unfavorable trade-off curves between unemployment and inflation; those with smaller regional gaps have trade-off curves closer to the origin.
3. Countries with large regional gaps tend to have economic fluctua-

tions of greater amplitude and a higher ratio of depression years
to prosperous years than those with small regional gaps.

Large regional disparities are a symptom of deep-seated disorders and
structural defects in the national economy; and there is no case on record
of such problems being remedied by measures to accelerate growth,
taken at the national level alone. All cases of wide regional disparity
giving way to dramatic regional convergence—including that of the
United States—are examples of regional policies designed to attack such
problems in the place where they exist. Thus there is every reason to
conclude that Malaysia's well-designed efforts to reduce regional disparities contributed significantly to the accelerated growth and generally
good performance of the national economy.

Apart from these general relationships between measures to reduce
regional gaps and improved performance of national economies, there
are some features of the specific Malaysian case that lead to similar
conclusions.

1. The several regional studies have added enormously to the stock
of knowledge of the Malaysian economy. The detailed information that
can be gathered by an interdisciplinary planning team, on the spot,
concerning natural and human resources, interactions and flows, is of
an entirely different order from that normally obtainable from published
national statistics.

2. The spatial structure is a fundamental aspect of the functioning
of any national economy. One cannot even do effective macroeconomic
policy formulation or planning without knowledge of the spatial structure; and this knowledge is most effectively garnered by the preparation
of regional plans.

3. Regional planning involves working on the spot with the target
population. It thus leads to far more realistic behavioral assumptions for
the analysis of the economy. One discovers who the real actors are who
determine the course of development, how they behave, and what they
are trying to do.

4. One also learns much more about the aspirations, values, ambi-
tions, and wants of the target populations. One can therefore construct
much more realistic welfare functions as a basis for policy decisions.

5. The knowledge accumulated by the various regional planning
teams, together with the constant interchange of information and ideas
both with the government and with representatives of the private sector, greatly improved the quality of decision making in both sectors.

6. The planning teams played an important entrepreneurial function. Planning on the spot always discloses previously unsuspected op-

portunities for profitable investment in both the public and private sectors. It must be remembered that some of the members of the teams were among the highest-ranking people in the world in their respective fields. Some had years of experience at top management level in private enterprise. Others were top-level scientists, engineers, or technicians. Such people are always on the lookout for good investment projects, and they nearly always find them. To take examples from Pahang Tenggarra alone, the team found hitherto unidentified opportunities for grazing cattle, for cultivating tapioca in marshy areas, for interplanting rubber with cocoa, for producing modular-design prefabricated housing. These were all private-sector projects, but until the on-the-spot technical and marketing studies had been undertaken, private enterprise had shown no interest in them.

7. The upsurge of interest in regional development in Malaysia coincided with a parallel explosion of interest among multilateral and bilateral donors. It was in this period that the United Nations Centre for Regional Development and the Regional Development Program of the United Nations Research Institute for Social Development were established, and many donors showed interest in financing regional development programs. Malaysia exploited this interest very adroitly. It is highly doubtful if Malaysia could have assembled such big aid packages during those years had the government not embarked on its regional development program.

Indeed, one may well ask whether Malaysia could have survived as a nation without the sort of regional policy that was pursued during the period 1970–1986, given the overlapping polarizations among societies, sectors, structures, and spaces outlined in this chapter. No Malaysian government can survive that fails to heed actual and potential race conflicts. Because these are defined in regional terms, no government can survive that fails to heed the need for astute and effective regional policy.

NOTES

[1]Zakaria Haji Ahmad, "The Political Structure," in E. K. Fisk and H. Osman-Rani, eds., *The Political Economy of Malaysia* (Kuala Lumpur: Oxford University Press, 1982), pp. 89, 96, 97.
[2]Mohamed Sulong, in Fisk and Osman, "The Geographical Setting," 1982, p. 25.
[3]Government of Malaysia, *The Second Malaysia Plan* 1971–75, p. 7.
[4]Ibid.
[5]Kamal Salih and Mei Ling Young, *Employment, Unemployment and Retrenchment in Malaysia: The Outlook and What is to be Done about It?* Paper presented to the Workshop on Industrialization in Malaysia at the Australian National University, 7–8 November 1985.

6Khalid Husin, "Resource Frontier Development in Malaysia: The Experience of Regional Development Authorities", RD, Seminar on National Development and Regional Policy, 1979.

7Benjamin Higgins, "The Unified Approach to Development Planning at the Regional Level: The Case of Pahang Tenggara," in Antoni Kuklinski, ed., Regional Development in Worldwide Perspective (The Hague, Mouton, 1976); "Perils of Perspective Planning: Pahang Tenggara Revisited," Nagoya, UNCRD, Working Paper WP 79-15, December 1982; "Development Planning," in Fisk and Osman-Rani, eds., The Political Economy of Malaysia (Kuala Lumpur: Oxford University Press, 1978), pp. 148–183; "CIDA in South-Southeast Asia," in B. Higgins and D. J. Savoie, Canadians and Regional Development at Home and in the Third World (Moncton, NB: Canadian Institute for Research on Regional - Development, 1988), Chapter 6.

8Benjamin Higgins, "Development Planning," in Fisk and Osman-Rani, 1982.

9Ove Simonsen, Regional Framework for Resource Allocation in Public Sector Programs (Nagoya: United Nations Centre for Regional Development, Working Paper 70-10), November 1979; Salih and Young, "Employment, Unemployment and Retrenchment in Malaysia.

10See Benjamin Higgins, "François Perroux," in Benjamin Higgins and Donald J. Savoie eds., Regional Economic Development: Essays in Honour of François Perroux (London and Boston: Unwin Hyman, 1988), pp. 31–47; François Perroux, "The Pole of Development's New Place in a General Theory of Economic Activity," ibid., pp. 48–76.

11Government of Malaysia, Fifth Malaysia Plan, Kuala Lumpur, 1986, p. v.

12Ibid., p. vi.

13Ibid., p. 43.

14Ibid., p. 21, and Minister of Finance, Economic Report 1988–89, Kuala Lumpur, 1988, p. 8.

15The comment was made in a seminar at the Australian National University in November 1985.

16Kamal Salih and Mei Ling Young, "The Regional Impact of Industrialization: A Case Study of Penang State," in T. E. McGee, ed., Industrialization and Labor: A Case Study of Peninsular Malaysia (Canberra: Research School of Pacific Studies, Australian National University, 1986).

17T. G. McGee, "Joining the Global Assembly Line: Malaysia's Role in the International Semiconductor Industry," in McGee, 1986, pp. 48–49.

18Ibid., pp. 46–47.

19Government of Malaysia, 1986, pp. 170–71.

20Ibid., p. 9.

21Minister of Finance, 1988, p. 8.

22Benjamin Higgins, "Trade-Off Curves and Regional Gaps," in J. N. Bhagwati and Richard S. Eckaus, eds., Economic Development and Planning: Essays in Honor of Paul Rosenstein-Rodan (London: Allen & Unwin), 1983; "Trade-Off Curves, Trends, and Regional Disparities: The Case of Quebec," Economie appliquée, 1976, Tome XXVIII, No. 2-3, pp. 331–360; Toward Growth and Stability in Construction (Ottawa: Public Works Canada, 1978); "Regional and National Economic Development: Trade-Off or Complementarity?" in Benjamin Higgins and Donald J. Savoie, eds., Regional Economic Development: Essays in Honour of François Perroux (London and Boston: Unwin Hyman, 1988), pp. 193–224.

CHAPTER EIGHT

Regional Disparities in a Large, Upper-Income Developing Country
Brazil

Brazil is at roughly the same level of general development as Malaysia and is growing at almost the same rate. In the World Bank list of 96 developing countries, ranked from poorest to richest, Brazil is seventy-fourth and Malaysia seventy-eighth. In 1985, Brazil had a per capita GNP of U.S. $1,640, Malaysia $2,000. The rate of growth of per capita GDP from 1965 to 1985 was 4.3% in Brazil and 4.4% in Malaysia.

In other respects, they are two very different countries. Brazil is one of the biggest countries in the world, bigger than Australia and conterminous United States. It has a population of 135 million. It is sometimes referred to as "the Colossus of the South." Malaysia is a small country with just over 15 million people. Malaysia is purely Asian. Brazil is significantly "American." Like the United States and Canada, it is in the New World and is a country of recent settlement, with a transplanted European society, originally mainly Portuguese and partly Dutch, but now very mixed. Germans and Italians constitute important parts of the population, whereas Japanese and Lebanese also play significant roles. Like the United States, it has a black population descended from imported slaves and a few remaining indigenous American Indians.

Racial feelings in Brazil are very complex. The Portuguese imported into Brazil their admiration for Moorish women, and even today the *mulatinha* (little mulatto girl) is much admired and, for some, is the standard of beauty.[1] There is much less open discrimination against blacks than there has been in the United States in the past. The discrimination is subtle. Blacks who manage to get higher education can rise to

237

the top of the ladder, but discrimination is there, nonetheless. Racial differences, however, do not play a major role in regional policy, as they do in Malaysia.

Brazil has a more advanced occupational and demographic structure than Malaysia. In 1980 only 31% of the population was still in agriculture, 27% was in industry, and 42% in services. There has been further structural change since 1980. Nearly three-quarters of Brazilians live in urban centers, about one-quarter live in São Paulo and Rio de Janeiro, over half of the population lives in cities of more than half a million. Given these facts, it might seem that Brazil should be regarded as a country already "industrialized"; but the tens of millions of people who still live in rural poverty make that classification a bit inappropriate.

The Brazilian national economy has special features and an unique history, which together have delineated its regional problems and informed its regional policy. In order to appreciate fully the nature of Brazil's regional policy, it is necessary to review briefly these features and this history.

THE PATTERN OF REGIONAL DEVELOPMENT: "BOOM AND BUST"

The failure of economic development in Brazil to bring moderately high levels of living to the Brazilian people as a whole is related to a "boom-and-bust" pattern of development. Each era of Brazilian development has had its own growing point in sugar, livestock, minerals, rubber, coffee, manufacturing, and each growing point has occurred in a different region.

Indeed, closely related to this boom-and-bust pattern of growth is Brazil's peculiar frontier history. As in the United States and Canada, Brazil's development has been associated with a moving frontier. But whereas in the United States the westward movement eventually settled, industrialized, and urbanized the whole country, and in Canada populated, industrialized, and urbanized a rather narrow band along the American border, Brazil's development involved a north to south "pogo stick" movement, in that it industrialized and urbanized only a few isolated areas on or near the Atlantic coast. The settlement of each space, and the creation of each city, was associated with a different sector, a different period of time, and a different group of entrepreneurs and workers.

SUGAR

The sugar industry established in the sixteenth century provided the first leading sector in Brazil. It was originally centered on the northeast, especially around Recife and Salvador. The sugar frontier was a large man's frontier from the beginning. Not only were the landholdings large; sugar mills as well in Brazil were large scale even in comparison to those in the West Indies. Per capita incomes in the sugar economy were high—according to Celso Furtado's estimates, about $350, in terms of current values. Moreover,

> this income per capita was evidently far higher than that prevailing in Europe at the time, and at no other period of its history, even at the height of the gold cycle, did Brazil regain this level of income.[2]

It is in any case certain that the Brazilian sugar industry was profitable enough to attract the interest of the Dutch, who occupied Salvador in 1624. They were driven out of Salvador relatively quickly, but it took longer to drive them out of Recife.

Thus the Brazilian sugar economy offered a significant market, which could have served as a focal point of growth for other regions of the country. In fact, however, it did not do so. Even within the northeast itself, its spread effects were small; its spread effects to the rest of Brazil were virtually nil. One reason was colonial policy; Portugal was determined not to permit the development of any activities that would compete with those already established in the Mother Country. It followed that the sugar planters spent much of their income on luxury imports that could not be produced within the colony; and what was left of their profits, they transferred abroad. The one sector that enjoyed significant spread effects from the sugar economy was livestock breeding, particularly cattle breeding. Beef was eaten by slaves in the colonies, and the sugar economy had great need for draft animals. However the cattle were raised in other areas of the northeast, not in other regions of Brazil.

SUGAR AS A "FOCAL POINT OF GROWTH"

With the wisdom of hindsight, we might now say that the Brazilian northeast was foredoomed to future economic stagnation the moment it embarked on a pattern of development in which sugar was the principal growing crop. Today sugar economies are in trouble the world over.

There are several reasons why this is so. First, sugar is a land-hungry and labor-hungry undertaking. It is a form of culture that comes close to "mining the soil"; some rotation with other crops or letting the land be fallow is necessary. Consequently sugar enterprises typically hold more land than is necessary to keep the refineries operating at capacity in any one year.

Second, sugar production is characterized by a high degree of seasonality. Planting, harvesting, and grinding together provide employment for only a few months in the year; but during these seasons, the requirement for labor is heavy indeed. During the "dead season," employment in the sugar enterprises themselves are affected. Secondary reductions in employment in transportation, shipping, and the like also occur because these service sectors are so heavily dependent on the movement of sugar. In the off season, workers drift into the cities in search of work they cannot find and become street beggars.

Third, sugar industry does not utilize the entire land area or the entire population of a region at any one time. It is therefore consistent with preservation of traditional peasant agriculture. In short, the cultivation and manufacture of sugar is not calculated to bring about technological progress that could spread to other parts of the country.

Finally, sugar is a product almost any country can produce, either from cane or from beets; and the income elasticity of demand for it is low and even becomes negative at high levels of income. Per capita consumption of sugar in industrialized countries is actually falling. In any case, even when sugar was profitable, such profits as were gained, were not reinvested in other sectors in other spaces of Brazil. Each successive boom was sui generis.

GOLD

The next boom was in gold. It was discovered in Minas Gerais in 1698, in Mato Grosso in 1719, and in Goias in 1725. The result was a gold rush. In the beginning, the mining frontier was a "small man's frontier," consisting of panning alluvial metal from the streambeds. A few sugar planters migrated to Minas Gerais, bringing their slaves with them to do the work of seeking gold. But gold did not provide a small man's frontier for long. It soon moved from panning to mining and became a capital-intensive, large-scale operation; the capital requirements, in slaves, imported food, and equipment were very high. Nonetheless, Brazil became for a time the world's leading gold producer. It did not retain this status for long. Gold exports reached their peak in 1760, by 1780 exports had been cut in half, and by the end of the century the boom was over. About the only spread effect was an increased demand for cattle, particularly for draft animals, and even this effect did not survive the collapse of the mining industry. As for the gold rush immigrants, most turned to subsistence farming.[3]

COFFEE

Coffee came to the rescue of Brazil but not to the rescue of Minas Gerais, Goias, and Mato Grosso. The center of the coffee industry was São Paulo, and later, states further south. Coffee was already being exported in the first half of the nineteenth century, but it became Brazil's principle export only in the last quarter of the century. Slavery had become a bit unfashionable by then, and the coffee manpower problem was solved by European immigration. In the state of São Paulo, European immigrants numbered 15,000 during the decade of the 1870s, and 600,000 in the 1890s. Coffee provided nearly half of Brazil's total foreign exchange earnings up to 1960 and is still the major single export. It is no longer, however, a leading sector. A good deal of land has been taken out of coffee, but development of faster maturing and higher yield strains and opening of new coffee areas have maintained production.

RUBBER

The rubber boom and bust was the most violent of all. This time the frontier moved to Amazonia, where production was entirely a matter of tapping natural rubber growing wild in the jungle. Expansion of the industry depended on success in attracting manpower into the jungle. Exports increased from an average of 6,000 tons annually during the 1870s to 35,000 in the first decade of this century. But then it was discovered that rubber trees planted in Malaya and Indonesia from Brazilian clones could thrive in much more accessible places, with much lower transport costs and abundant supplies of cheap labor. The Brazilian industry was doomed. The one serious effort to establish a plantation in Amazonia, in 1927, was a failure. The spread effects of rubber were, if anything, more restricted and shorter lived than those of earlier leading sectors.

Until recently, each of these sources of growth have produced a limited period of expanding activity, followed by stagnation or decline, with only limited impact on the rest of the country. The sugar industry in the northeast is now a problem industry, hardly able to hold its own in competition with sugar produced in other regions of Brazil and elsewhere in the world, whereas the world market fails to expand proportionately to world income. The livestock industry, similarly, now lags behind rather than leading the growth of national income as a whole. The mineral boom has passed, leaving ghost towns in its wake. The most spectacular of all "boom and busts" was the short rubber bubble, which has left behind a small high-cost industry, unable to meet even domestic requirements, and empty opera houses in Belem and Manaus. Coffee today remains a major export exceeded only by steel products, but it is no longer a major generator of growth for the economy as a whole. The new industrial development, however, is likely to continue.

All in all, in comparison with the other large countries of recent settlement (Canada, United States, and Australia), what is striking about Brazil is the failure of each successive wave of development, each based on a new commodity, to generate "spread effects," so essential to the widespread diffusion of high rates of growth among all sectors and regions of a country. The "ratchet effect," development in one sector and region encouraging growth in another, that growth in turn providing a basis for new expansion in the sector and region that started the process, has not yet occurred in Brazil. Except for a modest contribution of capital and entrepreneurship from the coffee sector to the recent industrial development, each new wave of growth has been almost entirely discrete. There has been very little transfer of profits and skills of the "leading sector" of one era and area to the "leading sector" of the next. The outcome is regional disintegration and "hollow frontiers," in contrast to the movements into the interior of Canada and particularly of the United States.

In Brazil, the most recent phase of frontier development has transported the modern sector almost intact from the east coast to the far west, leaving nothing but empty space in between. Western frontier cities like Campo Grande and Corumba are not noticeably different in amenities from those of cities of comparable size near the east coast. Yet they are separated from the east coast centers by hundreds of miles of almost wholly unsettled territory.

Indeed, in contrast to Malaysia, there are large metropolitan centers in every region; yet in this respect, too, the Brazilian case is less favorable than the North American or Australian one. The hinterlands of the big cities of North America and Australia represent some of the most intensively exploited areas in the country. But the great cities of Brazil, especially Rio de Janeiro and to a lesser extent São Paulo, are surrounded by land that is empty because it has been destroyed. Meanwhile, the frontier which is hollow, has moved farther and farther away from the market."[4]

Thus the outcome of this unique pattern of regional development is a country that is still largely empty, with population, industrialization, and urbanization concentrated in a handful of cities separated by large areas that are very thinly settled. Regional gaps remain—or have become—very large. (Table 29)

What, then, is the answer to the riddle of Brazil's unique record of boom-and-bust development? Although Portugal's embargo on industrial development provides an initial explanation, part of the answer also

Table 29. Per Capita Income by States (percentage of national average)

States	1947	1953	1956	1957	1958	1959	1960
Amazonas	94	67	76	78	72	66	68
Para	65	54	61	60	54	53	56
Maranhao	33	33	31	31	31	34	34
Piaui	37	25	25	28	26	28	29
Ceara	44	33	37	41	30	41	45
Rio Grande do Norte	53	41	46	48	40	52	57
Paraiba	43	37	41	42	38	46	54
Pernambuco	63	55	53	61	62	61	60
Alagoas	46	41	43	48	50	49	51
Sergipe	53	50	50	54	55	56	55
Bahia	53	46	46	48	50	51	56
Minas Gerais	77	80	81	82	75	75	71
Espirito Santo	67	83	80	76	66	65	64
Rio de Janeiro	100	101	107	97	96	95	95
Guanabara[a]	330	308	316	308	321	311	291
Parana	103	121	94	98	105	110	111
São Paulo	184	192	181	176	179	176	178
Santa Catarina	101	90	89	87	89	86	90
Rio Grande do Sul	122	120	130	125	118	116	120
Alta Grosso	79	114	110	84	94	71	78
Goias	46	65	59	54	54	57	55
National average per capita gross domestic product in U.S. dollars	225[b]	257	279	298	312	321	340

[a]Formerly the Federal District.
[b]For 1948.
Source. Werner Baer, *Industrialization and Economic Development in Brazil* (Homewood, IL: Richard D. Irwin, 1965), p. 170.

lies in Brazil's relative underpopulation. In most of the country, for most of the time, there was scarcely anyone to spread the effects to, and there was scarcely anyone to spread the effects.

LACK OF POPULATION AND LACK OF ENTREPRENEURS

Celso Furtado gives Brazilian population figures of 100,000 in 1600, a maximum of 300,000 in 1700, and 3,250,000 in 1800.[5] It was not until the nineteenth century that the population began to increase significantly. Even then, the rate of growth was only about 1.3% per year in the early decades (see Table 48 in Appendix). Birthrates were relatively low, and mortality—especially infant mortality—was high. In the early nineteenth century, a German geographer, Alexander von Humboldt, estimated a total population of only 4 million, of which less than 1 million were white. There were nearly 2 million blacks, and the remainder were Indians and mestizos. Italian, Portuguese, and Spanish immigration became important after 1850. German immigration reached its peak in the Hitler regime, 1934–1943, when it was 9.1% of the total, dropping to 4.1% in 1944 to 1953. In recent years, there has been heavy Japanese immigration, and today Japanese are the second largest group of foreigners in Brazil. However, immigration to Brazil has been a trickle in comparison to immigration to North America. Why?

The opportunities for economic self-advancement were simply not so apparent in Brazil. In North America access to land was relatively easy, but in Brazil the immigrant "found himself face to face with the established tradition of aristocratic landowner and tenant, of master and man."[6] The Brazilian frontier, like the Australian one, was a "big man's frontier." The initial investment in a sugar or coffee plantations was too large for a small proprietor[7]; the *colono* had little hope of accumulating capital on the required scale. Wages paid to the *colonos* were barely above subsistence level. Consequently immigrants to Brazil "sent back discouraging reports that must have compared poorly with stories of the quick wealth to be made in North America."[8]

Moreover, the concentration of landholding in the hands of a relatively small number of *fazendeiros* (estate owners) and the attitudes and values associated with this pattern of development were, for centuries, barriers to accelerated development in Brazil. Few *fazendeiros* were inclined to become industrial entrepreneurs, and as industrialization proceeded and other forms of wealth than land assumed increasing importance, conflicts arose between the new industrial bourgeoisie and the old landed aristocracy.

Brazilian entrepreneurs and managers as well as the *fazendeiros* also found it difficult to shift from sector to sector and from space to space. Consequently each new wave of development was not only based on a different leading sector, in a different space, but also involved a new set of entrepreneurs, who very often came in from abroad. Had it not been for large-scale immigration of people with capital and education during the 1930s and since the war, Brazil would be considerably less developed today.

Finally, an underlying reason for the big man's frontier and the difficulty in moving from space to space, was the hostile environment of much of the country—the impenetrability of its jungles, the dryness of its interior, and the great distances involved in new frontier development.

ADVANTAGES AND CONSTRAINTS FOR DEVELOPMENT

What, then, did the regional planners after World War II have to work with as a consequence of these conditions and this pattern of development? They had a mixed legacy: Brazil's underpopulation in relation to its resources presented bright possibilities; the problems of transport and communications, the chronic inflation, and the overlapping polarizations presented obstacles to be surmounted.

TRANSPORT AND COMMUNICATIONS

The environment and the consequent pattern of development has left Brazil with a colossal problem of transport and communications. Solving this problem has not been attractive for private enterprise and has led to what economist Roberto Campos, former minister of planning, has called "socialization by default." Until recently, at least, the unprofitability of providing infrastructure and the limits to indigenous entrepreneurship have led to vast amounts of public investment and public ownership: roads, railways, shipping, airlines, the iron and steel industry, and the petroleum industry. As late as 1965, public investment was estimated at 60% of the total. This situation was not a reflection of socialist ideology or political power of left-wing governments. Rather it reflects the lack of opportunities for small- and middle-sized private enterprise in a land of "hollow frontiers" and big man's frontiers, plus the daunting physical aspects of the development task. "Go West, young man" was never very good advice throughout most of Brazil's history.

CHRONIC INFLATION

In Brazil, inflation is as old as the country itself. The discovery of gold and silver in Latin America in the early sixteenth century swelled the European money supply and generated the "price revolution" of that century. The inflation was particularly rampant in Spain and Portugal, in whose colonies the gold and silver was found. And of course the inflation was rampant in their colonies, too. The inflation continued in independent Brazil, and in the early 1960s showed signs of becoming cumulative and turning into hyperinflation. The Castello Branco regime that came to power in 1964 succeeded in containing inflation for a time, and from 1965 to 1973 the rate of price increase fell to 23.2% per year. From 1973 to 1984, however, extremely high rates of inflation set in again, averaging 71.4% per year, and in recent years they have been higher still. The Brazilians have learned to live with inflation, and the system of indexing is so broad that no one social group bears the brunt of it. Nonetheless it is a constant problem, and all proposals for increased spending, including regional development programs, must be carefully scrutinized in terms of their potential impact on the rate of inflation.

OVERLAPPING POLARIZATION

There is in Brazil, as in Malaysia, an overlap of societies, structures, sectors, and spaces. The poorest states are in the northeast and Amazonia, the richest in the south central region, with the south and the thinly settled middle west (or central west) in between.

The sizable black population is more heavily concentrated in the northeast than elsewhere in the country, and the dwindling Indian population is more visible in the middle west and in Amazonia than elsewhere. In Amazonia there are still a few Indians living a traditional tribal life in the rainforest. The white population is concentrated in the south central and southern regions.

Until about 1960, when serious efforts to reduce regional disparities began, it could be said that the modern sector (plantation agriculture, mining and large-scale, capital-intensive manufacturing, and the services connected with these) was heavily concentrated in the south central and to a lesser degree in the southern regions. The traditional sector (small-scale, labor-intensive agriculture, cottage industry and handicrafts, small industry, and the services related to these) was concentrated in the northeast and Amazonia. The west was a largely unsettled frontier.

Concern for the extreme inequality of income distribution was not expressed in racial terms but rather in regional terms. In the 1960s, nearly one-third of the total population lived in the lagging region of the northeast, another 6% in Amazonia (the north). Because productivity was about four times as high in the modern sector as in the traditional sector, the differing proportions of modern and traditional sectors in different spaces gave rise to very large regional gaps. In 1960, the per capita GDP of Brazil as a whole was two and one half times as high as that of the northeast. The per capita incomes in the south central region were at least four times that of the northeast (see Table 29). The richest state, São Paulo, had a per capita income nearly seven times as high as that of the poorest state, Piaui.

REGIONAL POLICY

When official, formal regional policy began in 1959, with the establishment of SUDENE, the development authority for the northeast, it was not even regional disparities as such that had been the main concern. Rather it was the alternation of drought and flood and the tendency for peasants of the region to come to the south central region in search of food and employment when confronted with disaster in their own region. The early programs of the 1950s were as much disaster relief, designed to help and to keep the people where they were, as anything. The region was referred to as *o sertão* (the arid zone), and its problems were approached in much the same way as the similar problems of the African Sehel are approached today. Indeed, considering how dramatically regionalized the country is, it took Brazil rather a long time to arrive at a rational regional policy (see Fig. 16).

Thus when Brazilians began to think explicitly of regional policy in the years following World War II, and especially since 1960, it was inevitable that the policy would have three main facets: (1) opening up the remaining frontiers; (2) the provision of infrastructure, not only for the frontiers but for the existing settled areas; and (3) spreading the new industrial development to lagging regions. It is the last of these prongs in the three-pronged approach that offers most promise of achieving significant reductions in regional disparities. Brazil still has a mining

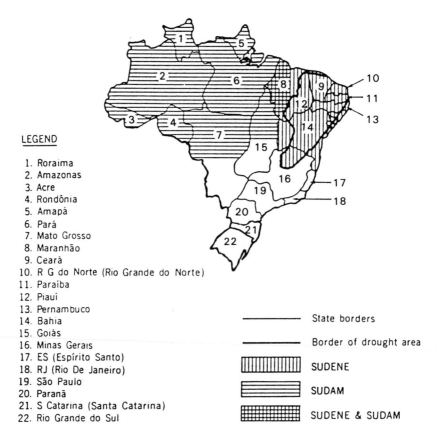

LEGEND

 1. Roraima
 2. Amazonas
 3. Acre
 4. Rondônia
 5. Amapá
 6. Pará
 7. Mato Grosso
 8. Maranhão
 9. Ceará
10. R G do Norte (Rio Grande do Norte)
11. Paraíba
12. Piauí
13. Pernambuco
14. Bahia
15. Goiás
16. Minas Gerais
17. ES (Espírito Santo)
18. RJ (Rio De Janeiro)
19. São Paulo
20. Paraná
21. S Catarina (Santa Catarina)
22. Rio Grande do Sul

—————— State borders

—————— Border of drought area

||||||||||||| SUDENE

≡≡≡≡≡ SUDAM

▦▦▦▦ SUDENE & SUDAM

FIGURE 16.   States of Brazil and areas of operation of Sudene and of Sudam (Sudene = northeast; Sudam = Amazonia or north).

frontier, but when mining yields high productivity and income it is always capital intensive, and its ability to absorb people into employment is limited. Brazil is now too far advanced to absorb many people into agriculture at incomes near the present national average, although some might be absorbed in new areas at incomes higher than those they earn now. But Brazil is in an unusually favorable position to invigorate lagging regions by attracting industry to their urban centers. A good many of Brazil's new hi-tech industries are "footloose"; transport costs and proximity to major markets are not primary considerations. The metropolitan centers of the lagging regions are not shabby small towns.

They are all large and graceful cities, on the seashore, with beautiful architecture and attractive town planning. Thus when the government decided to move its government-owned petroleum industry from Rio to Salvador, in the state of Bahia, the employees of Petrobras were not moving to "the sticks." Salvador is a city that many people, Brazilians and foreigners, visit each year for sheer pleasure. It is the eighteenth-century capital city with magnificent architecture and a vibrant present-day life. Salvador is not a "hardship post"; nor is Recife or Belem, or even Fortaleza. All these cities have amenities, from good restaurants and nightclubs to elegant clubs to universities, which can make them attractive to the scientists, engineers, and managers who are the core of hi-tech enterprises.

Apart from opening up frontiers and providing new infrastructure as interest shifted from sector to sector and from space to space, government concern for regional development in Brazil is a post-World War II phenomenon. The first official and formal expression of that concern was probably the provision in the 1946 constitution that "in the Economic Valorization Plan of Amazonia, the Union will apply, during at least twenty years, a specified quantity of not less than 3 percent of its tax revenue" (Article 199). It adds, "The States and Territories of the region [Amazonia] along with their respective *municipios*, will reserve for the same goal, annually, 3 percent of their respective tax revenues. The resources of which this paragraph concerns will be applied through the Federal Government."

Amazonia is the most vast of all Brazilian frontiers, with 59% of the country's total area and only 4% of its population. It is pierced by the mighty Amazon system and is still largely jungle. It has always captured the imagination of the Brazilian people. Yet for several years Article 199 was more honored in the breach than in the observance. Little was done in Amazonia, partly because of sheer technical difficulties of operating there and partly because the government in far-away Rio de Janeiro was more concerned with other matters. It was not until 1953 that the Superentendencia para Valorizacõ Economico do Amazonia (SPVEA), the regional development authority (*Superendencia*) for Amazonia was set up and a plan prepared. This first Five Year Plan was not yet implemented in 1966 because the Congress had not yet ratified it.

Thus it happened that the first "big push" in regional development took place, not in the mysterious and romantic north, but in the more mundane and calamity-ridden northeast. This region, where Brazilian development began, had become the country's biggest problem area. The people in the north were not clearly better off, but there were few of them. The northeast had one-quarter of the total population. It had long been known as a disaster area. There were parts of the region where there had been either drought or floods in 50 of the 100 years between 1835 and 1935. Even in years of relatively high rainfall, 90% of it fell between December and April. Yet as late as 1960 two-thirds of the population was on the land. In the sugar area around Recife, rainfall was relatively assured, but the sugar industry was stagnant, and that area was seriously overpopulated. In the early 1960s, it was estimated that to assure even a minimum per capita annual income of $100 for everyone in the area, it would be necessary to move 7.5 million people out of it. As it was, emigration from the northeast was high, and net population growth was well below the national average. Even so, the region's share of national income fell during the 1950s, and "regional policy" was largely a matter of disaster relief.

Then in 1959 SUDENE was established and quickly grew to be much the biggest regional development authority in the country. When visited in the mid-1960s, it had a staff of some 3,000 Brazilian professionals, assisted by some 150 American (USAID) experts and 120 United Nations experts. SUDENE's First Master Plan was published in 1960 and covered the three years 1961–1963. Although limited in scope and in its analysis, it was a development plan, as distinct from the disaster relief approach of earlier years. The Second Master Plan, for 1963–1965, was not much of an improvement. It was based on the implicit assumption that the problems of the region must be solved by measures taken within the region. It contained no analysis of intraregional or interregional trade, patterns of migration, or capital flows. The "two gaps" were not considered, costs and benefits of individual projects were not calculated, and capital requirements for achieving target rates of growth were not estimated. It was also much too small in scale to have any real impact on the region. SUDENE, and its sister institution, the Banco do Nordeste (a regional development bank), were very much still in the learning phase.

The Third Plan, for 1966–1968, was a good deal more sophisticated. It set a target growth rate of regional domestic product of 7%, designed to "diminish the inequality of income between the man in the Drought Polygon and his counterpart in the Center-South of the country" and "to promote the spatial and sectoral integration of the Northeastern economy, linking it more tightly to the national economy" (see Fig. 15). The scale of the development program in the third plan was roughly double that of the second plan. The Fourth Master Plan retained the 7% target for overall growth and added an ambitious target of 9% growth for industry. By that time, SUDENE, with a decade of experience behind it, had established a solid system of regional development planning and implementation.

Meanwhile things were beginning to move in Amazonia. In 1963 the Banco de Credito da Amazonia (BCA), originally created to finance the rubber industry, was converted into a regional development bank, comparable to the Banco do Nordeste. Its capital was provided by the U.S. government, the Brazilian government, and private investors. In its early years it promoted mainly agriculture, livestock, and agro-industry; but it also fostered mining and manufacturing. SPVEA also provided credit to small farmers at concessional rates for purchase of machinery and equipment and organization of cooperatives. Efforts were made to revitalize the rubber industry. A very important project, with the completion of the new capital city at Brazilia, was the construction of the 2,275 kilometer Brazilia–Belem highway, completed in 1960. This road opened up a vast area in the center of the country for farming and led to important mineral discoveries as well—much as railroad construction had done in North America in an earlier century. Other roads followed, designed to end the isolation of Amazonia and integrate it with other regions of the country. Water and air transport were also expanded with SPVEA assistance. Electricity plants and municipal water supply and sewage systems were provided with SPVEA finance and technical assistance. Private enterprises providing basic services, such as petroleum products, shipping, and airlines have been subsidized.

It will be noted that all these activities were highly pragmatic. It is perhaps easier to design regional policy for a frontier region such as Amazonia than for regions already settled. Almost everything is needed, and almost everything that is provided raises output and incomes.

In 1966 SPVEA was replaced by SUDAM (*Superintendencia do Desinvolvimento da Amazonia*) and the BCA by BASA (*Banco da Amazonia S.A.*) The change in titles did not seem to bring any fundamental changes in development strategy. SUDAM did attempt to resuscitate the rubber industry, substituting high-technology plantations for wild rubber, with modest success. Its main efforts, however, continued to be devoted to provision of infrastructure. Thousands of kilometers of new roads have been built. SUDAM also conceived the idea of rural growth poles, in a program called POLAMAZONIA, to set up agro-cattle and agro-mineral "poles." In so doing they were perhaps closer to the original Perroux concept of growth poles than were many of the urban "growth poles" in other countries, including Malaysia.

OTHER REGIONS

Regional policy in Brazil is not just a matter of striving to reduce regional gaps, and, accordingly, regional planning and regional development programs are not confined to the poorer states. On the contrary, all the richer states in the south and south central regions have their own development planning authorities. The State Planning Commission of São Paulo is among the most competent development authorities in the country. There is also the Conselho de Desenvolvimento do Extremo Sul (CODESUL), which prepares and implements development plans for the three prosperous states of the extreme southern region of the country: Parana, Santa Catarina, and Rio Grande do Sul. The organization of this council is of interest to people concerned with federal–provincial (or federal–state) relations in other countries. It consists of the governors of the three states, three representatives of the Union appointed by the president and the director-president of the Banco Regional de Desenvolvimento do Extreme Sul (the regional development bank established to supplement CODESUL and an executive secretary). Thus both federal and state interests are protected in the administration of the regional authority.

In Brazil there is general recognition that even the more prosperous states need planned development. The planning, however, is designed to aid and abet decision making and investment in the private sector, not to replace it. Concern for the welfare of people in lagging regions does not mean neglecting the interests of people in the more prosperous regions. The attitude is that there is more scope for raising productivity in the lagging regions than in those regions that are already dynamic, where technology is already advanced, and resources are already efficiently allocated. It is in this manner that regional disparities are to be narrowed, not by encouraging more rapid growth in the lagging regions *at the expense of growth* in the leading regions.

Regional development in Brazil has been a cooperative effort of the states, the regional authorities, and the national government. Because national development is regarded as an aggregation of regional development programs, it could not be otherwise, especially in a federal state. But by the same token, the national government has not hesitated to intervene when it felt that a state or regional authority was on the wrong track, or off the track altogether. Thus in 1970 SUDENE found itself unprepared for the renewed drought that struck the northeast in that year. The federal government then embarked on a new development strategy for the northeast, with increased emphasis on agricultural development, that largely sidetracked SUDENE's own program. They also prepared a special program for the São Francisco Valley. Two years later the national government prepared a 3-year plan for the northeast that replaced SUDENE's 5-year plan. This plan was followed by a national five-year plan (1975–1979) in which 37.7% of the budget allocated to the northeast was for social development, only 15.7% for infrastructure, and

14.1% for industry, a sharp shift from the strategies reflected in the series of plans prepared by SUDENE.

In fact regional policies in Brazil since World War II have not reduced regional disparities. What they have done is to prevent the gaps from getting worse in percentage terms. Growth rates in the poorer regions have been about the same as in the richer ones. More important, during most of the period the growth rates in all regions have been high, especially between 1965 and 1980. Given the obstacles that had to be overcome, that was no mean achievement.

CONCLUSIONS

When a series of Brazilian governments turned their attention to regional policy after World War II, they were confronted with a peculiarly unbalanced, disintegrated national economy. The so-called national economy, in fact, was a montage of loosely bound regional economies, not just in the sense that there were glaring gaps in per capita income among regions but as well that there were sharp contrasts in occupational structure and product mix and in ethnic mix. It could even be said that the different regions belonged to different centuries. There were also marked differences in current growth rates. Nor were these regional disparities a matter of "developed" and "underdeveloped" regions, as in Malaysia. Amazonia was underdeveloped, but the main problem area, the northeast, could be more accurately described as "overdeveloped" or "misdeveloped." It had already undergone four centuries of development, and in some areas was overpopulated.

The reaction to this situation has, on the whole, been a sensible and healthy one. In Brazil "regional policy" is "regional development." No region in the country, rich or poor, is without its development plans, programs and projects. There is virtually no perceived conflict between regional policy and efficient development of the national economy, as there is in Canada, for example. In the aggregate, regional policy is designed to assure more complete and more efficient utilization of resources, both natural and human, in all parts of the country.

It is an objective of national policy also to reduce regional gaps. However, there is no wish to achieve this goal by weakening the strong states. São Paulo is less clearly "the locomotive that pulls the other 20 States along" than when the Paulistas coined the phrase 20 years ago, but it is still the most dynamic state, and it is no part of regional policy to reduce that dynamism. Regional gaps are to be diminished, not by *redistribution* of income as a matter of social justice and political stability but by eliminating excess capacity and unemployment and improving resource allocation in the lagging regions. Nor is there opposition to migration as a solution to poverty and unemployment. The Brazilians are a highly mobile people, and internal migration has played a major role in the country's development. There is objection only to the poor and unemployed flooding the plantation and mining areas, and the great cities, in search of jobs that are not there and that cannot be provided there.

In Brazil, attacking regional gaps by decentralizing urbanization and industrialization makes good sense. All the industrial and urban growth cannot take place in São Paulo and Rio de Janeiro. These are already huge cities, with population growth too rapid to handle. São Paulo may well be the most modern city in the world; it makes Manhattan look like a village. Rio is not far behind, but both now suffer from congestion and pollution. Rio is squeezed between mountains and sea, can grow only along the coast, and is eating up its beautiful bay to reclaim land for freeways. São Paulo sits in a bowl, a recipe for smog.

Meanwhile, here are these gracious, vital capital cities in the lagging states. Why not use them? Petrobras can function efficiently in Salvador. Electronics firms can operate efficiently in Recife or Belem.

The scale of regional policy—planning and implementation—may well be larger in Brazil than in any country in the world. We have noted the size of staffs and budgets of the regional development authorities. There are, in addition, the state planning authorities and the city planning authorities. Within the Ministries of Planning and Finance, and within the Central Bank, there are also large numbers of high-level people concerned with regional policy. Indeed regional policy and planning are a major part of national policy and planning. One could justify replacing the term *regional policy* or *regional planning* by *decentralized policymaking* or *decentralized planning*.

One of the great advantages of the Brazilian approach to regional policy is that the regional authorities are involved in implementation as well as planning. Consequently, the planning itself is highly pragmatic and project and problem oriented. There is in the authorities a good deal of concern for technical problems, and engineers, architects, agronomists, hydrologists, and so forth outnumber the economists and econometricians.

Regional policy since World War II has been concerned with getting things done, with identifying good projects and assembling good programs, with encouraging and supporting private enterprise while being prepared to take into government hands things that need doing but private enterprise will not do. Hence regional policy has been less subject to whims and fads in Brazil than in some other countries. Brazilian regional planners may not have discovered brilliant new techniques for doing the professional planner's job. They have seen their task rather as year-by-year, month-by-month, day-by-day management of their regions, and thus, in the aggregate, of the national economy as a whole. From 1965 to 1980, at least, they managed it rather well.

IMPACT ON THE NATIONAL ECONOMY

Regional policy, together with other aspects of economic and social policy with which it interacts, has left the Brazilian economy and society with new strengths and old weaknesses. Let us look first at the strengths.

Self-Sufficiency (Independence) in Trade

Through the centuries, Brazil has evolved from a country highly dependent on both imports and exports, and with an extremely open economy, into a country that is among the least dependent on foreign trade in the world. In 1985, among the 10 countries on the World Bank list with per capita incomes between $1,600 and $2,130, only Argentina and Mexico had comparably low ratios of exports to gross domestic product: 16% for Mexico, 15% for Argentina, and 14% for Brazil. By 1986 the Brazilian figure was down to 6%, lower for that year than even the United States, with 8%. Because Brazil has a substantial trade surplus, the ratio of imports to GDP is even lower.

Brazil is a vast country with a large internal market, and has generated a good deal of development without going beyond its own borders. The domestic market is big enough (about 140 million people) to permit economies of scale and application of advanced technology for most products. Brazil has also made good use of import replacement strategies in the past, converting former imports into major exports once a high enough level of efficiency is achieved, as in the case of its highly successful automobile industry. However, the rise in the export ratio in recent years is a reflection of Brazil's increasing reliance on an export promotion strategy, rather than import replacement, as an "engine of growth." In the recent past, Brazil's exports have consisted largely of coffee and other primary products. As recently as 1965, such products accounted for 83% of exports; coffee alone accounted for 44%. In 1986, however, this figure had shrunk to 44%, and manufactures had expanded from 8% to 37% (see Tables A-11 and A-12 in Appendix). It is likely that at the present time manufactures exceed primary products in importance. Moreover, as in Malaysia, Brazil's manufactured exports are increasingly high technology. Although exports are still not a major portion of GDP, they are of considerable importance as "leading sectors."

High Rates of Growth

In most years since 1965, Brazil has enjoyed very high rates of growth of per capita income. For 1965–1985 the rate was 4.3%, as compared to 4.4% for Malaysia, an average of 3.3% for the upper-income developing countries as a group, 2.4% for the industrial market economies, and 1.7% for the United States. For 1985 and 1986 the growth of real GDP was over 8% and of per capita GDP over 6%. (Population grew by an average of 2.25% between 1970 and 1986). All major sectors except agriculture, which has been relatively stagnant, have shared in this rapid long-run growth. The growth of manufacturing has been particularly high.

Rapid Structural Change

The Brazilian economy has been transformed in less than two generations, and today it has the structure of an industrialized capitalist country. In 1950, over 60% of the labor force was still in agriculture, only 8.8% in manufacturing, and 9.9% in services. In 1965 there was still 48% of the labor force in agriculture, whereas industry had grown to 20% and services to 31%. By 1980 employment in agriculture had dropped to 27%, industry was up to 27%, and services to 42%. The modernization of the economy is even more apparent when expressed in terms of gross domestic product. In 1985, only 9.4% of GDP was produced in agriculture, 25.7% in manufacturing, and another 4.5% in construction (making 30.2% for industry) and 58.8% in services. The speed of structural change, and the explosion of industrialization, after 1960 is indicated by Tables A-12 and A-13 in the Appendix.

Perhaps even more important, manufacturing activities are concentrated in fields with relatively advanced technology and hence relatively high productivity. In 1980 the category with the largest number of employees was food processing, followed by metallurgy and machinery. The next in line are more traditional fields of manufacturing: clothing and shoes, textiles, and furniture; but then come electrical equipment, transport equipment, wood products, and chemicals. In 1986 the fastest growing industries were electrical and communications equipment, beverages, pharmaceuticals, plastics, capital goods, and machinery. The *London Economist Intelligence Service,* in its annual *"Country Profile: Brazil,"* states: "A major feature of the country's industrial development has been the rapid growth of the so-called 'dynamic' or technologically based industries. . . . By the mid-1970s these industries together accounted for over 59 percent of the value of production and 40 percent of industrial employment. Correspondingly, traditional industries . . . declined." The more technologically advanced industries, especially those in the electronics sector, were relatively unscathed by the recession of the early 1980s. [The "Profile" also points out] that "by mid-1985 a pattern of growth based upon the success of exports was giving way to one of response to a burgeoning domestic market."[9]

In an economy as riddled with regulations, controls, and public enterprise as Brazil's, it is virtually impossible to distinguish a genuine subsidy, in the sense of making costs lower or prices higher than a free market would bring, from interventions designed to counterbalance other interventions, and so create a situation simulating more closely a free competitive market. In any case, whatever the role of subventions, Brazil has been very successful in changing the structure of production and employment. For example, in the 1970s and again in 1986, the automobile industry produced approximately 1 million vehicles a year, and according to *The Economist "Profile,"* "the major firms involved have increasingly geared their production to the world market," and "by mid-1986 the industry had difficulty keeping pace with demand."[10] In general, exports have moved away from traditional primary products and toward manufactured goods. In 1986, coffee, long the major export, accounted for only 10.7% of the total, iron ore only 7.7%, and primary products of all kinds 41.2%. Manufactured steel products accounted for 11.8% of the total, transport equipment 9.3%, and manufactured goods, as a whole, 58.8%. On the import side, capital goods (24.1%) were approaching raw materials (34.2%), and the country was approaching self-sufficiency in energy; fuels and lubricants were down from 55.8% of the total in 1983 (energy alone constituted 71% of the value of imports in 1981) to 23.4% in 1986, mainly because of the development of hydro-electric power and offshore oil fields.

Low Unemployment

Underlying the growth and structural change is a record with re-spect to unemployment that could well be the envy of most indus-trialized countries. Despite the recession, (urban) unemployment did not reach 8% at any time during the 1980s, and in 1985 it was down to 5%.

Reduced Regional Disparities

I have left the question of regional disparities until the end of the list of "new strengths" because the picture is not altogether clear and is somewhat mixed. I have been unable to locate recent figures of per capita income by region or state, and therefore have been compelled to make a rough appraisal by means of proxy variables.

Table 30 shows that the Northeast, where the biggest effort was made, caught up a bit with the rest of the country between 1960 and 1968, but then retrogressed.

Figure 17 shows growth between 1970 and 1980 by state and region. Apart from the Federal District (Brazilia), which grew rapidly from a low base during this period, growth was heavily concentrated in the frontier

Table 30. Brazil: Comparison of Per Capita GDP
at Factor Cost, Northeast and Brazil

Year	GDP per capita, Northeast as proportion of Brazil (percentage)
1960	40.3%
1961	37.7
1962	37.8
1963	39.7
1964	41.9
1965	48.8
1966	47.7
1967	47.9
1968	48.1
1969	46.7
1970	43.1
1971	43.7
1972	43.5
1973	42.6
1974	41.7
1975	43.7

Source. Escritoria de Pesquises Economicase Administratives, Superintendencia do Desinvulvimento do Nordeste, and Fundacoã Getulio Vargas.

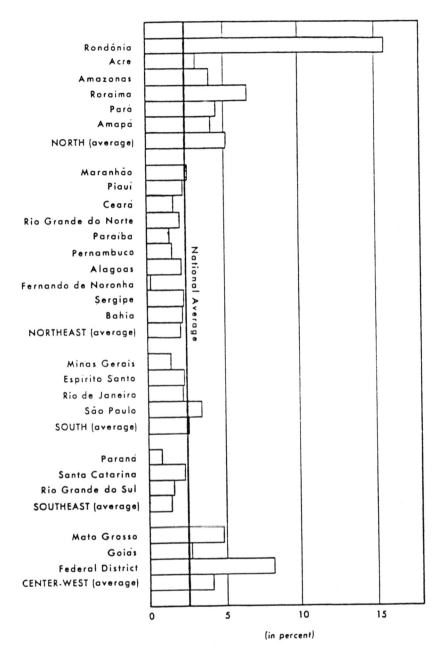

FIGURE 17. Average annual growth rates by region: 1970–1980. (Based on information from Secretaria de Planejamento da Presidência da República, Fundação Instituto Brasileiro de Geographìa e Estatistica, *Anuário Estatístico do Brasil 1980, 41*, Rio de Janeiro, 1980, 109.)

areas of the north and Mato Grosso in the west. São Paulo also grew more rapidly than the national average but not nearly as fast as the north or Mato Grosso. The Northeast as a whole grew at a rate slightly below the national average, except for the state of Maranhão, but it grew a good deal faster than the Southeast, and about the same as the South Central region apart from São Paulo. Considering the obstacles to growth in the Northeast, this picture might be regarded as a success story.

Unemployment rates by region show no very clear pattern (see Table 31), but it cannot be said to be concentrated in the poorer regions, as it is in so many other countries, including Canada. In 1984 and 1985 it was a bit higher in Recife and Salvador than it was on the average in urban centers, but so it was in Belo Horizonte, capital of one of the richer states. As may be seen from Table 32, the most rapid increase in urban employment between 1977 and 1983 took place in Belem, the slowest in São Paulo. Brasilia is of course a special case. Fortaleza, Salvador, and Recife all had significant increases in employment, whereas Rio de Janeiro as well as São Paulo suffered declines.

All in all, the scant data available suggest some degree of regional convergence in recent years. At the same time, it must be said that regional differences in the incidence of poverty persist. *The Economist,* in its *"Profile,"* states that disparities in income and wealth are "noticeably greater in the north east and in rural areas than in the south east."[11] It also reports a 24.6 year discrepancy in life expectancy of people born in Alagôas in the Northeast and those born in Rio Grande do Sul in the South.

Now let us consider the weaknesses of Brazil's regional policy.

Continuing Poverty

Brazil's continuing pockets of poverty bring us to the weaknesses in the country's development in recent decades. Although it has a regional aspect, the problem of poverty in nationwide. Indeed it represents the most notable failure of the military regime introduced in 1964. *The Economist* states:

> It is generally believed that 40 mn people live in extreme poverty. The World Health Organization reports that malnutrition is responsible for 69 percent of the deaths of children under five years old. One third of the population is believed to be malnourished, and as a result there are an estimated 15 million abandoned children in the country, mostly in urban areas. There is some evidence to support the view that disparities in income distribution have become greater

Table 31. *Unemployment Rates in Main Urban Centers*

Major cities	1980	1981	1982	1983	1984	1985	1984				1985			
							I	II	III	IV	I	II	III	IV
Rio de Janeiro	7.5	8.6	6.6	6.2	6.8	4.9	6.9	7.4	6.7	6.0	6.0	5.4	4.5	3.6
São Paulo	5.6	7.7	6.0	6.8	6.8	5.0	7.8	7.5	6.7	5.1	6.1	5.7	4.8	3.5
Belo Horizonte	7.6	9.0	7.0	7.8	8.3	5.7	8.9	9.1	8.0	7.1	7.5	6.2	5.2	4.1
Porto Alegre	4.6	5.8	5.2	6.7	6.9	5.4	7.6	7.9	6.9	5.3	5.8	6.2	5.6	3.9
Salvador	7.3	9.0	6.3	5.6	7.7	6.0	7.9	8.1	8.3	6.7	6.8	6.0	6.3	4.9
Recife	6.8	8.6	7.5	8.0	9.0	7.2	8.9	9.6	9.9	7.5	7.8	8.4	7.3	5.3
Average for urban centers[a]	6.3	7.9	6.3	6.7	7.1	5.3	7.7	7.9	7.1	5.8	6.3	5.9	5.1	3.8

Source. Brazilean Geographical and Statistical Institute (IBGE), monthly employment survey.
[a]Weighted according to the economically active population of each city.

Table 32. *Average Employment Index in Metropolitan Regions*
(February 1977 = 100)

	Industry		Construction		Commerce		Services		Total	
	1981	1983	1981	1983	1981	1983	1981	1983	1981	1983
Belém	115	110	130	118	115	121	122	130	119	121
Belo Horizonte	104	92	109	72	106	101	129	134	114	106
Brasilia	116	106	64	43	122	126	134	145	114	115
Curitiba	99	89	65	47	101	104	116	119	97	91
Fortaleza	104	104	90	75	110	108	126	137	112	113
Porto Alegre	99	91	83	70	129	138	126	132	109	107
Recife	105	93	135	82	106	108	128	133	116	107
Rio de Janeiro	89	75	95	69	126	133	114	113	104	96
Salvador	96	89	82	61	118	117	139	156	111	110
São Paulo	90	77	67	49	108	105	119	126	97	89

Source. Government of Brazil, Banco Central *Annual Report, 1983* (for 1981); *1984* (for 1983).

since the mid-1960s and particularly since 1980. . . . The distribution of income is such, in fact, that only about 80 mn of the population can be considered to make up the Brazilian market.[12]

These conditions with regard to income and its distribution are reflected
in an unsatisfactory situation with respect to education. Brazil's per
capita income must now be above $2,000 per year; but an estimated 25%
of the adult population is illiterate (1980). Only 10% of children continue
in school after the age of 10, and "the systems of secondary and higher
education are grossly inadequate for the requirements of an industrial
state."[13]

These shortcomings are to be explained partly by the very unsatisfactory social situation which the Branco government inherited
from its predecessors in 1964. But they are also partly to be explained by
an inadequate effort to improve the situation since. The Economic Commission for Latin America (CEPAL) report on public social expenditures
and poverty of October 1982 shows that in 1978 Brazil's social expenditures as a percentage of GDP were slightly above the average for Latin
America, but CEPAL also made it clear that it regarded the efforts of
Latin American governments to deal with the virtually universal presence of poverty and its related problems as seriously deficient.[14] It was
in the category of health and welfare that Brazil's expenditure compared
most favorably with the Latin American average. In the field of education, only the Dominican Republic and Uruguay had a lower ration of
expenditures to GDP than Brazil, whose ratio, at 2.3%, was far below
both the regional average and the regional target of 5%.

When we compare social expenditures with total expenditure instead of GDP, we find that Brazil's outlays for education were far below the average for the "upper-middle income" group in 1983, those for health and for "housing, amenities, social security and welfare" well above it. It is also interesting to note that Brazil's expenditures for defense (as a percentage of the total) were less than half the average for this group, and well below those of Argentina and Venezuela. The inadequacy of social expenditure does not seem to be explained primarily by an excess of military spending.

Rampant Inflation

The discussion of spending brings us to the second of Brazil's major economic weaknesses. In recent years, inflation has burst out of hand, and the entrenched system of indexing, at least on occasion, has become unstuck (see Tables 33 and 34). From 1965 to 1973 the authorities managed to hold the rate of inflation to an average of 23.2% per year. In the

Table 33. Brazil: Cost of Living and Minimum Wages

Major cities	Indexes (1978 = 100)			Growth rates				
	1983	1984	1985	1981	1982	1983	1984	1985
Nominal wage								
São Paulo	2,474	6,789	22,923	102.9	98.9	114.5	174.4	237.7
Rio de Janeiro	2,474	6,789	22,923	102.9	98.9	114.5	174.4	237.7
Belo Horizonte	2,474	6,789	22,923	102.9	98.9	114.5	174.4	237.7
Porto Alegre	2,663	7,307	24,673	102.9	98.9	114.5	174.4	237.7
Federal District	2,474	6,789	22,923	102.9	98.9	114.5	174.4	237.7
Recife	2,971	9,045	30,540	107.7	104.8	120.9	204.4	237.7
Consumer price index								
São Paulo	2,336	6,363	19,208	95.6	89.6	135.6	172.4	201.8
Rio de Janeiro	2,749	8,157	29,029	105.5	98.0	142.0	196.7	227.0
Belo Horizonte	3,179	10,592	40,801	104.6	95.7	136.3	233.2	285.2
Porto Alegre	2,954	8,652	28,180	112.0	96.9	141.0	192.9	225.7
Federal District	3,443	10,950	36,398	112.8	106.1	154.6	218.0	232.4
Recife	3,914	11,328	42,094	118.2	106.7	167.4	189.4	271.6
Real minimum wage								
São Paulo	105.9	106.7	119.3	3.7	4.9	−9.0	0.7	11.8
Rio de Janeiro	90.0	83.2	79.0	−1.3	0.4	−11.4	−7.5	4.7
Belo Horizonte	77.8	64.1	56.2	−0.8	1.5	−9.2	−17.6	−12.3
Porto Alegre	90.2	84.5	87.6	−4.3	1.0	−11.0	−6.4	3.7
Federal District	71.8	62.0	63.0	−4.6	−3.5	−15.8	−13.7	1.6
Recife	75.9	79.8	72.6	−4.8	−0.9	−17.4	5.1	−9.0

Source. United Nations Economic Commission for Latin America (ECLAC), on the basis of data supplied by the Central Bank of Brazil and the Getulio Vargas Foundation.

Table 34. Brazil: Average Wages in Industry (Base 1981 = 100)

	Average nominal wage		Consumer prices[a]		Average real wage	
	Index	Variation	Index	Variation	Index	Variation
1980	46.1	92.5	50.4	94.6	91.5	−1.1
1981	100.0	117.1	100.0	98.6	100.0	9.3
1982	212.6	112.6	200.4	100.4	106.1	6.1
1983	462.9	117.7	467.4	133.2	99.0	−6.7
1984	1,386.8	199.6	1,350.0	188.8	102.7	3.8
1985	4,827.8	248.1	4,367.1	223.5	110.5	7.6

[a]Extended national consumer price index.
Source. Getulia Vargas Foundation and Brazilian Geographical and Statistical Institute (IBGE).

next decade it rose to an average of 71.4% per year, and in 1985 the increase in prices was 255.5%. During 1986 and 1987, the rate was somewhat reduced again (see Figure 17 in Appendix). The foreign exchange value of the *cruzeiro,* which is determined through a combination of "crawling floats" and devaluations, depreciated steadily through the 1980s.

The inflation was not generated by prodigal government spending. For a military regime to spend only 4% of its total on defense, less than it spent on health and considerably less than it spent on either social security and housing or on economic services, shows considerable restraint. The ratio of total expenditures to GDP (1983), 21.4%, is lower than that of any industrialized market economy except Switzerland; and Brazil's ratio of budget deficits to GNP (3.6%) is lower than that of Canada, the United States, and the United Kingdom, the same as in France, and only slightly above Australia's (World Bank figures). Yet the money supply has expanded enormously, more than 300% in 1985, through a combination of cost push and a lax monetary policy. A sharp drop in the domestic savings ratio also contributed to inflation. The government has tried to maintain traditional indexing policies despite hyperinflation, with somewhat mixed success. Real wages fell in the early 1980s but rose in 1985 and rose again sharply in 1986.

Dependence on Foreign Capital and Mounting Debt

Despite its high degree of self-sufficiency, Brazil is not entirely cushioned against fluctuations in the world economy. It was affected by the recession of the early 1980s, and both GNP and income fell, although less than in other Latin American countries. Brazil's main form of dependency, however, has been her heavy borrowing abroad to finance her industrial expansion and overall development. Both public and private foreign debt have increased enormously over the past two decades. By 1986 Brazil, along with Mexico, was most heavily indebted among developing countries. In 1986 her debt services exceeded the total value of her exports.

Continuing Agricultural Lag

Recent governments have been little more successful than their predecessors in eliminating the agricultural lag. In the 1980s there have been years when the value of agricultural output scarcely grew and others when it actually fell. As the *Economist Profile* states:

> The performance of the agricultural sector reflects the extent to which government policies have tended to be oriented towards industrialisation and the development of other non-agricultural activities. Despite the fact that . . . Brazil remains one of the world's most important traders of agricultural produce, this sector of the economy has, with few exceptions, been starved of government resources. Agricultural techniques remain backward and yields are comparatively low; in many parts of the country little attention is given to manuring, seed selection or effective crop rotation. Large scale mechanisation has, until comparatively recently, been confined to areas of São Paulo and the Southern states, especially Parana and Rio Grande do Sul.[15]

This neglect of agriculture is a contributing factor to the continuing poverty and the increasing inequality of income distribution. The Figueiredo government has given higher priority to agriculture since 1980, with mixed success.

APPRAISAL

In the absence of detailed analysis, region by region, it is not easy to disentangle the role of strictly regional policy from other facets of economic and social policy in this recital of successes and failures in Brazilian development in recent years. On balance, it would seem that regional policy has been a significant factor in the successes and that the failures are primarily the result of macroeconomic and sectoral policies. Yet in a country where regional policy is such an important part of overall development policy, it cannot be totally exonerated of responsibility for some of the failure too. It would seem that regional policy has been directed mainly toward rapid industrialization, with considerable success. It would also seem that it has been too little concerned with eliminating pockets of poverty, improving levels of education and health, and raising levels of agricultural productivity.

NOTES

[1]Vianna Moog, *Bandeirantes y Pioneiros,* translated by L. L. Barrett as *Bandeirantes and Pioneers* (New York: Brazillen, 1964).

[2]Celso Furtado, *The Economic Growth of Brazil* (Berkeley: University of California Press, 1963), p. 25.

[3]Ibid., p. 130.

[4]Preston James, *Latin America* (New York: Odyssey Press, 1959), p. 482.

[5]Celso Furtado, *Formacão Economica do Brasil* (Rio de Janeiro: Fundo do Cultura, 1959), pp. 57–58.

[6]James, *Latin America,* p. 482.

[7]According to Furtado, the value of a sugar refinery was £15,000 at the end of the 16th century. The present equivalent would be several times as high. Investment in slaves must be added to this figure (Furtado, 1959, p. 60).

[8]Preston, *Latin America,* p. 403.

[9]*London Economist,* Intelligence Service, *Country Profile: Brazil* (1987) p. 32.

[10]Ibid., p. 34.

[11]Ibid., p. 9.

[12]Ibid., p. 9.

[13]Ibid,. p. 9.

[14]U.N. Economic Commission for Latin America, *Economic Survey of Latin America 1985* and *Gasto Publico Social y Pobreza en America Latina,*Santiago 1982, E/CEPAL/1.275.

[15]South America, *Economic Structure and Analysis,* The Economist Intelligence Unit (London), July 1987, p. 97.

APPENDIX

Table A-1. The Structure of the Regional Economies
(percentage of income of region)

Year	North	Northeast	East	South	Middle West	Total
1947						
Agriculture	29	37	25	33	49	
Commerce	18	21	18	14	13	
Industry[a]	24	13	17	22	10	
Services	11	16	17	13	13	
Transport and communications	8	5	8	8	6	
Financial intermed.	1	1	3	2	1	
Rents	1	1	3	3	1	
Government	8	6	9	5	7	
Total	100	100	100	100	100	
1960						
Agriculture	25	47	26	33	60	
Commerce	17	15	15	10	6	
Industry[a]	26	11	21	27	8	
Services	11	12	12	10	8	
Transport and communications	8	6	8	7	6	
Financial intermed.	2	2	3	3	3	
Rents	1	1	4	4	2	
Government	10	6	11	5	7	
Total	100	100	100	100	100	
1960 (percentage of total production in sector)						
Agriculture	2	15	27	51	5	100
Commerce	3	13	40	42	2	100
Industry[a]	2	5	32	60	1	100
Services	2	12	38	47	3	100
Transport and communications	2	9	40	47	2	100
Financial intermed.	1	5	39	53	2	100
Rents	1	4	35	59	1	100
Government	3	8	48	39	2	100

[a]Includes manufacturing industry, public utilities, and construction.

Source. Werner Baer, *Industrialization and Economic Development in Brazil* (Homewood, IL; Richard D. Irwin, 1965), p. 171.

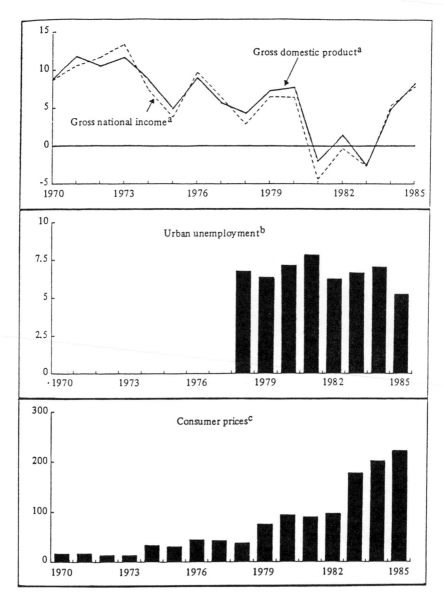

FIGURE A-1.   Brazil: Main economic indicators. (*Source.* United Nations Economic Commission for Latin America (ECLAC) and the Caribbean, *Economic Survey of Latin America*, 1985. [a]Annual growth rate. [b]Average annual rates in the metropolitan areas of Rio de Janeiro, São Paulo, Belo Horizonte, Porto Alegre, Salvador and Recife. [c]Percentage variation from December to December. Up to 1979, this corresponds to the consumer price index for Rio de Janeiro; from 1980, to the consumer price index for the whole country.)

Table A-2. *Composition of Value of Industrial Production According to Region and Type of Industry: 1949, 1959, and 1969 (percentage)*

Region	Year	Traditional	Dynamic A[a]	Dynamic B[b]
North	1949	67	31	1.8
	1959	62	37	1.2
	1969	68	31	0.7
Northeast	1949	86	13	1.2
	1959	70	20	1.3
	1969	60	35	5.0
South Central	1949	62	31	7.1
	1959	46	38	16.0
	1969	38	40	22.2
Brazil	1949	64	30	6.3
	1959	48	37	14.9
	1969	40	40	20.0

Value of production by type of industry (percentage of total)

[a]Nonmetallic minerals, pulp and paper, rubber, chemicals, etc.
[b]Mechanics, electronics, communications, transport equipment.
Source. Fundacão Instituto Brazileiro, de Geografiae E statistica, *Annuarios & statisticos do Brasil* (1949, 1959, 1969).

Table A-3. *Regional Distribution of Gross Domestic Product*

Region	1950	1960
North	2.25	2.20
Northeast	16.33	15.90
Minas Gerais and Espirito Santo	12.04	10.75
East central	51.55	50.48
South	15.87	18.22
Middle west	1.96	2.49
Total	100.00	100.00

Year (percentage)

Source. Fundacão Getulio Vargas.

Table A-4. Regional Distribution of Income Generated in Agriculture

Region	Year (percentage)					
	1950	1960	1961	1962	1963	1964
North	1.67	2.03	2.45	1.67	1.81	1.55
Northeast	20.26	22.14	21.42	23.56	23.78	23.75
Minas Gerais and Espirito Santo	18.48	15.45	14.01	14.92	13.16	15.04
East Central	33.98	27.52	28.28	25.08	27.18	24.75
South	22.29	28.18	27.74	27.87	27.41	27.14
Middle west	3.32	4.68	6.10	6.90	6.66	7.77
Total	100.00	100.00	100.00	100.00	100.00	100.00

Source. Fundacão Getulio Vargas.

Table A-5. Regional Distribution of Income Generated in Industry

	Year (percentage)					
	1950	1960	1961	1962	1963	1964
North	2.86	2.30	—	1.76	1.28	1.43
Northeast	10.34	8.24	—	6.91	5.08	6.30
Minas Gerais and Espirito Santo	8.22	8.09	—	7.15	6.67	6.98
East central	65.19	68.22	—	71.66	76.22	74.16
South	12.60	12.30	—	11.88	10.33	10.39
Middle west	0.79	0.85	—	0.64	0.47	0.74
Total	100.00	100.00	—	100.00	100.00	100.00

Source. Fundacão Getulio Vargas.

Table A-6. Annual Rate of Growth of Real Gross Domestic Product, at Factor Cost, by Region and Sector: 1947–1969

Period	A(N)	I(N)	S(N)	Y(N)	A(NE)	I(NE)	S(NE)	Y(NE)	A(SC)	I(SC)	S(SC)	Y(SC)	A(BR)	I(BR)	S(BR)	Y(BR)
1947–1953	-2.5	5.6	1.0	0.3	1.2	2.5	3.7	2.5	4.3	10.0	6.8	6.6	3.4	8.8	6.3	5.8
1953–1961	11.0	18.0	12.0	13.0	5.7	10.0	8.7	7.9	4.3	9.7	7.3	7.2	4.7	10.0	7.6	7.3
1961–1969	1.2	0.70	2.3	1.9	5.3	2.7	5.5	5.2	3.0	5.6	4.1	4.3	3.9	5.3	4.2	4.5
1947–1969	3.6	8.5	5.6	5.4	4.3	5.4	6.3	5.4	3.9	8.4	6.1	6.0	4.1	8.1	6.1	5.9

Notes. A = agriculture; I = manufacturing industry; S = services; Y = all sectors (GDP); N = north; NE = northeast; SC = south central; and BR = Brazil.

Source. Fundacão Getulio Vargas (FGV); Institutio Brazileiro de Economia (IBRE); Centro de Contas Nationais (OCN).

Table A-7. Northeast and Brazil: Annual Rate of Growth of Real Gross Domestic Product Per Capita, at Factor Cost

Period	GDP Total		GDP Per Capita	
	Northeast	Brazil	Northeast	Brazil
1960–1965	5.3	4.6	2.9	1.7
1965–1970	6.7	7.1	4.3	4.1
1970–1974	9.9	10.7	7.2	7.7
1960–1974	7.1	7.2	4.6	4.2

Source. SUDENE, FGV, and Instituto de Planejamento Economico e social (IPEA).

Table A-8. Regional Distribution of the Brazilian Population and National Income

Region	Population, percentage				
	1947	1949	1957	1959	1960
North[a]	4	4	3	3	3
Northeast	25	24	24	25	24
East	36	36	35	35	34
South	32	33	34	34	35
Middle west[b]	3	3	4	3	4
Total	100	100	100	100	100

Region	National income, percentage				
	1947	1949	1957	1959	1960
North	2	2	2	2	2
Northeast	11	11	10	10	11
East	37	37	36	36	34
South	48	48	50	50	51
Middle west	2	2	2	2	2
Total	100	100	100	100	100

[a]In the table, Bahia and Sergipe are included in the "east." If they were included in the northeast, as they are by SUDENE, the figures would indicate a slight decline in the region's share of national income between 1947 and 1960. The share of total population in the SUDENE "northeast" fell from 34.7% in 1950 to 31.6% in 1960.

[b]North includes the states of Amazonas and Para; Middle west, the states of Mato Grosso and Goias.

Source. Adapted from Werner Baer, *Industrialization and Economic Development in Brazil* (Homewood, IL: Richard D. Irwin, 1965), p. 169.

Table A-9. Composition of Value of Industrial Production According to Region and Type of Industry: 1949, 1959, and 1969 (percentage)

Region	Year	Value of production by type of industry (% of total)		
		Traditional	Dynamic A[a]	Dynamic B[b]
North	1949	67	31	1.8
	1959	62	37	1.2
	1969	68	31	0.7
Northeast	1949	86	13	1.2
	1959	70	20	1.3
	1969	60	35	5.0
South central	1949	62	31	7.1
	1959	46	38	16.0
	1969	38	40	22.2
Brazil	1949	64	30	6.3
	1959	48	37	14.9
	1969	40	40	20.0

[a]Nonmetallic minerals, pulp and paper, rubber, chemicals, etc.
[b]Mechanics, electronics, communications, transport equipment.
Source. FIBGE.

Table A-10. Exports: 1941–1984 (Coffee Shown Separately)

Year	Receipts from total exports	Receipts from coffee exports	U.S. $ 1,000, percentage coffee on total
1941	352,128	122,275	34.72
1942	392,955	105,742	26.91
1943	444,258	151,147	34.02
1944	577,026	209,165	36.25
1945	657,307	229,357	34.89
1946	984,725	349,819	35.53
1947	1,130,875	413,854	36.59
1948	1,180,461	490,672	41.57
1949	1,096,468	631,688	57.61
1950	1,355,467	865,483	63.85
1951	1,769,002	1,058,587	59.84
1952	1,418,117	1,045,305	73.71
1953	1,539,120	1,090,164	70.83
1954	1,561,836	948,077	60.70
1955	1,423,246	843,938	59.30
1956	1,481,978	1,029,782	59.40
1957	1,391,607	845,531	60.76
1958	1,242,985	687,515	55.31
1959	1,281,969	744,029	58.04
1960	1,268,772	712,750	56.17
1961	1,402,970	710,439	50.64
1962	1,214,185	642,682	52.93
1963	1,406,480	746,952	53.11
1964	1,429,790	759,915	53.15
1965	1,595,479	707,366	44.34
1966	1,741,442	773,522	44.42
1967	1,654,037	732,989	44.32
1968	1,881,334	797,258	42.38
1969	2,311,169	845,687	36.59
1970	2,738,922	981,806	35.85
1971	2,903,856	822,212	28.32
1972	3,991,219	1,057,104	26.49
1973	6,199,200	1,344,238	21.68
1974	7,950,996	1,002,002	12.60
1975	8,669,944	931,966	10.74
1976	10,125,736	2,398,284	23.68
1977	12,120,175	2,624,944	21.66
1978	12,650,633	2,294,490	18.14
1979	15,244,377	2,325,705	15.26
1980	20,132,401	2,772,920	13.77
1981	23,293,035	1,516,646	6.5
1982	20,175,071	1,854,353	9.2
1983	21,898,878	2,824,410	12.9
1984	27,005,336	2,564,136	9.5
1985	25,638,674	2,337,545	10.0

Source. Instituto Brasileiro do Café.

Table A-11. Active Population: 1960–1980

	1960	1970	1980
Total	48,828,654	65,862,119	87,811,196
Economically active	22,750,028	29,557,224	43,235,712
Agro-fishing activities	12,276,908	13,087,521	12,661,017
Processing industries	1,954,187	3,241,861	6,939,421
Construction industry	781,247	1,719,714	3,171,046
Other industrial activities	204,808	333,852	661,996
Merchandise trade	1,478,170	2,247,493	4,037,917
Transport and communications	977,345	1,167,866	1,800,243
Services	3,028,933	3,925,001	7,032,126
Social activities	755,043	1,531,563	2,971,100
Public administration	712,904	1,152,341	1,722,284
Other activities	580,383	1,150,012	2,238,562
Economically inactive	26,078,626	36,304,895	44,575,484

Source. Instituto Brazileiro de Geographia e Estatistica.

Table A-12. Rated Power: 1884–1985

| | Rated power | | | | Rated power | | |
| | Thermo- | Hydro- | | | Thermo- | Hydro- | |
Year	electric	electric	Total	Year	electric	electric	Total
1884	0,080	—	0,080	1933	159,301	658,316	817,617
1885	0,080	—	0,080	1934	163,349	665,307	828,656
1886	0,080	—	0,080	1935	173,430	676,699	850,129
1887	0,240	—	0,240	1936	179,255	745,726	924,981
1888	0,400	—	0,400	1937	192,381	754,629	947,010
1889	0,500	0,250	0,750	1938	214,743	214,917	1,161,660
1890	1,017	0,250	1,267	1939	224,060	951,976	1,176,036
1891	1,017	0,250	1,267	1940	234,531	1,099,346	1,243,877
1892	3,034	0,375	3,409	1941	242,243	1,019,015	1,261,258
1893	3,034	0,636	3,670	1942	247,022	1,060,646	1,307,668
1894	3,293	1,285	4,578	1943	248,275	1,067,275	1,315,438
1895	3,843	1,991	5,834	1944	257,239	1,076,969	1,334,208
1896	4,083	3,592	7,675	1945	261,806	1,709,827	1,341,633
1897	4,083	3,652	7,735	1946	280,738	1,134,245	1,414,983
1898	4,083	4,049	8,132	1947	282,973	1,251,164	1,534,137
1899	4,183	4,509	8,692	1948	291,789	1,333,546	1,625,335
1900	5,093	5,283	10,376	1949	304,331	1,430,860	1,735,191
1901	4,918	32,662	37,580	1950	346,830	1,535,670	1,882,500
1902	4,668	33,585	38,253	1951	355,190	1,584,756	1,939,946
1903	4,828	34,421	39,249	1952	325,585	1,659,216	1,984,801
1904	5,094	34,442	39,536	1953	385,321	1,704,152	2,089,473
1905	6,676	28,260	44,936	1954	632,301	2,173,226	2,805,527
1906	8,646	40,375	49,021	1955	667,318	2,481,171	3,148,489
1907	9,286	43,851	53,137	1956	674,721	2,875,284	3,550,005
1908	11,986	89,773	101,759	1957	764,471	3,002,940	3,767,411
1909	13,050	103,034	116,084	1958	769,280	3,223,820	3,993,100
1910	32,729	124,672	157,401	1959	798,992	3,316,208	4,115,200
1911	35,424	131,945	167,369	1960	1,158,057	3,642,025	4,800,082
1912	43,933	180,018	223,951	1961	1,396,301	3,808,851	5,205,152
1913	49,370	194,859	244,229	1962	1,603,200	4,125,573	5,728,773
1914	50,423	253,015	303,438	1963	1,875,561	4,479,507	6,355,068
1915	51,106	258,692	309,798	1964	1,946,000	4,946,000	6,840,000
1916	52,647	260,436	313,093	1965	2,020,200	5,390,800	7,411,000
1917	53,120	266,413	319,533	1966	2,041,800	5,523,800	7,565,600
1918	55,274	271,673	326,947	1967	2,255,000	5,781,100	8,036,100
1919	62,642	278,394	341,036	1968	2,372,000	6,183,300	8,555,300
1920	66,072	300,946	367,946	1969	2,405,000	7,857,500	10,262,500
1921	66,206	305,109	371,315	1970	2,405,000	8,828,400	11,233,400
1922	68,806	313,588	382,394	1971	2,426,000	10,244,400	12,670,400
1923	75,017	320,656	395,656	1972	2,258,000	10,721,000	13,249,000
1924	78,863	387,031	465,894	1973	2,859,000	12,495,000	15,354,000
1925	90,608	416,875	507,483	1974	3,241,000	14,285,000	17,256,000

(continued)

Table A-12. (Continued)

Year	Rated power Thermo-electric	Hydro-electric	Total	Year	Rated power Thermo-electric	Hydro-electric	Total
1926	120,660	489,282	591,942	1975	2,906,000	16,150,000	19,056,000
1927	110,732	539,108	649,840	1976	3,157,000	17,670,000	20,827,000
1928	130,829	576,607	707,436	1977	3,108,000	19,038,000	22,491,000
1929	138,589	621,747	760,336	1978	9,510,000	21,576,000	25,300,000
1930	148,752	630,050	778,802	1979	4,249,000	24,137,000	28,386,000
1931	153,325	646,086	799,411	1980	6,062,000	27,532,000	33,594,000
1932	155,926	649,518	805,444	1981	6,150,000	31,132,000	37,282,000
				1982	6,012,000	32,892,000	38,094,000
				1983	6,062,000	34,035,000	40,097,000
				1984	6,138,000	35,524,090	14,662,000
				1985	6,795,000	38,124,000	44,919,000

Source. Eletrobrés—SIEDE.

Table A-13. Estimated Population: 1830–2000

Year	Population 1,000 inhabitants	Year	Population 1,000 inhabitants	Year	Population 1,000 inhabitants	Year	Population 1,000 inhabitants
1830	5,343	1870	9,797	1910	22,216	1950	51,976
1831	5,425	1871	9,947	1911	22,687	1951	53,526
1832	5,508	1872	10,099	1912	23,168	1952	55,122
1833	5,592	1873	10,289	1913	23,660	1953	56,766
1834	5,677	1874	10,486	1914	24,161	1954	58,459
1835	5,764	1875	10,687	1915	26,674	1955	60,202
1836	5,852	1876	10,891	1916	25,197	1956	61,998
1837	5,941	1877	11,099	1917	25,732	1957	63,846
1838	6,032	1978	11,311	1918	26,277	1958	65,750
1839	6,124	1879	11,528	1919	26,835	1959	67,711
1840	6,218	1880	11,748	1920	27,404	1960	69,730
1841	6,313	1881	11,973	1921	27,969	1961	71,810
1842	6,409	1882	12,202	1922	28,542	1962	73,951
1843	6,507	1883	12,435	1923	29,126	1963	76,156
1844	6,606	1884	12,673	1924	29,723	1964	78,427
1845	6,707	1885	12,916	1925	30,332	1965	80,766
1846	6,809	1886	13,163	1926	30,953	1966	83,175
1847	6,912	1887	13,414	1927	31,587	1967	85,655
1848	7,018	1888	13,671	1928	32,234	1968	88,209
1849	7,125	1889	13,932	1929	32,894	1969	90,840
1850	7,234	1890	14,199	1930	33,568	1970	93,139
1851	7,344	1891	14,506	1931	34,256	1971	95,467
1852	7,456	1892	14,857	1932	34,957	1972	95,989
1853	7,570	1893	15,216	1933	35,673	1973	100,301
1854	7,686	1894	15,853	1934	36,404	1974	102,807
1855	7,803	1895	15,960	1935	37,150	1975	105,377
1856	7,923	1896	16,346	1936	37,911	1976	108,013
1857	8,044	1897	16,741	1937	38,687	1977	110,714
1858	8,167	1898	17,145	1938	38,480	1978	113,481
1859	8,291	1899	17,560	1939	40,289	1979	116,227
1860	8,418	1900	17,984	1940	41,114	1980	119,003
1861	8,547	1901	18,392	1941	42,069	1981	121,778
1862	8,678	1902	18,782	1942	43,069	1982	124,699
1863	8,810	1903	19,180	1943	44,093	1983	128,693
1864	8,945	1904	19,587	1944	45,141	1984	131,781
1865	9,082	1905	20,003	1945	46,215	1985	135,564
1866	9,221	1906	20,427	1946	47,313	1990	150,368
1867	9,362	1907	20,860	1947	48,438	1995	165,083
1868	9,505	1908	21,303	1948	49,590	2000	179,487
1869	9,650	1909	21,754	1949	40,769		

Source. Instituto Brasileira de Geografia e Estatistica, *Annuarios Estatisticas do Brasil, 1980.*

CHAPTER NINE

Conclusions

THE RISE AND DECLINE OF REGIONAL POLICY

Although some tentative attempts at regional development planning were made earlier, it was not until the 1960s that, with the exception of Great Britain, each of the countries studied in this volume launched major programs in this regard. What passed for "regional planning" before then was for the most part piecemeal, sporadic, and limited in scope, like the TVA in the United States, the town-and-country planning ventures in the United Kingdom and France, the efforts at decentralization in Australia, the early attempts at drought relief in Brazil, and resource development in Malaysia. Physical planning still played a major role, and there was little effort to apply either economic theory or development theory to regional planning in practice. The sharp increase in regional development activities in the 1960s and early 1970s was in each case a response to interrelated social, political, demographic, and economic problems, which show a similarity from case to case that is quite remarkable, considering the diversity of the countries covered.

In each case, too, there were similar, interrelated social, economic, demographic, and political motives. Equity and social justice were invoked on behalf of development policies for regions that lagged behind rising national prosperity. Large-scale rural-to-urban migration was cited by some observers as evidence that the market worked, but others viewed such migration as being socially disruptive and called for special development programs for regions experiencing heavy outmigration. There was a widespread perception that the rapid growth of already large metropolitan areas was creating net social costs that could be avoided by development in alternative locations and that there was inefficiency in terms of underutilized infrastructures in declining non-metropolitan areas. Thus economic rationales were given for regional programs that would promote the development of peripheral areas, lessen demographic pressures on the largest cities, and in general make all regions more productive. Politicians also saw advantages in taking credit for regional development policies benefiting their constituents; in France, reference was made to regional planning as *aménagement électoral du territoire*.

The regional policies pursued by the countries in question also had many similarities. The regions targeted for major development assistance were for the most part characterized by relatively high rates of unemployment and/or relatively low per capita incomes, though in France this approach was complemented by such other programs as the development of regional metropolises and industrial port complexes. Development assistance relied heavily on economic infrastructure projects and subsidies to capital, with some lesser attention to human resource development. Although comprehensive relocation assistance was discussed as a means to make interregional labor markets more efficient, virtually nothing was done in this regard because of a strong bias favoring the promotion of the movement of jobs to workers. Considerable formal efforts were made to encourage planning at the local and regional levels so that the planning process would be, at least in principle, a fusion of bottom-up and top-down participation. These attempts were frequently not very successful because of a lack of local and regional planning capability; and in some instances local elites resisted changes that potentially threatened the established order. There was also considerable resistance from senior permanent officials at the center to effective economic planning at the regional and local levels. This was as true in the case of Whitehall as it was, for example, in the cases of Ottawa and Paris. Thus planning formulation and implementation tended to be dominated by initiatives coming from the central governments.

It is still too early to evaluate the achievements of the regional policies of the 1960s because they were, explicitly or implicitly, directed toward long-term objectives. Though it was not evident at the time, with hindsight, it appears that some spontaneous processes were already moving in directions consistent with certain of these objectives; however, in the 1970s other factors radically altered the regional policy environment. The "favorable" spontaneous changes were first apparent in demographic data, which in turn probably reflected changes in the location preferences of people (on balance favoring smaller places at the expense of large cities) and of firms (manufacturing decentralization). More specifically, national population growth rates fell below projected levels, and "polarization reversal" occurred with respect to population distribution. Large metropolitan areas began to experience slowing growth rates and, in numerous cases, absolute decline. Meanwhile, many nonmetropolitan areas that had been experiencing net outmigration now had net inmigration, whereas still others at least had lower rates of outmigration. These phenomena, although consistent with regional policy objectives, nonetheless removed most of the demographic rationale for the need for such policies. The global economic crisis that began in 1973–1974 brought falling national aggregate growth rates, rising unemployment, and tight government budgets. Even though nearly all regions were adversely affected, old industrial regions were particularly hard hit. As regions increasingly contended for government assistance, the resources available became increasingly scarce. What resulted, in varying degree depending on the country, was a de facto abandonment of the long-term orientations of the regional policies of the 1960s for short-run "quick-fix" programs, such as public works, to cushion the effects of unemployment in the more distressed areas.

The retreat from regional policies in the 1970s in industrialized countries was not only a response to social and economic considerations. It also reflected changes in the political climate. (The story in the LDCs is different because, although they too suffered from the global recession, they did not abandon national development planning, nor the regional development component of it. Indeed, in many of them regional planning increased during the 1970s). The activism of the 1960s was replaced by renewed faith in the efficacy of market forces; the pendulum had swung once again from interventionism to noninterventionism as the guiding philosophy. It was pointed out in the introduction that a major thesis of this study is that regional policies reflect a mutual interaction between the socioeconomic evolution of a nation and the prevailing economic and social philosophy of the time. This proposition will now be considered in some detail in light of the principal social and economic objectives that have motivated the formulation and implementation of regional development policies.

THE RATIONALE FOR REGIONAL POLICY

In the industrialized capitalist countries (ICCs), "regional policy," and still more "regional planning," is perceived by many people as deliberate intervention in the functioning of the free market. By the same token, it is seen as an expression of dissatisfaction with the free market as an instrument for achieving economic and social goals. When viewed in this fashion, it is possible to approve or disapprove of "regional policy" as a *concept*, quite apart from any evaluation of the efficacy of specific policies undertaken by a particular government. The objectives toward which regional policy is thought to be directed include the following:

1. Promoting social justice, in the form of greater equality. This concept implies that the proponents of "regional policy" think that inequalities among social groups can be reduced by reducing disparities among regions. (Few would argue that social justice requires reducing gaps among regions, even if it takes the form of making the rich richer in the disadvantaged regions. Some regional policies may actually work that way, but they are seldom defended in such terms). It is therefore possible to oppose "regional policy" either on the grounds that it will not work to promote social justice or that the objective of greater equality is not acceptable if it means a reduction in efficiency for the national economy as a whole.

2. Reducing unemployment where it is most severe. It is hardly possible to oppose this objective on rational grounds, but one can (and some do) argue that a better way to reduce unemployment where it is heaviest is for the unemployed to migrate to more dynamic regions where unemployment is lower. Opponents of employment creation in lagging regions might accept "regional policy" in the form of assisted migration.

3. Eliminating pockets of poverty where they exist. The same considerations apply here as in "2" here, although it is conceivable that some would oppose the elimination of poverty as an objective if it means paying people "more than they are worth."

4. Promoting structural adjustment. Low productivity, inefficient, "traditional" industries tend to be concentrated in certain regions. Regional policy can be used to upgrade these industries. One could not rationally oppose this policy if it adds more to GDP than any other use of the same funds, but one can argue that the new, hi-tech, high-productivity industries should be established in those regions where their comparative advantage is greatest.

5. Realizing the development potential more fully. No one can rationally oppose this objective, if environmental issues are not involved and development is certain to add more to GDP than the cost, including interest. An ardent "marketeer" might argue, however, that development potential should be exploited wherever it is, and if the potential is greater (returns to investment higher) in a rich region, investment should be directed to the rich region rather than to poor ones.

These presumed objectives of "regional policy" are presented more or less in the order of importance attached to them in debate on regional policy in the ICCs. In short, many people in the industrialized capitalist countries identify "regional policy" with what many Americans call today *liberalism*, an interventionist economic and social philosophy based on a belief that government has a responsibility for assuring certain standards of social and economic welfare, as typified in practice by the Roosevelt, Truman, Johnson, and Trudeau administrations. In the minds of some, "regional policy" is also associated with a lack of faith in the market, an anticapitalist bias, and suspicion of private enterprise. Some also see "regional policy" as putting parochial interests above national interest.

Given such widely held views in ICCs, it is not surprising that disinterest in, or open opposition to, "regional policy" is stronger when the dominant sentiment in any such country is such as to bring a conservative government to power. We have seen such a move, with the predictable impact on regional policy, in every one of the five ICCs covered in this volume. Although the election of a Labor government in Australia and the failure to regenerate regional policy may seem at first sight to be a contradiction of this thesis, it must be remembered that a Labor government can be conservative, too, as the Hawke government has been: monetarist antiinflation policy, wage restraints (or "professional union bashing," as the left wing of Hawke's party would have it) privatization, and deregulation. During the 1987 election campaign in Australia, the conservative coalition struggled to occupy ground to the right of the Hawke government and still make some sense.

The antiregional-policy bias of conservative ideology seems to be a stool with these three legs: the belief that, at least in the long run, the free market is more efficient in bringing higher levels of welfare to the underdog than any kind of government intervention can be; the conviction that an underdog minority has no legal or moral right to thwart the overdog majority in the pursuit of its interests; and for some, the belief that a system of unbridled competition that brings the "best" people to the top is not only more efficient than any kind of welfare statism but is also morally superior. *Time* magazine, for example, in its issue of 12 June 1987 reports that the chairman of the Board of Governors of the Federal Reserve System, Allan Greenspan, holds this view, having been influenced by Ayn Rand. Clearly, as shown in Chapter 6, these attitudes are less prevalent in some developing countries.

How well the market is actually working in any country is of course a question of fact, although not a matter of facts that are easily ascertainable. The economics profession is by no means agreed on the question; economists who do not differ widely in basic political philosophy appraise the market differently. In his presidential address to the American Economics Association, Robert Solow put it thus:

> Some of us see the Smithian virtues as needles in a haystack, an
> island of measure zero in a sea of imperfections. Others see the
> imperfections as so many ticks on the thick hide of an ox, requiring
> only an occasional flick of its tail to be brushed away.[1]

But whatever may be the real truth about the relative harm done by
market failure and by government failure in particular countries, there
can be no doubt that "regional policy" is viewed as interventionism,
part of the package of a managed economy, in industrialized capitalist
countries. Consequently, people of different faiths regarding the market
economy and the managed economy will have different views regarding
regional policy, and regional policy itself will experience swings with
shifts in the balance of numbers in the two groups. As we have seen, in
LDCs most people take a more pragmatic view of regional policy, planning, and development, appraising these instruments of policy more
realistically on their technical merits or shortcomings. It does not seem
likely that the cycle in regional policy will soon disappear in the ICCs,
unless cycles in political viewpoint disappear first. History does not
provide us with grounds for expecting that to happen.

REGIONAL POLICY AND INDUSTRIAL STRUCTURE

Another major thesis of this study is that regional policies need to
be viewed in the light of changing industrial structures, as well as the
changing determinants of location. The general considerations presented in this regard in the introduction—which noted the increasing spatial
decomposition of production, the rise of "footloose" industries that
nonetheless depend on an innovative milieu, and the increasing importance of small- and medium-sized enterprises—were confirmed in detail
by the case studies. However, it is also instructive in this context to
review the theoretical locational assumptions that inspired many of the
regional policies and programs of the 1960s and early 1970s; to examine
critically why the results of this approach were disappointing; and to
suggest more promising research directions based on more recent
knowledge concerning the nature and significance of spatial-temporal
development processes.

Other than neoclassical theory, which essentially tends to justify
the laissez-faire conditions that most explicit regional policies are trying
to alter, no postwar regional development theory has been more influential than that concerning spatial growth poles. By the mid-1960s, it
was present in one form or another in all of the regional policies consid-

ered in this volume. Essentially, growth pole theory is oriented toward economic efficiency, but in a dynamic sense as compared with the comparative statics analyses of neoclassical theory. It embraced the notion that productivity can be increased by realizing the external economies of agglomeration (cost reductions resulting from factors external to the firm but internal to the polarized space) to be had by clustering infrastructure and directly productive activities rather than dispersing them thinly over wide areas. Regional policy, it was held, could induce growth pole development, which in turn would generate several interrelated benefits. First, the pole's own growth would directly promote regional development. Second, the growth pole would be a countermagnet, attracting migrants from lagging regions who might otherwise go to large, overcongested cities. Third, the growth pole would eventually produce positive "spread effects" in its hinterland. And finally, the growth pole would have a major relay function in the process of innovation diffusion through the hierarchical systems of cities.

Unfortunately, growth pole practice did not live up to the expectations of growth pole theory. What went wrong? To a large extent, growth pole initiatives were more paper policies than genuine attempts to implement the theory. Whatever the economic efficiencies that might be realized, it is politically virtually impossible to carry out a growth pole strategy in a democratic society. By definition, the implementation would leave out more places and people than would be included, which means that majority political support cannot be realized. What tends to happen is to keep the growth pole approach in name (lacking any other strategy) but to designate a large number of (often unpromising) places as growth poles, which satisfies the politicians but contradicts the economic justification for the policy. Moreover, there has been little positive evidence that induced growth poles—even if successful in themselves—necessarily generate many benefits for their hinterlands; the relevant linkages between growth pole activities and those elsewhere, to the extent that they exist, are usually widely dispersed geographically. Finally, the more general hierarchical diffusion of the innovation model has itself received little empirical support.

Although current regional policy discussions are not based on any one generally accepted grand theoretical paradigm, perhaps there is something to be said for an eclectic approach that provides flexibility in dealing with the different kinds of regional issues that arise among and within countries. Be that as it may, it should still be remarked that the product cycle concept, although not a general theory of regional development, has nonetheless proven to be a valuable tool in analyzing spatial-temporal regional development processes. Theoretical variants in terms of profit cycles and process cycles have essentially the same spatial outcomes. This approach basically argues that in the early phase of a product's development, the most important location factors are scientific–engineering skills and the presence of external economies (universities and research laboratories, major transportation and communications linkages, producer services, amenities that attract skilled personnel, etc.). If and when a product reaches the stage where its technology is widely known and it can be manufactured in long, routine production runs, then competition forces firms to seek out cheap—and usually unorganized—labor, though large amounts of capital may also still be required. In spatial terms, this implies that the relatively sophisticated operations of the early phase of the cycle will be carried out in those places that have the appropriate milieu: California's Silicon Valley, Boston's Route 128, Paris and its southern suburbs, the southeast of England, Sydney, and Melbourne, São Paulo, and the Kuala Lumpur Port Kelang corridor are among the more dramatic examples. In contrast, routine, standardized operations will be performed in peripheral areas of industrial countries or in newly developing countries.

It should also be pointed out that although the product cycle concept was initially formulated in the context of manufacturing, it also applies to office activities, which, in contrast to manufacturing, are rapidly growing in employment. Relatively sophisticated office work and functions requiring frequent face-to-face contacts are performed in large cities, whereas routine "back office" activities are increasingly being decentralized.

What are the major regional development policy implications of the product cycle? First, because areas involved in the initial phase—typically large service-oriented cities—continually spin off activities as they become standardized and routine, these areas must continuously innovate to replace old activities with new products and processes. Failing this, even a Silicon Valley could eventually become an old industrial region. Second, in industrial countries, peripheral areas that have based their growth on decentralized activities are likely to find this a fragile foundation for genuine regional development, especially in view of competition from newly developing countries with even cheaper labor. Third, it is possible for a country or region to begin the development process by initially taking on activities in the mature phase of the product cycle, but then to shift gradually the nature of its product and process mixes in favor of more sophisticated activities with greater skill requirements and higher wages. This has been done in such countries as South Korea, Malaysia, Singapore, Hong Kong, and Taiwan, as well as in certain regions within industrial countries—parts of the U.S. South and some areas in the west and south of France, for instance. The nature of this process, which often involves endogenous small- and medium-sized enterprises, deserves more careful study in view of its obvious relevance to the destinies of many peripheral regions.

THE FUTURE OF REGIONAL POLICY

In addition to the ever-present need for a better understanding of processes of regional development and decline, there is still a need for explicit regional development policies in each of the countries that have been considered. Even the most conservative of governments recognizes this and publicly supports some form of regional policy. If one views the immediate future in the context of the postwar era—and indeed of the century as a whole—the general socioeconomic and political climate may well be due for a new swing in the direction of greater activism. Already in the U.S. setting, Robert Lawrence, a prominent student of sectoral policies, recently concluded that

> It is time to recognize that the problem now faced by the United States is declining regions, not declining industries" [and that] clearly the concept of industrial policy is merely diverting our attention from what I think is the more fundamental question of why some regions decline while others rise.[2]

Clearly, also, this evaluation applies to the other countries that have been examined.

Lawrence goes on to argue that "because America's problems are regional rather than industrial, it is appropriate to develop policies at the state level. Federal coordination could be improved, but the states must play a larger role."[3] In fact, however, the states and local governments have been playing a larger role in development policy, not so much because they have been encouraged to do so by the federal government but because federal revenues have been diverted to military expansion and servicing the national debt.

More generally, the national experiences that have been surveyed here indicate that for regional policy to be successful, it is essential that regional and locally elected officials and community leaders be involved in all phases of the planning process. Uniform policies and programs conceived and implemented in a top-down manner do not effectively respond to the differing problems and opportunities of diverse regional economies. On the other hand, completely decentralized regional planning results in unequal and often inefficient competition among regional (states, provinces) and local authorities and development organizations. Inequality arises because of differing degrees of planning capability. The richer areas have more sophisticated planning staffs and greater financial means for promoting development than do the poorer areas. Competition among regions and localities also leads to a profusion of financial subsidies and expensive investments in industrial parks—though today smokestock chasing is less fashionable than the pursuit of high-technology activities. Subsidies represent a diversion of resources from other—and perhaps more vital—community needs; and even if they do bring new jobs, the relevant firms are likely to be marginal. Industrial and science parks likewise have important opportunity costs, and the odds are high that they will be underutilized if they are used at all. Moreover, the product cycle is just as operative in high-technology industries as in traditional industries. Thus many "high-tech" jobs involve a relatively unskilled, inexpensive labor force performing routine assembly tasks.

One result of the lack of any real central government involvement in regional policy in the United States

> has been an uneven performance by communities, states, and regions. With the severe erosion of the federal aid that once promoted equality between a Connecticut and an Idaho, for example, the national picture is increasingly one of prosperity in some areas and poverty in others. Pressure is building for the federal government to take some action to alleviate the disparities. But for the time being, state and local officials see no way out but to fend for themselves.[4]

This could, however, defeat the very purpose of a conservative government determined to pursue national economic efficiency goals. State building could in time become as widespread as province building is in Canada. Canadian provinces, particularly slow-growth provinces, have become convinced that discriminatory federal policies have obstructed their development. They have as a result put in place a host of competing economic development schemes. There have been many occasions in which the competitive actions of several provinces have harmed the national economy.[5] With all provinces setting up competing incentive schemes, the resulting distribution of investment has not changed greatly, but the overall government cost has been greatly increased. Another example is discriminatory procurement policies on the part of the provinces that tend to view economic development as a zero-sum game in which the winners are identified on a case-by-case basis in highly regional terms. There are thus important reasons of economic efficiency for the federal government to be directly involved in promoting regional economic development. Unless a central government in a federation makes some efforts to equalize economic activities, it runs the risk of seeing states or provinces attempt to do so at a great cost to the national economy.

In time, the same could well apply in the United States. Quite apart from this and the various economic and rational arguments for and against regional policy outlined earlier in this chapter, there are always strong political reasons for central governments to put in place regional policies and programs. Some governments may at times wish to disengage from regional policies. They may well do so or at least cut back considerably in regional programs. But shortly after, they—or a newly elected government—are as likely to proclaim a "new commitment" to regional development.

We saw, for example, that the British Conservative government was not able to realize a fundamental rethinking of British regional policy once in government, even though in opposition, Mrs. Thatcher and leading members of her party had called precisely for such an approach.

There are now various forces at play leading governments into regional policies and programs. In the introductory chapter, we noted that potentially footloose activities have increased in importance, especially in the case of scientifically oriented, high-technology firms for which the transport costs of inputs and outputs are small in relation to the total value of their products. Multinational companies now have greater flexibility than ever to locate new production facilities. Governments, of course, know this full well. They have responded by putting in place a "web" of incentive schemes to lure new plants to locate in their countries. Frequently, such schemes have a regional bias. Governments that profess complete faith in the free market as a guide and mechanism for resource allocation and economic growth quickly discover that not all governments have similar faith and, unless they also put in place regional programs, they are not likely to be able to compete effectively for new economic activities with other countries.

For some countries, there are also other forces, often operating beyond their immediate control, favoring the establishment of, or at least support for, regional programs. Member countries of the European Economic Community, for example, must have regional development programs to take advantage of the community's substantial regional development fund. Unless they have such programs, they will forego community funds earmarked for them.

There are also, as we have seen in this volume, "practical" political reasons for having regional policies and programs. Such reasons have compelled even very conservative governments, such as that of Thatcher in Great Britain, the military régime in Brazil, and the Mahatir government in Malaysia, to retain regional programs. Doing away with regional programs may well upset a country's delicate regional political consensus and threaten national unity.

Experience has shown that even a reduction in regional programming can fuel regional alienation that, if nothing else, can prove very costly for the government at the next national election. Experience has also shown that governments will intervene to promote regional growth. It is true that one government in particular may well wish to reduce its commitment to regional development. However, it is likely to be temporary, or the government will likely be replaced in time by another with a strong commitment to regional policy. A leading proponent of neoclassical economics recognized this and observed that governments will intervene in regional development and will not "stand idly by and allow the unfettered market to call the adjustment tune."[6]

The question is not so much whether governments will intervene. It is rather how they will intervene. This volume has revealed a host of possible regional development measures. Some were common to all countries surveyed. Various types of incentives to attract firms to locate in designated regions is one. The growth center concept is another. Others, however, could only be introduced in countries with appropriate political institutions. One can hardly imagine, for example, that the kind of centralized control on investment intentions exercised in France and Great Britain would be accepted in a federal system of government of the kind found in Canada, Malaysia, and Brazil.

The search for new solutions, for new measures for regional development, is well under way in many countries. We have seen of late new interests in community development, entrepreneurship, knowledge-based development, and in new education and research facilities for traditionally less developed areas. New government measures have also been introduced, ranging from special enterprise zones in Great Britain and the United States to special regional development agencies in Canada. We are likely to see still more new measures in the near future in the different countries surveyed. These measures will invariably be a product of past efforts, of existing political and administrative institutions, and of new thinking by social scientists in the economic development field. In short, the search for solutions to regional disparities will continue.

REGIONAL DEVELOPMENT AND THE MACHINERY OF
GOVERNMENT

Hand in hand with the search for new measures to promote regional development is a search for the right government organization to
promote regional development concerns inside government in the policy and decision-making process. This volume reveals countless government reorganizations for regional development in all countries surveyed. Great Britain tried time and again to find the proper government
organization to integrate regional and national economic planning but
was never successful. In Canada, a recent Royal Commission on Canada's economic prospects observed that

> The most obvious manifestation of this failure [i.e., the federal gov-
> ernment regional development policy] is apparent in the constant
> rearrangement of the federal bureaucracy, first, to bring regional
> interest in a single department, then to encourage all departments to
> consider regional implications and, finally, to drift back to a single-
> ministry concept.[7]

A former Canadian cabinet minister responsible for regional development added, after a lengthy review of his departmental policies and
programs, that the problem to be resolved was as much one of defining
an appropriate government structure as it was one of formulating the
relevant policies and programs.[8] The situation, it would appear, is not
unique to Canada; scholars in other countries have also noted the problem.[9] Yet precious few studies exist on the issue, which remains a per-
plexing one for government decision makers.

Some students of regional development are also suggesting that we
have not paid sufficient attention to the impact of the machinery of
government on the policy formulation process. It has been suggested,
for example, that government structures play an important role in shaping policies. "Government organization is a determinant of national
policy . . . precisely because the manner in which the government is
organized affects the distribution of authority, power and influence in
ways that are not politically or policy neutral."[10]

In the regional development field, in particular, how a government
organizes itself will have a significant impact on its policies and programs. Perhaps more than in any other policy field, a government's
regional development policy, if it is to be effective, must be flexible and
must be able to accommodate changing circumstances. No one can pre-

dict either the regional development opportunities or the problems that may surface in the future. To deal with this situation, regional policies and programs should be flexible enough to accommodate virtually any kind of initiative, however different one may be from another. This necessary flexibility in turn requires an organizational structure capable of introducing program changes quickly.

The first issue a government must address is to decide what priority it wishes to give regional development. Those like the Thatcher government that decide to deal with the issue on an ad hoc basis and provide assistance only to desperate and isolated cases can turn to a small line department or agency. The agency will need a program capacity to deal with such special cases as the sudden closure of a region's single industry plant and widespread layoffs that happen to be concentrated in one region of the country.

Presumably, programs will not be ongoing. They will be applied to selected cases and only for the time it takes for designated regions to go through the necessary transition and adjustments. Over time, other regions will be designated, and the agency will have to move on to these areas and adjust programs to correspond to local economic circumstances. Popular initiatives to deal with ad hoc cases have included schemes for early retirement of affected workers, wage subsidies to firms employing laid-off workers, and special development grants to firms wishing to locate in the designated region. Thus the agency will need a planning capacity to come up with necessary schemes that can be revised to correspond with local requirements. It will also require a capacity to deliver the initiatives, often through local or on-site offices.

Generally, however, governments have had more ambitious regional development policies. Publicly at least, they talk about the need to mount concerted and coordinated attacks on regional problems. That is, a cross section of government departments and programs ought to be sensitive to the government's regional development priorities and use their resources accordingly. It is precisely when governments define their regional development objectives in these terms that particular attention ought to be given to the organization of their administrative structure.

In describing the problems he encountered in promoting regional development measures inside government, a senior official commented that "it's like pulling against gravity." There is no doubt that the traditional bias of administration favors national and sectoral policies. Departments are traditionally organized along sectoral lines so that officials in a Department of Agriculture, for example, will perceive problems from a sectoral rather than a spatial or regional perspective. They are more likely to highlight general issues, such as the credit position of farmers, water supply problems, and sudden drops in commodity prices than to look at the diverse problems in a particular region. Line departments have long histories of looking at situations from a narrow sectoral perspective. In short, their overriding concern is the economic health of the sectors, not of the various regions.

For their part, central agencies tend to look at the overall economic health of the national economy. More important, however, they have developed a gatekeeper capacity and understandably are more preoccupied with evaluating and frequently stopping new initiatives suggested by line departments than with coming forward with new ones themselves. The concern, for instance, of treasury officials is managing the government's expenditure budget and improving management practices in government. They are unlikely to propose new ideas to spend more money.

It is important to bear in mind that the regional development policies and programs of a government are sustained by support at the political level and by the officials who deliver the programs. Support from politicians representing economically depressed regions, in particular, is crucial for the continuation of regional development programming. The electoral campaign platforms of national political parties, either right or left leaning, invariably include a section on the need to stimulate economic development in slow-growth regions. It is unlikely that on their own, the bureaucracy or permanent officials, taken as a whole, would promote or even sustain regional development programming. This volume, among other studies, makes that clear.

How then should a government organize itself to translate this political-level commitment into concrete measures and support inside government? In ICCs where the concept of regional development authorities has not caught on, the debate is likely to revolve around two organizational models—line department versus a central agency.

Having a line department responsible for regional development holds important advantages in that government responsibility clearly lies in one department and with one minister. Problem regions will quickly identify with the department and will know precisely whom to turn to when encountering difficulties or potential opportunities.

From an administrative point of view, a line department can bring all regional programs together and thereby bring a sense of coherence to a government's strategy. Program expenditures budgets can be struck, and a minister with his or her department can become responsible and

CHAPTER NINE

accountable for them. Officials dedicated to regional development are brought together under one roof, thereby providing a "critical mass" of expertise for the government. From a policy perspective, it also means that the political head of the department can participate at Cabinet meetings with a clear and unencumbered mandate to come forward with measures to promote regional development.

Designating a single minister and department for regional development can also be particularly beneficial in a federal system. State governments can turn to the department, not only for signing agreements to promote regional development, but also to coordinate their efforts with those of the central government. For example, the department can provide provincial governments with a point of contact in the national capital. It can also explain provincial positions or development initiatives to concerned federal departments and, in turn, explain to provincial or local governments emerging policy and program proposals of the various sectoral departments of the central government.

But the single line department approach is not without opponents. By definition, it is suggested, a single department can never mount a concerted and coordinated effort at promoting regional development. If responsibility for regional development is to be governmentwide, how can it be properly delegated to a single minister and a single department? A traditional line department will never have the influence to coordinate and, if necessary, direct the activities of several departments and agencies at any one time, even less so on a continuing basis. The minister of a line department sits among his or her equals at the Cabinet table. They or their officials compete on an equal footing with other departments for a bigger budget and for an expansion of their sphere of influence. The line department can hardly rise above interdepartmental competition to play a coordinating role, simply because other departments will not let it for fear that it would gain an edge in the competition. Other departments are also unlikely to be eager to tailor their programs or their budgets to contribute to the objectives of the regional development department, risking the expansion of its influence, growth, and prestige—possibly to the detriment of their own self-interest. Quite naturally, officials of other departments have their own objectives and priorities to promote, and it would be rare, indeed, if they had enough resources left over to contribute to those of another department. Moreover, a line department with a regional development mandate could well lead other departments to dismiss all regional concerns, arguing that there is a department already responsible for them and that any problem should be turned over to it.

If governments are serious about mounting a coordinated and governmentwide regional development effort, then they must look to organizational models other than the single line department. One such alternative is the central agency. A central agency responsible for regional development holds important advantages.

Unlike a line department, a central agency can legitimately claim to be able to rise above interdepartmental competition. It can also claim to bring a multidisciplinary approach to regional problems. If a particular region has an unrealized agricultural potential, for example, the agency can turn to the Department of Agriculture for intervention. It can also do the same with every other government department. With a capacity to cut across sectoral or jurisdictional lines, the central agency can present itself as remarkably flexible to regional problems and opportunities.

A central agency also has the capacity to make regional concerns central to a government's policy and decision-making process. As departments come forward with economic development strategies, the agency is able to bring them all together, view them in their totality, and assess them from a regional perspective. The agency is thus in a position to direct departments to amend their strategies to reflect regional circumstances and to revise their programs to deal with particular problems.

However, the idea that a central agency should perform this function is also not without opponents. To some, the notion that everyone should be responsible for regional development means that in the end no one is responsible. A central agency with no budget and no program capacity, it is suggested, cannot properly be held responsible for regional development. Central agencies also have another important drawback. Generally, they are not held in high esteem by line departments. They are considered to be the gatekeepers of the treasury and are perceived as having an excellent capacity to "shoot holes" in a proposal but little ability to come forward themselves with new concrete initiatives. Certainly, for a central agency to promote regional concerns would mark a departure from its traditional role. Line departments are likely to be skeptical, at least for some time, of the ability of a central agency to play an advocacy role.

A question that will need resolution is whether such a new central agency should be given a budget or a regional fund to which line departments can apply. If the agency has no fund to support new measures, it is not likely to meet with much success in launching new initiatives. Departments will see little reason to work with the agency unless there are clear advantages to do so, including bigger budgets and programs. Accordingly, the establishment of a special regional development fund will likely be necessary to ensure that new activities and initiatives are launched.

However, the establishment of a fund might well in itself raise some questions and in some ways contradict the objective behind the establishment of a central agency for regional development. Sectoral departments, for example, may be tempted to continue with their regular programming and turn to the regional fund whenever they have to deal with regional problems. Any attempt at mounting a coordinated effort at promoting regional development could thus be as difficult as it would be with a line department approach.

The one place where a central agency approach has, comparatively speaking, met some success in the past in promoting regional development is in France. DATAR was able, among other things, to direct departments to initiate new measures in selected regions. It did not have two competing mandates to contend with, one for regional development and the other for managing the expenditure budget. In addition, the agency was successful not so much because it was a central agency but because of the political support and the program instruments it was able to secure.

All in all, there are several features that are essential for any successful government organization for promoting regional development. There should be an advocate at the Cabinet table who can speak from a clear and unencumbered mandate. In addition, despite the drawbacks, governments should put aside a special regional development budget or fund to support new measures. Without such a special fund, even more problems are created—great ideas for new initiatives may well surface, but they are likely to remain just that if no resources are available. The same would be true for any sector. For instance, unless a department with its own budget is established for agriculture, it is unlikely that the country's agricultural sector will see new government initiatives.

The question that remains unanswered is whether the minister responsible for regional development should head a central agency or a line department. General theory on the role of central agencies holds that they should be neutral and objective and should not appear to be competing for resources normally available for allocation to line departments. The theory provides for a neat and tidy division of responsibility, with central agencies acting as the "honest broker" among competing line departments.[11] For the purpose of managing the expenditure budget in an orderly fashion, the theory has proven quite successful in practice.

Where it runs into difficulties is when governments are confronted with a problem that requires flexibility and a capacity to cut across sectoral or jurisdictional lines. Traditional line departments do not have the capacity to cut across jurisdictional lines, and experience has shown that they are not able to mount a comprehensive multidepartmental effort at promoting regional development. Line departments have another important shortcoming in their entrenched tradition of doing things a certain way. To have to deal with established routines is frustrating in a situation that requires quick action, an important consideration in the regional development field.

The question, then, is how can government organize itself so as to be both flexible and able to coordinate the efforts of various line departments? One option would be to establish an agency or department that cuts across jurisdictional lines, that has solely a regional development mandate, and that manages an especially constituted regional development fund.

The agency would be responsible for defining regional development strategies, for negotiating these strategies with line departments, and with other governments in the case of a federal system, and for ensuring a regional dimension in government policies and programming. But the agency's capacity would go beyond that. It could provide special grants from the regional fund to line departments as an incentive for them to do new and needed things.

Such an agency should be fully entrepreneurial and should make efforts to avoid falling into established routines. In the absence of proposals from line departments, it should develop them internally. It should initiate new programs as required, when line departments are unable to respond quickly. It should transfer a new initiative to a line department as soon as it is mature enough to stand on its own and the department understands the objective of the program so that it would not choke it with tradition.

The agency should also facilitate the integration of regional, national, and sectoral economic planning. A word of clarification regarding the regional perspective in national policies is in order. Regional perspective is frequently contrasted with a sectoral perspective, where the national economy is viewed both as a collection of industrial sectors with total output that equals GNP in the same way as the total output of the regional economy equals GNP.

How then can the regional perspective be integrated into national policies? Should a series of national sectoral policies be developed and then modified to fit the regional strategies, or should regional strategies be developed and subsequently modified to incorporate sectoral considerations? In our view, both should be developed simultaneously so that neither has the upper hand. National governments have traditionally started with a sectoral strategy. Yet this approach has contributed little to national economic cohesion or to easing of interregional tensions in the great majority of the countries we surveyed. Attempts at defining a national industrial strategy have been viewed as helping the most developed regions.

The formulation of national policies incorporating both sectoral and regional perspectives at the outset would permit a comprehensive pulling together of both concerns early in the process. Such an approach might encourage officials to analyze regional comparative advantages and development opportunities in ways that make interregional and intersectoral trade-offs as clear as possible. Failure to go beyond a regional "add-on" approach will only invite inappropriate and ad hoc measures to stimulate economic development. The development resulting from such efforts is likely to be superficial and short term. This book has shown time and again and in different countries that this is so. Solid, lasting, and self-sustaining regional development requires an integration of national and regional economic development planning. Unless governments put in place an organizational structure and policies to accomplish this, they are likely to be even less successful in promoting regional development in a rapidly changing world than they have been over the past 30 years when economic circumstances were more predictable.

As illustrated by the Brazil and Malaysia cases, a good many developing countries have opted for a regional development authority format. This is true both for countries with unitary and those with federal constitutions. In the latter case, the state or provincial government with jurisdiction over the region in which the authority operates will have some representation on the board or steering committee of the authority. Usually, however, such authorities have a good deal of autonomy, with their own budgets and their own management. Such authorities seem to be less favored in industrialized countries, although the new regional agencies in Canada bear some relationship to regional development authorities.

Part of the reason for the greater reliance on such authorities for the administration of regional policy in developing countries is that teams provided through foreign aid programs play a greater role in regional planning there than independent, tailor-made teams assembled to plan development of regions, which are not political units, do in industrialized countries. Moreover, foreign aid agencies engaged in preparation of regional plans usually provide further technical and capital assistance to implement them, a fact that gives such authorities a degree of independence from the central and state or provincial governments of the country concerned that is clearly impossible in the industrialized countries. Nonetheless, there are great advantages in the format found in developing countries. The staffs of such authorities have a continuity of interest in and contact with particular regions that is rarely found in industrialized countries in the administrative units concerned with implementing regional policy, and such a system is less likely to become bogged down in relations between central and state, provincial or local governments.

NOTES

[1] Robert Solow, "On Theories of Unemployment," *The American Economic Review*, March 1980, Vol. 70, No. 1, p. 2.

[2] Statement by Robert Lawrence in "General Discussion," in William J. Adams and Christian Stoffaës, eds., *French Industrial Policy* (Washington, DC: Brookings Institution, 1986), p. 194.

[3] Ibid., pp. 194–195.

[4] John Herbers, "With Federal Cuts, It's Each Locality for Itself," *New York Times*, 14 June 1987, p. E4.

[5] See, among many others, Donald J. Savoie, *Regional Economic Development: Canada's Search for Solutions* (Toronto: University of Toronto Press, 1986), Chapters 2 and 10.

[6] Thomas J. Courchene, "A Market Perspective on Regional Disparities," *Canadian Public Policy*, Vol. VII, No. 4, p. 513.

[7] See Canada, Minister of Supply and Services, *Report*, Royal Commission on the Economic Union and Development Prospects for Canada, 1985, p. 215.

[8] André Raynauld, ed., *Seminar on Regional Development in Canada* (Montreal: Centre de Recherche en Développement Économique de l'Université de Montréal, 1980), p. 42. This discussion borrows heavily from D. J. Savoie, "Organizing Government for Regional Development," *Government and Policy*, Vol. 4, 1986, pp. 481–490.

[9] See, among many others, J. Friedmann and W. Alonso, *Regional Policy: Readings in Theory and Applications* (Cambridge: MIT Press, 1978), pp. 3, 8.

[10] See P. Aucoin and H. Bakvis, "Regional Responsiveness and Government Organization: The Case of Regional Economic Development Policy in Canada," *Research Report 37* (Toronto: University of Toronto Press and Royal Commission on the Economic Union and Development Prospects for Canada, 1985), p. 53.

[11] See, among others, H. Heclo and A. Wildavsky, *The Private Government of Public Money* (London: Macmillan, 1981), Chapters 2 and 3.

Index